THE PAPERS AND ADDRESSES OF

WILLIAM PRESTON FEW

WILLIAM PRESTON FEW

THE PAPERS AND ADDRESSES OF

WILLIAM PRESTON FEW

LATE PRESIDENT OF DUKE UNIVERSITY

Eruditio et Religio

*"Consider that I labored not for myself only,
but for all them that seek learning."*
—Apocrypha: Ecclesiasticus, xxxiii, 17

Edited, with a Biographical
Appreciation, by

ROBERT H. WOODY

DUKE UNIVERSITY PRESS
MCMLI

Copyright, 1951, by the

DUKE UNIVERSITY PRESS

Printed in the United States of America
By the Seeman Printery, Inc., Durham, North Carolina

PREFACE

THE TIME is too near for a definitive biography of William Preston Few or for a detailed history of Trinity College and Duke University during his administration. Nevertheless, it seems appropriate to print some of President Few's addresses and papers. They contain nothing sensational and little that is strikingly original, but they represent the best thought and the calm and reasoned opinion of a wise man who devoted forty-four years of concentrated effort toward the building of an educational institution and the improvement of society by the process of teaching and learning. The original text of President Few's writings included in this volume is followed except for typographical errors or minor stylistic changes to conform to present practices. In the case of unpublished writings the best copy has been followed. Editorial comment has usually been omitted except to identify the source. The papers are arranged chronologically.

The biographical sketch included in this volume is tentative. It attempts to present a fair and rounded view, but I realize that we are still too close to the subject to be completely objective. To draw up the final balance sheet is beyond my purpose. Furthermore, the appraisal is based upon a selective rather than an exhaustive study of correspondence and collateral material.

President Few was an unduly modest man, and the little he had to say about himself tended to be rather formal and impersonal. He kept himself in the background. This is seen in the preliminary chapters of his history of Duke University on which he was engaged at the time of his death. For several reasons, however, it has seemed best that his story be told in his own words as far as possible, and some of his letters are quoted at length. I have tried to let him speak for himself. Biographers find that the outer, external aspects of a man are easy to grasp, but that the inner soul, the hidden man known only to himself, is difficult to discover. Particularly is this true of the quiet, introspective man of pensive mood, who is untroubled and serene within his own soul.

Many hands have contributed to the making of this volume. Members of the faculty and staff of Duke University too numerous to enumerate here, and others associated with President Few off the campus, have been uniformly helpful in answering questions and supplying needed information. Shortly after President Few's death the Reverend Dr. Marion T. Plyler, a distinguished minister of the Methodist Church and a lifelong friend of Dr. Few, began to collect material for a life of Few and a history of the founding of Duke University, a much more ambitious undertaking than is here attempted. This material has been generously placed at my disposal (it is now deposited in the Duke University Library), and it will need to be consulted by any future biographer, especially for its reminiscent quality and the sense of devoted loyalty which pervades it.

Mrs. Mary Thomas Few, President Few's widow, has been sympathetic and helpful as well as remarkably patient throughout the unduly delayed preparation of this volume. Miss Ellie

Few, a younger sister, has kindly contributed family letters and other data as well as her recollections. The Reverend Eugene Few, a nephew, contributed genealogical data and other material. Benjamin F. Few, also a nephew, who lived with President Few while a student at Trinity, recalled for me a number of incidents concerning his uncle.

Dean Francis M. Rogers of the Harvard Graduate School supplied data on Few's graduate record; Professor S. Frank Logan, Registrar of Wofford College, generously gave time he could ill spare to searching the file of the Wofford *Journal* and the late President H. N. Snyder's correspondence. President Walter K. Greene of Wofford College, President J. R. McCain of Agnes Scott College, Professor Edwin Mims of Vanderbilt University, and Professor Edgar W. Knight of the University of North Carolina, all contributed information and thoughtful comment. Vice-Chancellor William H. Wannamaker of Duke University has kindly reviewed with me his forty-year association with President Few as pupil, teacher, and Dean of Trinity College and Duke University. Dr. Alice M. Baldwin, former Dean of the Woman's College, has read the biographical sketch with constructive insight, and I am deeply indebted to her. Joseph P. Breedlove, former Librarian, and Robert North Wilson, Charles W. Edwards, Gilbert T. Rowe, and A. S. Pearse, all professors emeriti, have kindly discussed with me their long association with President Few. I have made generous use of the excellent biography, *John Carlisle Kilgo, President of Trinity College, 1894-1910,* by Paul Neff Garber, now a Bishop of the Methodist Church.

Mr. T. F. Southgate, son of James H. Southgate, a former Chairman of the Board of Trustees of Trinity College, recounted for me some incidents in the life of President Few. I am indebted to the Manuscript Department of the Duke University Library for many courtesies, and to Miss Mattie Russell of that department for calling important documents to my attention. Professor W. T. Laprade, a member of the faculty during all of President Few's administration, has read the manuscript and as Director of the Duke University Press has been helpful in many ways. I am indebted also to Mr. Ashbel G. Brice, Professor Laprade's successor as Director of the Press, and to Mr. Norman Knox and the staff of the Press, for painstaking care in seeing the volume through the press. No formal acknowledgment can express the measure of my thanks to my wife, Louise Wills Woody, for her constant encouragement and for a candid reading of the manuscript.

This memorial has been sponsored by the Trustees of Duke University and has been under the special charge of a committee consisting of the Reverend W. A. Stanbury, Bishop W. W. Peele, and Mr. G. G. Allen. It is fair to state, however, that the editor is responsible for errors of fact or interpretation.

President Few's life and character are his best monument, and his part in the building of Duke University is recorded for the ages. It is natural that I have written with a sense of deep respect for his memory, but I have sought to keep within the facts of history and to give no cause for the making of a legend. Few's life was so intertwined with Duke University, however, and his spirit so much a part of its life, that he inevitably becomes a part of its tradition. He lived not for the judgment of history, of which he would have had no fear, but for the good he could do for the causes of humanity. To those who have benefited from his ministry in the past or who may feel his influence in the future this volume is dedicated.

Robert H. Woody

Duke University
November 6, 1951

CONTENTS

[ix]

ILLUSTRATIONS

WILLIAM PRESTON FEW

1867-1940

A BIOGRAPHICAL APPRECIATION

WILLIAM PRESTON FEW, President of Duke University, died of a coronary thrombosis at the Duke Hospital on October 16, 1940, after a brief illness. He was nearly seventy-three years of age; he was the first President of the institution to die in office since Braxton Craven in 1882. For forty-four years President Few had been associated continuously with Trinity College and Duke University, first as Professor of English, beginning in 1896, as Dean from 1902 to 1910, as President of Trinity College, 1910-1924, and as President of Duke University, 1924-1940. He was the first Dean and fifth President of Trinity College and the first President of Duke University. His body was the first to be placed in the crypt of the University Chapel.

I

President Few was a native of South Carolina, but his forbears had been associated with the very section of North Carolina in which their descendant was to cast his lot. The first Few to come to America from England was Richard, a Friend, who

[3]

settled in Chester County, Pennsylvania, in 1682. William Few, the first of the family in North Carolina and the great-great-grandfather of William Preston Few, came south from Maryland in 1758 and purchased land in Orange County near Hillsboro on the Eno River. This William Few (1714-1794) was a colonel in the Revolutionary War, and his son James became an unenviable hero of the Regulator movement when he was captured and hanged by William Tryon, the Royal Governor of the colony, after the Battle of Alamance, May 16, 1771. The Regulator movement was a loosely organized rebellion against economic and social injustice and had its center in Orange County. James Few was not one of the principal leaders, and historians have uniformly condemned Tryon for this arbitrary act, done without trial, although it is said that the victim was twice offered a reprieve if he would take an oath of allegiance. James Few left two infant children, twins, who were barely three months old. Tradition has it that the boy, William, was reared by James's brother Benjamin; the girl, Sarah, later married a Methodist minister, John Gavin, of Augusta, Georgia. Just before the American Revolution the grandfather of young William had moved to a Quaker settlement, Wrightsboro, in Richmond County, Georgia; a son, Colonel William Few, represented Georgia in the Continental Congress, in the Convention which framed the United States Constitution, and in the United States Senate, and two other sons, Major Ignatius Few and Colonel Benjamin Few, became officers in the patriot army. Major Ignatius Few married Mary Candler, the daughter of William Candler, a neighbor in the Wrightsboro settlement, and they became the parents of Ignatius A. Few, the founder of Emory College, with which the Candler family of Georgia became so intimately associated. Colonel William Few, mentioned above as United States Senator from Georgia, was one of the founders and a member of the first board of trustees of the University of

Georgia, and he was later a president of the National City Bank of New York.

Just when William, the son of the Regulator, James, and the grandfather of William Preston Few, removed to Georgia is not known, but at an early age he had crossed over into South Carolina and settled in upper Greenville County. In 1832 he was one of the founders and a trustee of the Jackson Grove Camp Ground. A bridge over the South Tyger River and Few's Chapel, of the Methodist denomination, are said to be named for him. One of the sixteen children born of his union with Sarah Ferguson was Benjamin Franklin Few (1830-1923), who was a graduate of the South Carolina Medical College in Charleston and who served as an assistant surgeon in the Confederate Army. In 1863 Benjamin Franklin Few married Rachael Kendrick (1840-1922), a cousin, and she became the mother of his five children, two girls and three boys. Benjamin Franklin Few was mustered out of the Confederate Army in 1865 near the Bennett Place, a few miles from the future site of Duke University and near to the place where his great-grandfather had had a mill on the Eno River a century earlier. After the surrender he returned to South Carolina, where he settled in a rural community called Sandy Flat, in Greenville County, to practice his profession. It was here that William Preston Few was born, December 29, 1867.

Young Few grew up in a typically rural South Carolina environment where the leanness of the economy permitted few luxuries. The debacle of war and defeat and the political, social, and economic upheaval that was ironically called Reconstruction had left the times sadly out of joint. Genteel poverty was an ever-present reality for many, although Dr. B. F. Few was a man of some property as well as a profession, and his five children obtained at least a college education. South Carolina during Reconstruction was surely not the best of all possible worlds. Happily, a small boy's world did not encompass the doings of the legislature in Columbia or even in Washington, and Wade Hampton's "redemption" of the state from "radical" rule by the Negro-carpetbag-scalawag regime probably made no more marked impression on young Few than did the decayed economy of the state or the social revolution which followed emancipation and the enfranchisement of the black man. While the political events of Few's youth prepared the way for the "solid South," there is no reason to think that the drift of his mind was toward the "Bourbonism" of Charleston and the low-country any more than toward "Pitchfork" Ben Tillman and his "wool hat" boys of the up-country. It is probable that he grew up with a less fervid interest in politics than did his contemporaries and that he never came to have the traditional faith of the South in the political solution of complex problems.

II

As a child "Billie," as his parents and intimates called him—he was known at college as "Will"—was rather quiet and more introspective than most. At an early age he committed himself for life to the Methodist Church when he joined the Jackson Grove congregation which his grandfather William had helped to organize in 1832, a few miles from the Sandy Flat community. It is recorded in the family Bible that he was "Baptised into" the Jackson Grove Church with his older brother, Robert, and his younger sister, Sallie, on September 10, 1871. Religion never ceased to be a formative influence in his life. Many years later, when speaking at the centennial celebration of this same church, he reportedly said: "When a boy I walked down the aisle of this church to join the Church and to commit my life to the service of God and humanity, and I have never failed to follow the gleam from that day to this."

Family ties were always strong with Few, but as a boy he seemed to be closest to his mother; from her he received his early education, although he did attend one or two of the short sessions of the Gum Springs school near his home. She is remembered as having a singularly sweet, quiet, and patient nature. He later wrote: "I was an invalid boy. I spent most of my time with my Mother, the rest with a dearly loved horse and dog. She, and they in their way, literally loved me back into life. I have ever since loved horses and dogs and I have carried through all my life a deep sense of devotion to my Mother." He was near thirteen years of age before he was able to attend school. The family tradition suggests that the urge to become a teacher or preacher was felt by him at an early age, when he would enter a room and proudly announce: "I am going to be my mother's preacher."

Few attended the high school in Greer, South Carolina, to which town his father had moved, and he came under the influence of J. W. Kennedy, later president of Presbyterian College, and J. M. Manly, later a distinguished professor of English at the University of Chicago, who is said to have given him his first impulse to scholarship. His father had the first drug store in Greer—housed in the first brick building—and he helped to build the first Methodist church in that town. It was natural then that young Few should enter the Methodist college of Wofford in near-by Spartanburg.

He was a freshman in the fall of 1885; he graduated in 1889. Benjamin Wofford, the chief benefactor of the College, was still around and able to affix his tremulous signature to Few's diploma, as did the other trustees and the members of the faculty. The catalogue shows a rather rigid regime of mathematics and astronomy, physics, chemistry and geology, English language and literature, Latin, Greek, German and French, and metaphysics and political science. The trifles sometimes found in the modern curriculum were not needed by a serious-minded student who is said to have been a sophomore declaimer, a junior debater, and whose graduating speech was on "The Benefits of Reading." He was pleased to become a member of the Chi Phi social fraternity and the Preston Literary Society. He was one of the founders and Literary

Editor of the *Journal,* at that time the Wofford literary monthly. His name appears on the first issue, January, 1889, along with that of E. D. Smith (later Senator "Cotton Ed"), who was Editor-in-Chief. Few's contribution was an article on the "Wofford College Reading Room," which he modestly initialed and in which he refuted the charge that colleges were not practical. "There is nothing," he said, "that tends more to bring young men in contact with the outside world than does the reading room. Here they touch elbow with the leading writers and thinkers of the day." This was his only contribution to the paper. He later wrote:

I remember as if it were yesterday the movement to launch *The Journal* and the actual launching of it. I had hoped to do a good deal of work for the new paper but unfortunately for me I was ill a good part of that year. I was absent at one time for three months. When I returned I was obliged to give whatever I could give to my college studies. . . .

Few liked his studies and his professors, and he made friends. He wrote home to his mother, "Old schoolmates are about the best friends a man ever has. This is one good feature of school and college life." His letters of this period are of sufficient interest to justify extended quotation. The success of his first year as well as his appreciation of the opportunities he had are evident in the letter to his mother, June 11, 1886:

I have finished the Fres. Class at Wofford College with Final Distinction on every study. Stood my last Ex. today on Eng. and made high First Grade. In fact I do not believe that I missed a single question. I was [not?] feeling well and got tired and quit before I wrote enough on one or two of the questions. . . . However it was not very hard. All the class passed except three men. About 5 or six will get Final Distinction. We, no doubt, have the best class in College at present. . . . During this week I have prepared and stood three exs. read two books and went visiting on Monday night, and have not been feeling well at that. I did not study a great deal for any of my exs. this time.

[8]

Although I have taken a good stand in my class I have not neglected outside work. Have read twenty nine good books and have tried to improve myself in various other ways. I feel very well satisfied with my years work. I believe that it has been worth all that it has cost. Now for the next three months I am going to try to enjoy myself as much as possible, and build up socially and physically. I am undoubtedly weakest at these two points. . . . A man ought to try to be as symmetrical in character as he can. . . . All the members of our fraternity are going to ride on Monday afternoon. I am going with Miss Mary Moore. It will be Few & Moore. . . . I am anxious to see you all. Especially will I be gratified to come home again to the bosom of my dear Family, from whom I have been separated a good part of the present year. I feel that I owe to you all, especially to my dear father and mother, a debt of gratitude that I can never pay. I sincerely hope that we may all have a pleasant and happy future. I shall ever do all in my power to add to your happiness and peace, and may I never give you any sorrow, or any regret for doing what you have done for me. . . .

The last report card for his first year had a remark appended, apparently by President James H. Carlisle: "We hope to see him and his brother in October. We want such students."

The next fall he had not lost his enthusiasm for school. He wrote his mother from Spartanburg, October 14, 1886:

I have a good deal more work to do this year than last, but of course a Soph. is expected to be able to do more than a Fresh. The studies of the Sophomore year are more interesting than those of last year. The higher up a boy gets the better pleased he is apt to be. We are studying new Physics (natural philosophy) & Trigonometry and they are very interesting. We are also higher in Latin & Greek and in a few days I will begin the study of Old English & Anglo Saxon. . . . I am going to try to learn all I can without hurting myself. . . . I play tennis almost every afternoon, and I am beginning to enjoy it. . . .

The next month he wrote to his father:

I have not got very much to do—at least my work is comparatively small tonight. I spoke this morning on the rostrum. It excited me less than usual. I have to debate Friday night. This outside work makes college work a great deal harder. About the school you want me to take—if you can get no other job I will be perfectly willing to teach school. I would prefer to do something else after going to college all year. . . . One of the boys who has been staying in this room has left. . . . So there are only 3 in the room now. I was rather glad when he left. The boys left are nice fellows and very congenial to me. . . . I cannot leave on Friday at any time without neglect of duty. I am censor in Society, and I want to discharge the duties of this, the first regular office to which I have ever been elected, as well as I can. I don't know that it is any great honor to hold this office, but I am mindful of the fact that he that is faithful in little things will also be faithful in great things. I am much interested in several departments of my work. I am delighted with Trigonometry, the first branch of Maths. that I have been especially fond of. It opens up a wide field. I also like very much Natural Science. The experiments, etc. are very interesting. Prof. [Daniel Alston] DuPré is one of the first men of this college. . . .

Just after his return to the College from the Christmas holidays he wrote to his mother, December 30, 1886: "The work to be done is truly great, but if one can take it easy and do faithfully every duty as it comes, the time can be spent pleasantly and profitably. . . ." It was just at this time that his report card said of his work in English, "Best scholar in class."

He continued to find plenty to do. He wrote to his father, February 27, 1887: "I was very busy all of the last week—worked harder than I have this year. It is a big job to prepare for ex. on about 80 pages of Greek. I have re-read a good part of it. Have done about all that I can do. . . . I am getting on very well in every way. My health has been very good. . . ." Friday, May 13, 1887, was the day for the annual sophomore exercise which consisted mainly of speeches and recitations. The program which Few enclosed to his mother the next day shows that his speech, "The Puritans," was from

Lord Macaulay. He commented with some satisfaction on the occasion:

> The Sophomore Ex. is over. It passed off very, very nicely indeed. I spoke without much excitement. I don't believe I was excited as much as I usually am when I speak before the students and profs. I received a right good pile of flowers—two of the baskets were very pretty. Ellerbe gave me a very nice book. The audience was about as large as it usually is on such occasions. I enclose a programme. . . . I have not yet begun to review for examinations. I expect to do as little of this as possible. At this season of the year a student, who has been at work for a long time, feels very little like studying. . . . Miss Lou asked me to tell you that, if you had been here, you would have been proud of me. They tell me here that I made the best speech of the evening; but I don't know whether they mean it. I certainly got through better than I had ever expected. This is a very pleasant day. . . .

One of Few's fellow-speakers on the occasion was E. D. Mouzon, later a distinguished and eloquent Bishop of the Methodist Church.

The next fall "Billie" was back a Wofford and was feeling old enough and wise enough to give his sister Sallie, also away in school and probably homesick, some helpful advice. On October 6, 1888, he wrote:

Of course, we don't find everything like we might wish it to be. . . . We might all have remained at home and led an easy and listless life, but we never would have done any good for ourselves or for any body else. For my part I will say, that it is my own choice and I am willing to pay the price. We all, anyhow, have to bear whatever circumstances may happen to encompass us. Nothing is truer than the philosophy which says, "To bear is to conquer our Fate." I have accepted this as my philosophy. . . . I know you are going to make the best of your surroundings, and tough it out until better things come. The time of feasting comes after the days of labor. "No cross, no crown." . . . . I like the new prof. of Eng. very much. He is very clever and nice. . . .

The next month, however, he was expressing to this same sister a somewhat more mundane view:

I like long cold nights, when I can sit by the fire and read while the wind is whistling around the corners of the house, or the rain is pattering on the roof. Then I can go to bed, sleep soundly, and snooze till late in the morning in a warm, comfortable bed. That's fine living. I venture this prediction: We are having a happier time now than we shall ever see after we have passed beyond the stage of school-boy and school-girls. We shall doubtless look back upon our school life as the green spot in memory, and will often, but vainly, long again for the happy days we spent at school. We should not forget this in the stress and labor now laid upon us. We must enjoy ourselves, as well as pore over books. I am more and more convinced that not all, or even the best part, of our education is gotten from books. These are but aids to the great study of nature and human life . . . . We are going to publish a college journal here. I have the honor to be one of the editors of the first issue. . . .

Later that winter he had to drop out of school for a time on account of his health. His report card for February 1, 1889, however, gave his grades as "Satisfactory" despite several absences, including "Absent from Prayers, 14 times," and President Carlisle remarked, "We all regret his necessary absence. He is missed, by students and Professors." The medal "Billie" won for his graduating oration on "The Benefits of Reading" he gave to his mother.

III

Very likely Few had decided to become a teacher before he finished college. After his graduation in 1889 he taught one year at St. John's Academy, Darlington, South Carolina. The pleasures and difficulties of the schoolmaster are seen in his letters to his sister. Shortly after his arrival in Darlington he wrote, October 3, 1889:

I see very little difference between this country and Greenville or Spartanburg. I don't feel any special difference in the climate. The land is not altogether as hilly, tho it is not as flat as I thought

I should find it. I could hardly tell I am in the low country if I only had some mountain water to drink. I miss this more than anything else. We drink altogether artesian water, and that is not very pleasant to the taste. For several days I suffered for want of good water, but I am beginning to get accustomed to it. I suppose it is healthy anyhow. . . . We have a nice school house and beautiful grounds; but the negroes have a finer house than ours—I mean a larger house. I am well pleased with my boarding place. Have a nice room, plastered and carpeted, a good table, with good shelves for my books. Have a good lamp and get good fare at the table. I am well pleased with the town and people. . . . We will fall to the work next week in dead earnest. . . .

After the labor of a month he wrote:

I am simply and surely the hardest worked man you ever saw. I sometimes thought I had been hard worked while a student, but I have six things to do now where I had one to do then. Rushing into a school like this with no experience and with no technical training was a risky thing. "Fools rush in where angels dare not tread." I am going to keep my head above water, if there be any possible chance. I have just returned from the Presbyterian church whither I went to preaching for the first time tonight. The preacher is slow till it hurts. . . . But I do have to be very dignified and look wise like an owl. Here is a great objection to the school-master's work: He must pretend to know everything. This keeps me on my tiptoe, for I lack a heap of knowing it all. Indeed I never have been so burdened with my insignificance as of late. . . . My work here is very pleasant, barring the afore mentioned fact that it is frightfully hard; and I suppose I am getting on as well as could be expected. It is needless to say I cannot please everybody, and who, pray, can. I am standing up remarkably well under the work. I have been feeling better since coming here than I have felt in a long time. . . .

Another month went by, things improved, and to sister Sallie he wrote in a philosophical vein:

While, as I become more used to my work, it grows lighter, still I have my hands abundantly full. I ought to rejoice in it, however; for it is a blessing for one to have his hands full enough

[13]

to keep him out of mischief. I think I am making a creditable record here; but I am playing a new role all round. I have to mingle with people and in society generally more than I have ever done. I don't know whether I have ever learned the art of living with others, and I must now go at it and improve all the talents I have along this line. If you would care for a bit of advice, I could advise you to cultivate whatever of talent you have on this score. You, I judge, are about on an equal with me in this matter. You have little opportunity, I fear; but be sure to improve all you have. We have been taught to regard this as an insignificant thing. It is insignificant in itself, and for that reason it is by some cried down; but it smooths one's way in life very much, if there is something more substantial in character to back it up. This is good counsel, if I must say so, and the longer you live the more you will feel it to be true. . . . While I have many things in school to vex me, there are a great many occurrences that are amusing. I think I could give you something to stretch your sides; but it is to [*sic*] cold at my desk, and I must get my feet to the fire . . . .

At the end of his first year he was invited to teach in the Wofford College Fitting School, the Wofford preparatory school, where he remained for two years as an instructor in Latin and English. On September 11, 1890, he wrote to Sallie, still in school at Williamston Female College: "Have been getting out my clothes this morning and Ma is patching them up for me. I want to leave next Tuesday. I don't look with any pleasure to the task of fitting up a room in which to live. . . ." Two months later he reported:

I am doing the best work of my life. My school duties are arduous, but besides I am doing a full year's work. I am working with Prof. Snyder in Eng. & am studying Latin fr. H. M. I put all my spare time on these & that is the reason I write so little. I think I am doing well with my classes and my health was never better. I enjoy a game of tennis nearly every afternoon.

Professor Henry Nelson Snyder, later president of Wofford, remembered Few at that time as "a tall, thin, shy, timid man" with all the makings of a scholar.

[14]

IV

After two years of teaching in the Fitting School, where one of his pupils was William Hane Wannamaker, later Dean of Duke University, Few decided to do advanced work in the field of English; in September, 1892, he entered the Graduate School of Harvard University. He may have been influenced to select Harvard by his friend, Professor Manly, who had received his Ph.D. from Harvard in 1890, and by the fact that Harvard had an exceptionally strong English department. The difficult transition from a small church school with an enrollment of perhaps 150 to Harvard was made successfully; in 1893 Few received the degree of Master of Arts, in 1896 the degree of Doctor of Philosophy, both in Modern Languages. During this time he held one of the Townsend Scholarships, founded by Miss Mary P. Townsend of Boston by a bequest "the income of which is to be used for the benefit of indigent scholars." He took courses under Professors F. J. Child and G. L. Kittredge in Shakespeare, Old English Literature, Bacon, Milton, Chaucer, Anglo-Saxon Poetry, Beowulf, The Metrical Romances, The English and Scottish Popular Ballads, and German Mythology. Under Professors von Jagemann and Sheldon he had courses in Germanic and Romance philology among others. In all the courses for which there is a record the grades are about evenly divided between A and B. Once he wrote home, "I have been a good deal of a 'grind,' as they say here. I have stood the strain as well as I could expect." His unpublished thesis was "On the -*ing* Suffix in Middle English with Special Reference to Participles and -*ing* Verbals." A portion of the thesis was printed in very distinguished company in a memorial volume marking the completion of Professor Child's fiftieth year at Harvard. His explanation of the development of the modern participial ending -*ing*, by analogy with verbal endings, is probably the correct one, but not enough of his dissertation was published to attract attention.

The record of Few's work at Harvard is impressive, for it was done under the handicap of illness. Again the letters to "sister Sallie," then teaching at Duncan, South Carolina, are revealing. Writing from "32 Felton Hall, Cambridge," January 8, 1893, he referred to the difficulty of keeping up his correspondence and continued:

We can only do so much anyhow and if we do this, without hurrying and straining it is a thousand times better. I have not yet learned much about how to work, but I hope I have learned this much: never to be in a hurry and never to strain myself unduly. It always results in more harm than good. I have frightfully hard examinations to stand here. They begin in two weeks, but I am going to take things easy. The examinations are awfully hard and long. Sometimes I think I have undertaken to do too much; but such thoughts I put away from me, and do not write them in any spirit of complaining. . . . Once when I was at Darlington, sick and greatly overworked, out of the despair of my heart I wrote to Dr. Carlisle [President of Wofford]. He answered me in a note such as only he can write, and he quoted this from Thomas Carlyle: "Learn to devour the chagrins of your lot." This is a lesson all of us greatly need to learn. We have to accept our lot as it is & make what we can of it. I have often pondered how I could best be of help to you all. I knew of no quicker way than the method I have adopted. Perhaps somebody else could have done better. I have to work with the limitations that have been put upon me. Maybe after all, things will work out better in our lives, if we be true to ourselves. . . . And always feel free to write to me about anything that concerns you nearly, and you may be sure of a brother's sympathy and a brother's counsel. I am not sociable by nature, and I have not showed my love for you all, as I should have done, and yet I know I love you all dearly as a son and as a brother. If we were perfect, healthy characters we should not need to write to each other in this strain; but very few of us can claim to be this, and I have written in this way hoping that you will receive it as a sincere expression of my heart. . . .

Again he wrote of the examinations:

I must confess to being pretty well tired out, but I don't know that that will do me any harm. Tonight I am as tired from walking as from any other cause. . . . This is the last week of mid years. I hate to be forever talking about these abominable examinations. It sounds rather boyish—I know you are tired of hearing of them; but one thing is sure, you can't be half as tired of them as I am. They are perfect nuisances. I shall be glad when this week is past. Now I am so sleepy that I can't hold my eyes open. I cannot write a letter tonight. I should put it off till tomorrow, but I shall be busy all day long. . . . Don't blame me, but blame the hardness of my present circumstances. . . .

Two years later he was writing his sister, who by this time was Mrs. M. L. Marchant, Jr., of Greer, South Carolina:

This is the first letter I have been able to write in some time. I finished examinations on Friday. I think I got through pretty well this time. Today I have enjoyed a good rest with nothing hanging over me to disturb my peace of mind. . . . It has been as cold as 'git out' . . . . the mercury went way down, from ten to twenty degrees below zero. It was next to impossible some days to walk very far. The wind was so cold, & the snow was blown into your face, to such an extent that we could not stand it long. But it is much better now, and I am hoping it may remain so. . . . I have a cold in my left eye lately & it troubles me yet. I am giving it a good rest tonight . . . .

He later wrote of his experience at Harvard:

I found the climate of Massachusetts hard on me, and it was with great difficulty and personal sacrifice that I stayed there through four years. Of these four years I missed a great deal of time. I sat at one stretch for three months in the dark— a good part of it in the Massachusetts General Hospital—suffering with inflammatory rheumatism which seriously affected one of my eyes. Ill health interfered seriously with my life and work there, as, in fact, it has handicapped me throughout life . . . . until about 1924 I had had bad health all my life.

It was this consideration, primarily perhaps, that caused me to turn my face towards the "Sunny South" after I had finished at Harvard in 1896. I therefore welcomed word from President John C. Kilgo, whom I had known in South Carolina [once he had written from Wofford, "Mr. Kilgo, the agent for Wofford College, preached a very good sermon in the Methodist Church today . . . ."], inviting me to Trinity to serve one year in place of Edwin Mims, who was given a year's leave of absence to study at Cornell.

v

Thus a young man of twenty-eight, whose most apparent assets were a Ph.D. from Harvard and an ambition to establish a place for himself in the educational world, had a temporary appointment in a little-known institution with an uncertain future. If Few undertook to appraise the prospects by an examination of the past history of the College, he probably found little to inspire immediate confidence. Trinity College had its origin in the joint efforts of the Methodists and Quakers of Randolph County, North Carolina, who in 1838 had established a school which became known as Union Institute. From the beginning it was a hard struggle. Braxton Craven, who had succeeded Brantley York as Principal in 1842, thought the school could accomplish more by training teachers in preparation for the much-discussed program of public education in North Carolina. Accordingly, the school became Normal College in 1851. Results were meager; the educational boom did not materialize, with the result that the North Carolina Conference of the Methodist Episcopal Church, South, was asked to take over the school, and in 1859 it became Trinity College. It barely survived the Civil War, in fact was closed during the last year of that conflict, but in the fall of 1865 it reopened under the leadership of Braxton Craven, who remained President until his death in 1882. After that members of the faculty served as executive heads of the institution (except during 1883-1884, when M. L. Wood was President) until John Franklin Crowell, a native of Pennsylvania and a graduate of Yale, was elected President in 1887. Crowell was a man with ideas and energy, and his impact was felt in many ways by a people who were a little too provincial to accept him entirely. His work was of lasting benefit, however, and was generously praised by his successors. President Few remained his lifelong friend and was always appreciative of his services to Trinity College. Crowell's most important contribution, perhaps, was his decision to persuade the Trustees to get the school out of its rural environment. In 1890 Trinity College, aided by a gift of $85,000 from Washington Duke, whose son Benjamin Newton had become a Trustee the previous year, and by a gift of sixty-two acres of land from Julian Shakespeare Carr, started a building program in Durham, and in September, 1892, the College opened its doors in that city. Durham, a city of the New South, then approaching a population of 8,000, was to make its development along industrial lines. It was expected to grow, and the College might well grow with it. "The society of Durham," read the Trinity catalogue, "is cultured and elegant yet free from any of the evils that poison social life." But the country was already in the throes of a severe economic depression, and it seemed to be impossible for the College to raise urgently needed funds from its Methodist constituency in spite of a generous matching offer from B. N. Duke. The College was in debt, faculty salaries were in arrears, and there was a real possibility that the school would have to close. Moreover, there was faculty opposition to Crowell, who did not feel that he had the full support of the Trustees, and the Methodists had been critical of his introduction of organized athletics. He became convinced that the state's religious leaders "failed to see the importance of progressive methods and policies in intermediate and collegiate education." Despite the refusal of the Trustees to accept his resignation, he left the institution in May, 1894.

Crowell's successor, John Carlisle Kilgo, of South Carolina, was probably the most powerful preacher and dynamic personality—though "not an impressive figure of a man"—ever to be connected with Trinity College. He had attended Wofford College for one year—his only year of formal college education; then he taught school briefly before he joined the South Carolina Conference and became a Methodist circuit rider. He so distinguished himself as a preacher that Wofford College, the Methodist institution in South Carolina, asked him to become its financial agent in 1888. In this position, which involved contact with the agencies of the Methodist Church and with the patrons of the school as well as the raising of an endowment, he was phenomenally successful. After 1890 he taught part-time at Wofford as professor of metaphysics and political science; at the same time he was being tutored privately by Professor Henry N. Snyder, later president of Wofford, and in 1893 he was awarded the M.A. degree.

Kilgo had not been the first choice of the committee to find a President, but when he arrived in Durham in the summer of 1894, it was generally realized that a President had been found. The people liked his pulpit eloquence, his plain manners, his vigorous personality, and his zeal for the causes of the church and education. Kilgo was given to strong convictions positively expressed, and some of his views created a good deal of alarm. His emphasis upon Christian education under the auspices of the church and his tacit alliance with the Baptists of Wake Forest were noted by the state-controlled institutions; his attempts to raise the standards of the public-school system of the state were received unfavorably; in an age of agrarian discontent and trust busting he was looked upon as an agent of the vested interests, especially when he spoke critically of Thomas Jefferson; and the mere fact that his benefactors, the Dukes, were openly and unashamedly Republican was enough to justify nearly any suspicion slyly planted in receptive minds. Given the generally static outlook on education and the many tensions produced by the economic and social discontents prevalent throughout the South and the strong and dominating personality of Kilgo, it was perhaps inevitable that he should become something of a storm center.

The new President brought with him ideas about education which were based upon his observation and experience in

South Carolina. He was convinced that the emphasis should be upon Christian education and that the leaders of the church were not sufficiently aware of their obligations in that respect. He was convinced "that a great college could not be built in the South upon popular subscription, because . . . the average Southerner could not visualize the large amount of money needed for higher education." Somehow sources of great wealth would have to be tapped. He was convinced that educational standards would have to be raised. "In the South," he said, "we have no educational system, and the public is open to all the frauds possible to money-conceived plans. Because of this we suffer in the educational world. A College in the South means anything chartered by a Legislature." Furthermore, he visualized more and better education for women, which he thought should be on a co-educational basis. Kilgo was earnest and zealous, but he was not narrow in his thinking. He was for progress and improvement and the creation of wealth and opportunity in the South; he was not provincial or sectional in his outlook—he wanted Trinity College even though small (it had a faculty of ten and 150 students in 1894—and a liberal estimate for all expenses was $200 annually per student) to be national in aims and interests—and he consistently opposed rigidly sectarian education. "There is a vital difference," he declared, "between denominational education and Christian education carried on by a denomination."

In 1908, shortly before he left Trinity to become Bishop, he said: "If Trinity College were a sectarian college, if its chief aim was to advance the denominational interests of the Methodist Episcopal Church, South, then I would not waste my time and labors upon such an unworthy project." The broad lines of policy laid down by Kilgo during his sixteen years as President of Trinity were carried forward by his successor. Kilgo had built upon the foundation laid by Crowell, and there were probably no essential differences in outlook so far as higher education was concerned between Crowell and Kilgo. Few in his association with Kilgo may have modified Kilgo's notions in minor respects, but it is probable that there were no great differences in their thinking on educational matters. Few's education was broader; he was more the scholar, but on the need for a thorough Christian education which would meet the approval of the public there was a close agreement. Few did not claim to be an innovator; he was always aware of his obligations to Kilgo, as he was to Crowell; in his quiet and persistent way, however, he was more nearly able to approach the true ideal of genuine scholarship.

VI

It was natural that Kilgo should turn to his young Wofford friend when he needed a temporary replacement in the English department. Kilgo was eager to strengthen that department; he was apt to be sensitive about criticism of Trinity, and he was inclined to be direct in his methods; thus when he heard that Dr. Thomas Hume of the faculty of the University of North Carolina had spoken slightingly of Trinity, he wrote to him, June 24, 1896: "It has reached me . . . that you make the statement that Trinity College is two years behind the University in English. I feel it but just that you know that you are quoted as making this statement, and that you have the opportunity to explain it. . . ." Professor Hume was on vacation, did not receive the letter at once, and therefore made no immediate reply, whereupon Kilgo wrote a second letter, July 9. Two days later Hume, having received the first letter, replied cordially that he had not made the statement attributed to him. Nevertheless, the addition of a young Harvard Ph.D. to the Trinity English department would not go unobserved at Chapel Hill. Mims, whose place Few was taking, probably had little to do with Few's appointment; he wrote to Kilgo in August: "Please write me *at once* Few's address (also his initials). I wish to write to him right away."

As it turned out, Few's appointment was not temporary. At the end of his first year Kilgo reported to the Trustees:

Dr. Few . . . has impressed himself not only on the College community, but on the entire town as a man of superior ability. It was the desire of all to retain him in the College, but our income did not warrant the undertaking. I placed the matter before Mr. B. N. Duke, and through his munificence the College has been given a new chair in English, making this department in Trinity the strongest in the state, if not in the entire South.

Within the family circle modesty was not required, but there was more than a note of satisfaction on President Kilgo's part—as well as on Dr. Few's, no doubt. The fact is that Kilgo, in the words of a contemporary, had been "charmed with Few from the very beginning." There is a hint that Mims, who had been close to Kilgo, found it necessary to move over and make room for Few. It is likely enough that, in view of their differences in educational background, Kilgo found Few a useful consultant in the work of Trinity College; it was soon evident that Few was interesting himself in general educational matters. He did not lose interest in the world of literature then or later, but the promise of further research, suggested in a note to the published extract from his thesis, did not materialize. Rather, as the papers collected here show, Few's publications, mostly in the *South Atlantic Quarterly*, were on the broader aspects of educational problems. His creative talents were turned in another direction than individual scholarship.

Few early became acquainted with the members of the Duke family. He knew and admired Washington Duke, and he was a close and lifelong friend of Benjamin N. Duke. He knew Ben more intimately than he did Ben's younger brother, James Buchanan, and there can be little doubt that Ben's influence was the most important single factor, with the possible exception of Washington Duke's original interest, in the creation of the Duke Endowment. Ben's wealth, as well as his interest in it, was not nearly so great as his brother's, but in proportion he was probably even more generous in his benefactions than was J. B. Duke. Ben spent much more time in Durham, he was quiet and retiring in disposition, and, like President Few, had more than his share of bad health. Their outlook must have been much the same and their affection genuine and reciprocal. Few later wrote of his first contacts with the Duke family:

The Dukes were already interested in Trinity College when I came here in 1896. This interest perhaps began at the time when Mr. B. N. Duke went on the Board of Trustees of the College, in 1889, while it was still at old Trinity in Randolph County. The first definite recollection I have of the Duke family was one evening when I went to call, I think in company with R. L. Flowers and Jerome Dowd. There were among others present a small boy and a small girl, Angier and Mary. Their interest in Trinity College, particularly that of the little girl, was intense; and finding at that time so much indifference, if not opposition hereabouts, I was deeply impressed and soon became attached to the whole B. N. Duke family, and through them to the Washington Duke family. Besides Mr. W. Duke, I came to know there Miss Anne Roney, her niece, Miss Florence Roney, and Mr. [Washington] Duke's granddaughter, Mary, daughter of Mr. Duke's only daughter who married Robert E. Lyon, now Mrs. J. E. Stagg. . . .
I, and others of us, maintained cordial and close friendly relations with all these persons through a long period of years. We were all interested alike in Trinity College and its causes. Miss Anne Roney gave the funds for the valuable Shakespearean collection now in the Duke Library. She also gave the fountain in front of the East Duke Building on the Woman's Campus, and they were both helpful in many other ways. . . .

One summer young Angier, B. N. Duke's son, was sent with Few on a trip to the West; occasionally, Few played tennis with Mary Duke, Angier's sister. It was remarked in those days that Few was frequently seen in the afternoon riding out with members of the Duke family. Sometimes he would hitch up B. N. Duke's ponies and take the children for a drive. It was probably with the Duke family primarily in mind that the Trinity College catalogue stated with reference to Durham: "No Southern town is blessed with larger hearted philanthropists."

VII

The contacts which Few, a young bachelor, made with the College and its friends were no doubt pleasant enough, but his main job was to teach. For all its obscurity and insignificant size, the Trinity faculty was an excellent one; several of its members were, or became, distinguished scholars and teachers. As a teacher Few was competent, thorough, exacting, but not exciting to the merely average student. His lectures were analytical and factual rather than enthusiastic. To some he seemed a little cold-blooded. He was without question a scholar, and he had mastered the spirit and method of the best in English literature, but he was at his best before superior students or adult audiences. The classroom for him was no place for theatrics. Showmanship was never one of his talents. His colleague, Mims, on the other hand, was more buoyant and more entertaining and inspiring to the freshmen and sophomores. Together, however, Few and Mims made a great team. Besides the general courses, Few gave alternate courses in Shakespeare, Chaucer, and Anglo-Saxon literature. It was not easy, as any teacher will realize, to interest every student in the contributions of Norman French to the English language or to make plain the intricacies of French philology. The requirements of his Shakespeare course were described in the catalogue of 1897-'98:

Five plays of Shakspere read carefully and critically in class, and all the other plays assigned in a conjecturally chronological order for outside reading. Two hours of classroom work are devoted to a minute interpretation of five plays, and one hour is given to lectures in Shakspere's works. The class is required to write a weekly report on assigned topics selected from the play read during the week.

[25]

The description of the Chaucer course read:

The greater part of the Canterbury Tales, the Parliament of Fowles, and the Legend of Good Women are read. Due attention is paid to pronunciation, grammar and metre, and some consideration is given to medieval literary history.

Not "crip" courses, surely, and the sort of factual and analytical instruction received from Few may have been just what was needed by the students under him. His examinations were in keeping with the courses: specific questions, and quotations for analysis and identification. His scholarship was recognized by students and faculty alike, and it was generally agreed that upperclassmen should elect work under him.

Few always insisted on simple fundamentals or first principles. An idea of how this was applied in the field of English may be gathered from his brief remarks at the third annual meeting of the Southern Association of Colleges and Secondary Schools, which he attended at the University of Tennessee, November, 1897:

I think the teachers in schools ought to pay a great deal more attention to written work than has ever been done. There is a tendency among Southern students to be decorative and uncommonly loose-jointed in all kinds of writing and speaking, and I think there ought to be a very earnest and strenuous effort . . . . to teach boys to set down their thoughts on paper simply, earnestly, and honestly. I think all boys in schools ought to be required to write a paper every week.

At one time it was customary for the faculty to give a series of public lectures on subjects of their own choosing. Few's lecture, the sixth of a series, delivered March 31, 1900, was not fully reported by the Trinity *Archive*. A few years later, however, the *Chronicle* gave a full report on his Shakespeare lecture on "The Formative and Consoling Power of Great Poetry," and it added: "The lecture was not as well attended as was expected." Though small, the audience was "exceedingly appreciative." It is said that Few knew most of Shakespeare by heart, and those who heard him speak on that or related subjects outside the classroom were often deeply impressed.

Few's notion of the inspirational value of literature, as well as his didactic tendencies, may be noted in a letter of advice on literary matters, probably written from Harvard, to his younger sister Ellie:

I should like to see you enthusiastic over Wordsworth and the rest of them, but not foolishly so. I think it a desirable thing that we should hold genius sacred, & yet these are only men and we want to judge them as such, praising and blaming as we feel inclined. Personally I believe I like Wordsworth almost as well as any English poet of this century. He holds a high place in the second rank of poets. Learn when he lived & any thing about his life you can find out. You might find his name in the encyclopedia at [the] Drug Store. Write & tell me all you read, how you like it & why. And tell me any difficulties you meet with. But enough of this. The rest of the family will have to look off while you are reading the above. I am only too glad to be through with my examinations. I don't like them a bit. . . .

Another letter to a brother or sister, possibly written some years later, suggests:

Read that little book of poems sometimes. The first time you read it begin at Part IV. Read the first piece [,] look in the index under the name of the author & read then all the poems in the volume by him, & so on through. The ones that are most significant to *you* read & read anytime during the next fifty years. It will help you to fill your life with what is beautiful, tender, & good, & will be of more value to you than you can perhaps estimate . . . .

Few was a man of independent judgment on literary matters. In October, 1899, he reviewed in the *Archive*, under the title "A North Carolina Poet," a book by Professor Benjamin Sledd of Wake Forest College. His object was to call attention to a book which had been issued about two years before by an author of "genuine poetic talent" and which had been overlooked by many. "It is always a difficult matter," he wrote, "for any of us, except the most highly endowed and the most liberally and sanely educated to appreciate at their real worth the things and men about us." He continued, "those who would understand and appreciate literature—that highest product of man's life, the flower of experience, the countenance that is in the face of all knowledge" must "be free from personal and local bias" if they would "make a just estimate of anything that concerns human life." He always related literature to life. Perhaps his appreciation of literature may be best summed up in words which he applied to Sidney Lanier:

Literature is not a science but an art, and the most human of all arts. This most human of all arts should not be approached in the spirit with which one would approach the investigation of facts. Literature does not, like the study of mere things, make its appeal solely to the mind, but to the imagination and to the feelings. The student of literature should not be simply a student, he needs something of the nature of a lover. . . .

He [Lanier] had the enthusiasm of all fine-souled men for good and beautiful things, whether in art, in nature, or in human conduct.

Few remained a teacher for many years after he assumed full administrative duties. He was listed in the catalogue as "President and Professor of English" as late as 1920. In September, 1912, the *Chronicle* reported: "President Few announces that he will devote more of his time this year to teaching than he has for the past four years. He intends to return to active work in the department of English." The comment was added: "President Few is a profound scholar, a most capable teacher, and one of the foremost students of Shakespeare in the South." Few wrote to a friend in 1917: "I always give one three hour course and usually do as much as six hours of teaching."

VIII

It seems probable that Few early decided to cast his lot with Trinity. He liked the South; the situation at Trinity was in keeping with his Wofford background and his attachment to the church; his friend and associate, Kilgo, was President; the need for the work that could be done at Trinity was evident; and the prospects were good for a further strengthening of the College. Few was ambitious, but not in a narrow, personal way. Perhaps the most striking thing about him was his intense devotion to the institution with which he was connected. His was an ambition for success and accomplishment that clearly transcended material concerns. A letter to President Kilgo from Morehead City, June 18, 1900, is unusual but its sincerity is evident:

I can say without a tinge of cant that my chief ambition now is to help on in my little way the great work we have begun at the College. You, of course, knew that already, but perhaps it won't hurt for me to say it again at this time, and to assure you that the treatment I have received during the dark year from the College and from my personal friends in and at the College has bound me to the College with a love that is one of the passions of my life. I hope to spend a good part of my days in attempting to pay the debt of gratitude I owe and I shall be happiest when I am set to do unpleasant tasks for the College.

We do not know whether this was an intimation of the deanship to come, but the reference to "the dark year" undoubtedly was to Few's recurring eye trouble. The *Archive* in February, 1902, mentioned that Dr. Few had been kept from his College duties for several days on account of his eyes. He then made a visit to his home in South Carolina and returned much improved but was "still unable to assume all of his regular duties." Years later, when President Few was trying to persuade one of his former faculty members to return to Trinity at a reduction in pay (the maximum salary was $3000), he wrote: "When I stood where you now stand, I was willing to take the chances; and I have never regretted it. I believe more than ever in the future of Trinity College, and I should be very glad if you, too, could take some risks; but I am obliged to leave that to you."

During Few's first year at Trinity he served on the Library Committee. Soon he was placed on the Committee on Admissions, the Committee on Athletics, and was serving with President Kilgo on the Committee on Courses of Instruction. The catalogue of 1900-1901 announced him as "Manager of Athletics." No one thought of Few as an athlete, of course, but he had played baseball and tennis at Wofford, and all his life he retained a keen interest in sports. He is reported to have taken pleasure in defeating at tennis his friend Frank C. Brown, Professor of English, who came on the court in perfect attire and with the latest equipment only to be trounced by the inelegant and probably awkward Few, who never removed his high collar. For many years Few was fond of horseback riding (for a long time he had a five-gaited trotting horse named "Squire"), as well as walking, but neither he nor his fellow administrators, W. H. Wannamaker and R. L. Flowers, ever learned to drive an automobile. For many years he walked the mile to the post office every afternoon, and his long stride and swinging arms were a familiar sight. He did not swim, but he sometimes took groups of boys from the Methodist summer home at Lake Junaluska on camping expeditions. He enjoyed visits to the Southgate Cabin, the country retreat of the chairman of the Board of Trustees, and it was here that he later wrote his inaugural address.

While he was Professor of English and Manager of Athletics, he was giving some thought to the larger aspects of the local situation. In an article on "Trinity College and Her Present Opportunity," printed in the Trinity *Archive*, November, 1901, he touched on themes to which he was to recur again and again in future years. Among other things he said that it was to "the well equipped and well endowed college that we must look for all education reforms." "The most important function of a Southern college," he thought, was "to teach." Here there was an "immense deal to be done and the competent workers . . . few." The purpose of a liberal education was to make "cultured men, to form the manners, the morals, and the character of its students," and some elective subjects, rather than "an iron-cast curriculum," would aid in that process. He was convinced that a liberal education required strong scientific departments, that laboratories, museums, and libraries were "absolutely indispensable adjuncts to college instruction." But again he came back to the teacher, who "must not only be a thorough scholar to begin with," but "must remain to the end a painstaking and enthusiastic student." "Perhaps no kind of intellectual worker is more useful than the scholar, but it is sure that none gets less remuneration or less notoriety," although it was clear that "every advance in civilization has been dependent on the influences which have proceeded from seats of learning."

IX

In the summer of 1901 President Kilgo on the insistence of the Trustees took a European vacation. During his absence the administration of the College was under Professors W. H. Pegram, R. L. Flowers, and W. P. Few. In 1902 Kilgo reported to the Trustees:

The growth of the College makes it necessary that the administration shall be in the hands of an authoritative head. It frequently occurs that the President of the College must be absent . . . . I therefore suggest . . . the propriety of the election of a Dean, who shall fill all the functions of what is ordinarily known as the vice-president of an organization.

Thereupon three of the Trustees, Robert L. Durham, Joseph G. Brown, and Andrew P. Tyer, on stationery from the President's office, recommended the appointment of a Dean "who shall be invested with all the authority of the President in his absence." There is no direct evidence that Kilgo recommended Few for the position, but it is difficult to imagine a man of Kilgo's personality recommending such an appointment unless he was sure of harmonious relationships with the new officer,

[31]

When the Trustees met it was first moved that the selection of the Dean be referred to a special committee. But immediately, the records show, the committee idea was dropped; Few was nominated and the motion carried, June 3, 1902. The new Dean—"Dean Billie," Kilgo called him—got no immediate increase in his $1600 salary, which was the same as that of most of the other professors.

About this same time it became known that there was a movement to elect Kilgo a Bishop in the Methodist Episcopal Church, South. James H. Southgate, the chairman of the Trinity Board of Trustees, wrote to B. N. Duke of his concern that the College might find itself without a President. He was very anxious that Kilgo remain another four years. "We need him inexpressibly and to lose him means that we cannot duplicate him and that the College may be several years finding a man who can even approximate him." It was very probably in Kilgo's mind, in making Few Dean, that he should be training a successor. After this Few could be seen in his rocking chair on the porch of his South Carolina home in vacation time studying the Bible and making notes because, as he said, his biblical education had been deficient.

The position of Dean was a new one at Trinity, and the duties of the office were not specifically defined, but Few immediately accepted it, and his appointment seems to have been received with satisfaction. Probably little change was made in the ordinary routine of things. A committee of the faculty usually handled disciplinary problems. In 1907, after Kilgo had been away some two months for his health, the *Chronicle* commented: "During his [Kilgo's] vacation Dean W. P. Few acted as President and managed the affairs of the college in an entirely satisfactory manner." After Few was elected President in 1910 the *Chronicle* remarked that the office of Dean had been filled by him "with the utmost efficiency and success" and that "for a number of years President Few had received wide recognition as an authority on the best practice in college administration."

x

Trinity's progress to some extent was a matter of passing from crisis to crisis. The removal to Durham and the near bankruptcy, followed by Crowell's resignation and Kilgo's election, ushered in a series of crises, nearly all centering in the person of John Carlisle Kilgo. Few found himself associated with a man who not only had constructive ideas about education and Trinity College's place in it and progressive ideas on the development of Southern society, but who had a positive and vigorous way of expressing his ideas. By the time Few joined the faculty Kilgo was the center not only of attention but also of attack. His insistence upon higher educational standards met a mixed reception from the smaller denominational schools, even within his own church, and his emphasis upon Christian education, as opposed to the secular—in the realm of higher education, that is—put him in disfavor with the supporters of the state institutions. His stress upon quality, not numbers, seemed out of keeping with current practices, and the idea that student loans were much better for worthy students than free scholarships smacked of an aristocratic carry-over from the days of the Old South, when free public education was not widely accepted. He even thought that the state did not owe everyone a higher education. He had a low regard for politicians and they for him.

His pride in the fact that he did not belong to a political party—in view of the political climate of North Carolina—bordered on treason. He was openly accused of voting for McKinley, and his animadversions on Bryan and the sixteen-to-one business were bitterly resented. Because the College accepted money from the Dukes, and sometimes stock in the American Tobbaco Company, the so-called Tobacco Trust, he was denounced as having sold out to the trusts, to the cigarette interests, and having become a corrupter of youth. The fact

[33]

that he enjoyed a good cigar put him among the plutocracy. When he advanced the notion that the development of Southern industry, for which the Dukes were doing much, would do more to improve and strengthen the South than the labors of all the politicians, he was accused of defying public opinion and destroying his own institution—which could stand only so long as it was supported by public opinion. If he hinted at the evils of demagoguery or insisted upon the right of a man to think for himself and to be free from the narrow sectionalism of an archaic past, he was accused of going against the faith of the fathers. And if he dared to speak of the elevation of the colored race (Booker T. Washington's first speech from the platform of a white Southern educational institution was made at Trinity College on invitation of Kilgo) and especially if he suggested its need for liberal education, as opposed to technical, he was given no credit for a wise attempt to advance the South by a mutual and sympathetic understanding between the races. His public utterances were not always as carefully phrased as they might have been, and he was misquoted and his words distorted or put into a different context by his enemies. He was especially subject to attacks by the press, ranging all the way from a paper of one of the Methodist Conferences to perhaps the most influential daily in the state under the editorship of a man who later became distinguished for his supposed liberalism. In short, Kilgo was denounced by the liberals as an ally and stooge of great wealth (he had sold the College lock, stock and barrel) and by the conservatives as a recipient of the devil's gold. He was finally attacked by one of his own Trustees, and the man who unsuccessfully sued him for slander in a famous legal action was a broken-down Methodist minister whom he had befriended. As Paul N. Garber states in his biography of Kilgo: "During the period from 1894 to 1910 Kilgo was not the only Southern leader who held advanced political, social, and economic opinions, but he was unique in his determination to build an educational institution where these views could be freely discussed."

Neither Kilgo nor Few, so far as we know, ever used the term "New South" in the Henry A. Grady sense, but it was in that spirit that they visualized the triumph of progress and prosperity and intellectual freedom over sectionalism, partisanship, and denominational bigotry. Kilgo was vindicated by the courts and loyally supported by the Trustees, and there is no reason to doubt that he had the admiration and sympathy of his protégé and Dean. But the young Dean was not pugnacious by temperament, and he may have felt somewhat apologetic because of the embarrassment which Kilgo, with something of the spirit of the zealot, brought to Trinity. It was Few's nature to shun the limelight and to accomplish by indirection rather than by frontal assault the good which his judgment approved. Few was always aware of the power of public opinion; he did not want to get so far in advance of it that harm would be done to the causes he had at heart.

The atmosphere which pervaded Trinity College and the spirit of those associated with it may be epitomized in the remarks of James B. Duke to Walter Hines Page, former Trinity student and future ambassador, when he came to dedicate the new library donated by Duke in 1902: "Tell them every man to think for himself." It was just a year later that William Garrott Brown, an able historian and sympathetic interpreter of the South, made a tour of the South and published his observations in a series of letters to the Boston *Transcript* under the title of the "South at Work." Brown was a native of Alabama, a Harvard friend and roommate of Few, and probably Few's most intimate friend outside his own family. Once they had gone on a camping trip together to the White Mountains, and they remained the closest friends until Brown's untimely illness and death. Under date of March 3, 1904, the readers of the *Transcript* were told that Durham, North Carolina, was a young and vigorous city but that it made little fanfare of either dress or entertainment. "Better still, there is less bigotry and more tolerance of various kinds than in many a bigger and older community one could name. . . . The new industrialism and commercialism which they [the Dukes] stand for has proved to be the strongest impulse towards liberalism ever awakened in North Carolina. These men are . . . devoted to freedom and [are] guardians of the plain man's opportunity. . . ." He added, the Dukes have endowed Trinity College "as no other Southern college ever has been endowed by private benefactors."

A week later Brown was to point out in a letter from Pinehurst that Trinity had become obnoxious to men high in office or in party authority because she had refused to be the tool of the politicians. He mentioned that Trinity had already separated itself from other colleges in the state by enforcing higher standards for admission and by its stand against intercollegiate football. "It was therefore generally regarded as an innovator and the ultra-conservative forces in the State were ready to array themselves against it." At the College there was ample evidence that the faculty and students were in full sympathy with the progressive ideals of the administration. Edwin Mims, Few's colleague in the English department, had written in the Trinity *Archive* in 1901 that Kilgo, in keeping away students not properly prepared, had "tried to put Trinity in line with that great educational movement that has been led so wisely and so successfully by President Eliot, of Harvard University." "I have never seen a body of college professors," he added, "who had just the same interest in building up their departments and in the making of scholars and men." There were many evidences that this loyalty of the faculty to their work and to Trinity was not a transitory thing; it seemed to be deepened by the vicissitudes through which the College passed. In 1906 Dean Few was writing to B. N. Duke: "I believe I never saw a body of men more thoroughly banded together by a great purpose than the faculty of Trinity College. We are laboring with your assistance to make this a mighty power for truth and right that will continue long after we have ceased to work."

XI

The most famous instance of the loyalty of the faculty to Kilgo and to the College as well as to the ideal of academic freedom and the right to a free expression of opinion, however contrary it might be to majority sentiment, was the famous Bassett case. Dean Few had a small but important part in that affair, which became a landmark in the history of the institution as well as in the fight for academic freedom in the South. The matter can be stated only briefly here, but it is discussed in detail in Gerber's *John Carlisle Kilgo* in the chapter called "A Test of Academic Freedom"; Josephus Daniels's side is given in *Editor in Politics* in the chapter "I Am Hung in Effigy."

John Spencer Bassett, the professor around whom the controversy raged, was a native of North Carolina, a graduate of Trinity who had returned to Trinity after receiving his doctorate at the Johns Hopkins University. He came to be recognized as probably the most distinguished historian North Carolina had produced. In 1902 he founded and became the first editor of the *South Atlantic Quarterly*, a literary journal of some distinction, which published contributions by President Kilgo, Dean Few, and other members of the Trinity faculty as well as by those not connected with the College.

In the issue for October, 1903, Bassett published an article written by himself called "Stirring up the Fires of Race Antipathy." It was intended as a dispassionate discussion of some aspects of the race problem in the South. Bassett inquired into the reasons for the growing antipathy toward the Negro race evident in many pieces of restrictive legislation, and he deplored the fact that the Negro issue had been seized on by the

[37]

politicians. He predicted that the Negro race would continue its struggle toward equality, and he hoped that any conflict between the races would be confined to the political sphere; in any case, a spirit of conciliation on the part of the whites and wise leadership on the part of the Negroes was desirable. In the course of his remarks Bassett pointed out that Booker T. Washington, the Negro leader and educator from Tuskegee, was not a fair example of what the Negro race might become; he was "an exceptional man," so much so that "we cannot in reason look for his reproduction in the present generation." He used this sentence: "Now Washington is a great and good man, a Christian statesman, and take him all in all the greatest man, save General Lee, born in the South in a hundred years; but he is not a typical negro." This sentence in particular— inserted while reading the proof, probably as the result of a race incident at Hamlet, North Carolina—as well as the entire article in general was seized upon by Josephus Daniels and the *News and Observer* and subsequently by almost all the press of the state in a violent denunciation of Bassett, Kilgo, the Dukes, Trinity College, and those who would send their sons to that institution. Such an article would scarcely cause the lifting of an eyebrow today. In a subsequent interview Bassett explained that he "had no thought of social equality" between the races, and the word "greatest" as used with reference to Booker T. Washington "had been given a mean- ing which I did not have in my mind. I had only reference to one's capacity to break over fearful impediments and achieve success." But the explanation was not accepted; the scent had been whiffed, and the hue and cry was on.

There is neither the space nor the inclination to give here more than a sample of the vituperation hurled against Bassett. Daniels inquired: "Does he pray with his face turned toward Tuskegee?" Further he said that if the "ideas in the Bassett article become widespread, then the civilization of the South is destroyed. He has committed the only unpardonable sin."

Other papers said that there could be no doubt that Bassett was crazy, that he had a "measly mind," that he was a "spectacular viper," that he had more mouth than brains, that he had "a streak of black blood down his back," and that he should be given a chair in a Negro educational institution. It was made to appear that Kilgo and the Dukes were responsible for Bassett's utterances. Thus the attack was broadened, and the opportunity was taken to get at Trinity through Bassett. *Webster's Weekly*, Kilgo's perpetual and bitter critic, said "that Duke's money has made it possible for Trinity's teacher of history to fling defiance in the face of Southern ideals and call on the young men of the South to forsake the faith of their fathers and worship at the shrine of a negro." Another paper said: "But since Trinity has been tobacconized, Kilgoized and republicanized with a Duke for a ruler we can probably look on the jabberings of this idiot with less contempt. He is the product of the theory of his own institution." Trinity was called the Chicago University of North Carolina, "a nursery of freaks." Daniels, with his characteristic self-assurance, asserted that "Kilgo has made blunder after blunder, denounced good man after good man, exhibited a spirit of venom and proscription . . . spit upon this tradition and shown contempt for that sentiment dear to the hearts of old-fashioned Methodists." The real enemies of Trinity, he said, were the men in the faculty "who write and speak things that are false, absurd, fantastic, egoistical, malicious—give utterance to the sentiments that shock the best sentiments of the state"—and thus the students and Trustees, patrons and preachers, "from a false conception of loyalty," uphold a wrong cause. "The friend of Trinity College is he who would apply the remedy necessary, not failing to use the knife. A surgical operation separating Dr. Kilgo and Dr. Bassett from all connection with the institution will save it to the state and to the Church. This paper," he felt it necessary to remind his readers, "has always been the friend of Trinity College." Daniels's attitude in the

Bassett case may help to explain why his paper came to be referred to as "the official organ of the unrelated prejudices of North Carolina."

Aside from the Durham newspapers and the *Biblical Recorder*, edited by Josiah W. Bailey, only the *Progressive Farmer*, edited by Clarence Poe, the Charlotte *Daily Observer*, and the *Caucasian*, a Republican newspaper, adopted a sympathetic attitude, and they as well as the two Methodist papers were inclined to deplore Bassett's ideas though defending his right to hold them.

The upshot of the matter was that Bassett offered to resign if the Trustees requested it. Neither the public nor all the Trustees were quick to see the real issue of freedom of speech and of academic freedom. As Walter Hines Page, a former Trinity student and rising star in the world of journalism, put it in a letter to B. N. Duke, the correctness of Bassett's opinion was "a question of no importance. But it is of the highest importance that a professor from Trinity College should be allowed to hold and to express any rational opinion he may have about any subject whatever. . . . We need many things; but first of all we must have absolute freedom of thought and expression." Later he wrote:

When we win this fight, you may forever afterwards be sure that *Trinity College will be free*—and *everybody will know that it is free*. Liberal people all over the United States will rejoice and congratulate the college. Every really great & free institution in the whole country will rejoice; and Trinity will stand higher than it could be made to stand by many years of good quiet work. It is a *great* chance—a chance to show the whole world that there is at least one institution in the South & in North Carolina that is free. It will be the best thing that could happen for the State and for the South.

Former President Crowell, Bishop Warren A. Candler, alumni of Trinity College, and others wrote in a like vein.

When the vituperation was at its worst, J. B. Duke reportedly said to Kilgo: "This man Bassett maybe has played the fool and oughtn't to be on the faculty, but he must not be lynched [fired]. There are more ways of lynching a man than by tying a hempen rope around his neck and throwing it over the limb of a tree. Public opinion can lynch a man, and that is what North Carolina is trying to do to Bassett now. Don't allow it. You'll never get over it if you do." But it was uncertain what the Board of Trustees would do; it was known to be divided; and public feeling was running high. When the Trustees met, December 1, 1903, Kilgo appeared before them with a long and eloquent plea on behalf of academic freedom. Unknown to the Trustees, Kilgo had prepared his letter of resignation to be presented in case of an adverse decision by the Trustees; he had individual sealed envelopes containing the resignation of each member of the faculty in case Bassett were asked to resign; he had also a document "signed in the order of official seniority by every member of the faculty, except one, who is & for several days has been out of town." Dean Few's name stood midway in the list of twelve names. Two sentences of the document read:

We are willing to risk our future standing for the great principle of free speech and to accept all the consequences of this choice. For we believe that our chance to build up here eventually a great institution among the colleges of the world will be far better if we stand for truth and freedom than if we silently consent to yield our minds to any sort of intellectual bondage.

Oddly enough, just at this time, when Kilgo was bringing all his eloquence and the faculty all its *esprit de corps* to bear in behalf of academic freedom, Josephus Daniels was writing to Kilgo's old enemy, Judge Walter Clark: "I want to write an editorial for Sunday's paper showing Kilgo's policy for suppressing free speech and trying to drive out and ruin men who express opinions hostile to his position or criticize him. I would be glad if you would write me down every instance of his proscriptive policy that you can recall and greatly oblige."

[41]

As it turned out, however, neither Kilgo's resignation nor those of the faculty were presented. A committee of the Trustees to whom Bassett's letter was referred, after a full discussion before the Board, retired from the room. In some fifteen minutes the committee returned with its report, which was finally adopted. Bassett's offer of resignation was declined, and the principle of academic freedom was asserted. The statement on academic freedom presented by the Trustees' committee had been prepared not by the committee, but by Dean Few with the assistance of his friend William Garrott Brown, who happened to be his guest at the time. The following is the statement in full:

We, the Board of Trustees of Trinity College, duly conscious of the charge committed to us, and moved by a single desire to promote those high and beneficent purposes which the College is set to cherish, have at all times exercised our best care in the tasks belonging to our office. We have had before us the offer of Dr. John S. Bassett to resign his professorship of History, and it is made clear to us that it was not presented out of a voluntary decision to sever his connection with the College, but that it was tendered under coercive influences from the outside, and because of a feeling that his further connection with the College might bring injury to it. Candor impels us to admit our regret that Professor Bassett has expressed certain opinions which give offense to many, and we are glad to find that these opinions were expressed solely on his own authority, through a medium which is in no sense an organ of the College, and not at all in his capacity as a college official, so that neither this Board nor the College can be held in any way to have approved or countenanced them, or to be in any degree responsible for them.

On the contrary, it clearly appears that the faculty and the students disagree with certain of Professor Bassett's opinions—so far as we can ascertain, unanimously. Neither do we agree with them. Nevertheless, both faculty and students, with equal unanimity, have manifested their desire that this Board decline to accept Professor Bassett's offer of his resignation, and for the following reasons, which seem to us high and vital, we do decline to accept it.

1. Any form of coercion of thought and private judgment is contrary to one of the constitutional aims of Trinity College, which is "to cherish a sincere spirit of tolerance." We prefer to exemplify this virtue rather than hastily set it aside and thus do violence to a principle greatly esteemed by all men of noble feeling.

2. We are particularly unwilling to lend ourselves to any tendency to destroy or limit academic liberty, a tendency which has, within recent years, manifested itself in some conspicuous instances, and which has created a feeling of uneasiness for the welfare of American Colleges. Whatever encourages such a tendency endangers the growth of higher education by intimidating intellectual activity and causing high-minded men to look with suspicion upon this noble profession. We cannot lend countenance to the degrading notion that professors in American Colleges have not an equal liberty of thought and speech with all Americans.

3. We believe that society in the end will find a surer benefit by exercising patience than it can secure by yielding to its resentments. The search for truth should be unhampered and in an atmosphere that is free. Liberty may sometimes lead to folly; yet it is better that some should be tolerated than that all should think and speak under the deadening influence of repression. A reasonable freedom of opinion is to a college the very breath of life; and any official throttling of the private judgment of its teachers would destroy their influence, and place upon the college an enduring stigma. For it is not the business of college professors to provide their students with opinions. American college students would generally resent such dictation if it were attempted. It is the business of colleges rather to provide for young men the material, the knowledge, and the training which will enable them to form and defend their own opinions. Neither, on the other hand, is it the business of governing boards like ours to prescribe opinions for professors. The same broad principle holds both in the college and the state. While it is idle to deny that the free expression of wrong opinions sometimes works harm, our country and our race stand for the view that the evils of intolerance and suppression are infinitely worse than those of folly.

4. The matter which has engaged our attention is of more than local interest and will be far-reaching in its results. It is hard to commend even the slightest measure of coercion or suppression

of opinion to the people of this country. But we are particularly regardful of the reputation of the commonwealth from which Trinity College received its academic privileges. We are jealous of its good name, and mindful of its historical struggles and sacrifices in the cause of free speech and freedom of conscience. To subject any citizen of North Carolina to any form of coercion or persecution for his opinion's sake would be to misrepresent the state, to foster a suspicion of its tolerant spirit, to set our people in a false light before the world. Rights which were bought with blood and suffering must not now be endangered for want of patience, tolerance, and a noble self-restraint. Nor would we do anything which may seem to imply that the social order of our Southern states in general needs to be defended from criticism with any weapons but reason and the truth.

5. Trinity College is affiliated with a great church whose spirit and doctrines are tolerant and generous, and a due regard for the teachings and traditions of this Christian society requires us to exercise our judgment in harmony with its spirit and doctrines.

Viewing the matter in the light of these wider interests, and finding that there is no complaint against Professor Bassett's moral character, his scholarly fitness, his energy, his competency as a teacher, or his command of the confidence of his classes, we are sure that duty requires us to decline the offer of his resignation. Great as is our hope in this college, high and noble as are the services which under God we believe that it is fit to render, it were better that Trinity should suffer than that it should enter upon a policy of coercion and intolerance.

It was not generally known that Dean Few was the principal author of this statement; he seems to have been singularly free from the criticism directed at Kilgo and others during this episode. But he must have taken some pride in his part in this affair; though the public was not aware that he figured in it, he sent Wallace Buttrick, Secretary of the General Education Board, a copy of the Charlotte *Observer* in which the proceedings of the Trustees were reported. Buttrick, thanking him, said, "You very well know how heartily we are rejoicing over the great victory for freedom of academic thought which you have achieved at Trinity College." Such a statement from such a source probably did a good deal to ease the sting of public criticisms. The liberal tradition as evidenced in the Bassett case had the complete sympathy of the Dukes. Few wrote in "An Expression from the Faculty" on the death of Washington Duke in 1905, "He never hampered us with a small idea or a personal wish or preference. His voice was always for the true and the right, and always against the narrow, the bitter, the sectional, the partisan. . . ."

Eventually Bassett resigned to accept a chair at Smith College, but he retained a warm feeling for Trinity and for Few and his other associates. The *Chronicle* printed an interview with Bassett at the time of his departure in which he stated that "Trinity feels its debt to the great spirit of progress in the South more than any other institution which I know of in the South. . . ." He went on to say that Trinity's mission was "to lead in the process which keeps thought in the South cosmopolitan." Dean Few was elected by the faculty to succeed Bassett as manager of the Library. Some years later Few was to assist Bassett in gathering material for an article on William Garrott Brown, published in the *South Atlantic Quarterly*, of which Few was then one of the editors.

The *News and Observer* reported the decision of the Trustees on academic freedom with headlines which read in part: "Dr. Kilgo Loosed Vitriolic Floods upon the Press of the State and upon The News and Observer in Particular. Begun Reading Headlines from the Latter and These Aroused the Only Unanimous Applause of the Trustees." Daniels never seemed to grasp the real significance of the Bassett case with respect to academic freedom; when writing his memoirs a generation later, he had nothing to retract; there was nothing to justify Bassett in "opposing the majority opinion in North Carolina." He made two concessions, however: that those who opposed Bassett's article "were more intemperate in denunciation of it, because of the surrounding conditions, than we would have been at any other time"; and that Bassett, after he got "away from the pro-trust environment and anti-Jefferson policy then permeating Trinity and approved by the Dukes, . . . developed into an able teacher of history and sound economics, such as Jefferson and Jackson and Wilson incarnated." Few, on his part, always held to the opinion that majorities could be wrong, an idea he was wont to express in the phrase "the gusts of unwisdom that inevitably arise from time to time in all democracies." His connection with the Bassett episode illustrates his readiness to take a firm stand for what he thought right and also his care not to be involved in personal controversy. He would not yield on principle, but he never made an issue on a matter of personal prerogative, nor was he apt to rush into a quarrel not his own. He seldom made pronouncements outside his own sphere.

XII

Few was entirely happy in his work at Trinity, and his relations with Kilgo were warm and close. Though their backgrounds were similar, in personality and characteristics they were almost diametrically opposite, and it is likely that they complemented each other to an unusual degree in their joint educational endeavors. They were alike in their thoughts about Christian education and the necessity for moral training, and they were in agreement on the Trinity ideals and the program for the future. But where Kilgo was dynamic and aggressive, not to say pugnacious on occasion, Few was quiet, soft-spoken, scholarly, a man of the study. Kilgo was essentially a preacher, eloquent, moving, and on fire for the Lord; Few was essentially a teacher, never used the rhetoric of eloquence, and perhaps lacked the power to make a purely emotional appeal. Kilgo as he grew older became more conservative in his religious outlook, turned more to the faith of his fathers, developed a passion for creed that amounted to partisanship; Few was essentially a mystic, touched by the Quakerism of his ancestors, with a clear faith in God as revealed in the heart of man—not a matter of creed or outer manifestation, only of the inner soul in touch with the infinite. Kilgo was at his best before the multitude, Few was the wise man of the inner councils; Kilgo was inspirational in his approach, Few quiet and retiring to a fault. Kilgo was unconsciously an egotist, Few not even conspicuous in his modesty. Kilgo was inclined to be elemental and direct; Few was a more complicated individual, in many ways very articulate and yet seldom able to give full expression to his genuine love for people. His emotions and feelings were fine and strong, and the tender side of his nature was a powerful, though sometimes concealed, influence. There was about him something of the tenderness and intuitive quality of a woman. Few had a reverence and respect for Kilgo, perhaps even a dependence upon him; events were to prove that Kilgo and the Dukes had a faith in and fondness for the young Dean.

In the summer of 1908 Dean Few in company with Professors C. W. Edwards, W. F. Gill, and W. H. Glasson made a trip to Europe, landing in Scotland and spending most of the time in England and France. Few was evidently reluctant to leave Kilgo and Trinity, for he wrote to "My Dear Mr. President":

I am leaving today for New York, where on Saturday I take passage for Europe. Stress of circumstances has prevented my giving thought to this matter. If out of your experience you feel like offering any advice to me dictate it & send it to the care of Harvard Club, 271 W. 44th St., New York. I will send you a European address from New York & I hope you will be good enough to send me a word occasionally.

You at least will believe that I dread the trip immensely. I had far rather stay here with my people or help your work in North Carolina, but I must go through with it.

I am sending to Flowers today the rest of my grades & also the letter to the papers on the athletic situation. I wish I might have sent both earlier; but for once I believe I can say I have done my best. Please read the paper and make any changes that may be needed. I wrote it in great haste & I am sure it needs doctoring. . . .

Following the summer in Europe, which he probably enjoyed more than he anticipated, for he spent some time in the Shakespeare country, he resumed his academic life at Trinity. That winter the *Chronicle* reported the Lincoln anniversary meeting of the Trinity College Historical Society where Few read an appreciative and able paper on "Lincoln's Personality and Style," which is printed in this volume. In September, 1909, at the beginning of school, Dean Few spoke in the Y.M.C.A. Hall to "quite a large crowd of students, both old and new men." That fall he became one of the editors of the *South Atlantic Quarterly* along with W. H. Glasson, Professor of Economics. He remained an editor of the *Quarterly* until 1919, although he was less active in its general management than was Professor Glasson.

XIII

As previously mentioned, in 1902 there had been some talk that Kilgo would be elected Bishop, and there was some uneasiness among the Trustees. By 1906, however, there was not only confident expectation that Kilgo would be elected, there was also an acceptance of the situation on the part of the Trustees. Benjamin N. Duke wrote to former Governor Thomas J. Jarvis:

I note with pleasure that you are a delegate to the General Conference . . . , and am glad that you will do what you can to make Dr. Kilgo a bishop. I agree with you that his election would be a blow to Trinity College, but we could not let that stand in the way of his promotion. . . . I trust that you will leave no stone unturned to bring about his election.

Again Kilgo failed of election, largely as a result of the organized opposition of his North Carolina enemies, who distributed anonymous "literature" which contained elaborate, if not pungent, discussions of "Kilgo's use of tobacco, his relationship to the trusts, and his legal difficulties in North Carolina." Nevertheless, his friends looked forward to the next General Conference, which was to be held in Asheville.

On December 9, 1909, Benjamin N. Duke wrote to Kilgo: "I trust that Conference will have enough sensible men in it to do the right thing when the election of the Bishops takes place." All of which suggests that no great uneasiness would be felt if the office of the President of Trinity College became vacant, and that a successor was available.

As a matter of fact, Wallace Buttrick, of the General Education Board, had written Few in the spring of 1909 that he, Buttrick, had mentioned his name "in connection with the presidency of a University in Iowa." Few, in reply, frankly disavowed any interest in the place and stated: "I believe that circumstances have conspired to give Trinity College an opportunity rare among men to do a piece of constructive and lasting work in moulding the life of a whole people. I should therefore not be willing to consider leaving here unless it were under most extraordinary circumstances. . . ." The *Chronicle* reported in March, 1910, that Kilgo had talked in Chapel on what it takes to make a good college president. He was reported to have said that it takes men and money to make a college, and that a president must be a good beggar. Money should be used, as at Trinity, in the spirit of helping a student, "but not to make him a bulletin board for the advertising of the charities of the institution."

Kilgo was consecrated a Bishop in May, 1910, and when the Trustees met in June he presented his resignation as President. There is no official evidence that he suggested Few as his successor, but there is no doubt that Few had his support as well as the complete approval of Benjamin N. Duke. Duke was not present at the Trustees' meeting, but on June 6, 1910, Few was elected President. On July 1, the day Kilgo's connection ceased, Few wrote to D. W. Newsom, Treasurer of the College and Secretary to the Board of Trustees, that he regretted his "enforced and extended absence," but that he accepted the position with its "great and arduous responsibilities. I shall do my level best to make the College serve in all possible ways the causes of men."

A few days after Few's election one of the Trustees wrote to Kilgo that he was pleased with the way the Trustees disposed of the matter:

I went to Durham with a feeling that I would vote for Dr. Few with reluctance. When I ascertained that the Dukes favored Mr. Few, and when I understood that you favored Mr. Few, my attitude toward him changed. You very successfully and wisely touched upon the importance of the Trustees paying some special attention to what Mr. Ben Duke wanted and what he did not want, and what he approved of and what he did not approve of. The wisdom of this suggestion of yours, [*sic*] to the Trustees was subsequently demonstrated. Dr. Few has only one weakness as I see it. He is not a popular orator. It is, however, like you say, he is a genius in every other respect.

He added that he would like to have an orator, such as Plato Durham, connected with the College. Perhaps Bishop Kilgo was especially appreciative of the further comment: "The fact that you are to remain in Durham is a source of great satisfaction to me. You[r] remaining there will in a great measure, [*sic*] eliminate the objecton to Dr. Few as a public speaker."

The *Chronicle* in its next issue after Few's election had a comment on the new President:

It has been frequently rumored that Few would be made President, which was only an indication of his fitness for the position. While the Trustees were holding forth Monday night until past midnight, a crowd of students were gathered in the halls to see what would be the results of the meeting, and it was with a feeling of joy that the news of the election of Dr. Few was received . . . . sure that Trinity College will continue to make rapid strides under his wise guidance and it will not be many more years until she will be really and truly the "Harvard of the South."

Buttrick wrote Few: "We are all rejoicing that you have been chosen to the Presidency of Trinity College."

[50]

Few's first talk to the students as President at the opening of the fall term dealt with a closer relationship between faculty and students. This was always a matter of concern to him. Few had the keenest interest in the individual student, and he had a natural tendency to rate the heart of a man above his head; yet there was lacking in him something of the personal magnetism needed to close the gulf between professor and student. Only those who gradually learned to know Few esteemed him at his best. As a matter of fact, Trinity probably had less need for organized student-faculty relations than many another institution, for the size of its student body, the caliber of its faculty, and the serious attitude of most of the students had tended to center their interests on the campus, its people, and its work. Nevertheless, President Few suggested a faculty committee on social organization to keep in touch with each boarding house (the College then having no general dining hall) to see that good food was provided and that a healthy social spirit prevailed; there should be a committee to visit the sick; the daily inspection of all dormitories was proposed; and the students were cautioned against extravagance.

A year later, when thanking Benjamin N. Duke for his gift of $10,000 to be applied to Road and Campus improvements and his offer of an additional $5,000 if needed, President Few expressed what was probably his constant attitude toward his new job: "I am beginning a new chapter in my career, and I am going to take a new lease on life. I am very glad to have a place where, under fortunate circumstances, I can engage in useful work."

XIV

President Few's inauguration, November 9, 1910, was a much more elaborate affair than Trinity College was accustomed to seeing. The town joined with the College in providing entertainment. The mayor issued a proclamation, and a special train was operated between Durham and Greensboro for the convenience of delegates and guests. Among the more than three hundred delegates and special guests were the presidents of the University of Chicago, Harvard University, Vanderbilt University, and Tulane University. The West Duke Building, which was almost completed, was presented to the College on behalf of the donor, Benjamin N. Duke, and after the inaugural an elaborate luncheon, provided by a caterer from Washington, was held in the building. Mrs. James E. Stagg, the granddaughter of Washington Duke, gave a similar luncheon at her home, Greystone, for the wives of delegates and other guests. That evening a reception was held at the home of Mr. and Mrs. B. N. Duke, the present University House.

The inaugural itself took place in Craven Memorial Hall. The President's address, which was characterized by Elmer E. Brown, United States Commissioner of Education, as one of "extraordinary frankness and insight," was on Few's "conception of the college in southern development." He suggested no radical break with the past. On the contrary, he found that "the way has been marked out by my predecessor and that the College has only to go on to the completion of the tasks it has already set before itself." It was a call for liberal education, Christian education, with emphasis upon "self-cultivation and wholesome living," the development of the whole man rather than the specialist. The Southern college must be "given a free hand" if it was to be "a leader for conservative progress" and able to disregard "the voices of political expedience and pliant opportunism." He felt that colleges in the South must be capable of "resisting the imposition upon them from outside of ideas that would hurt them," that would unfit them "for doing the very service to which they seem by circumstances to be ordained." And there should be no "temptation to strive for bigness." "The greatness of a college," he always thought, "depends not upon the size of its plant or the number of its students, but upon the quality of the men who teach and the quality of the men who learn, upon its ideals and its influence." At Trinity, he concluded, "we are immensely concerned that it shall be a shining place where high-minded youth may catch aspirations to true character and genuine excellence, and whence into this vast experiment in democratic government that is being tried out on the American continent, there shall go a long succession of men who have been trained to think straight and to think through to right conclusions, and who have been made strong by the power to know the truth and the will to live it."

President Lowell of Harvard remarked at the luncheon that a good deal had been said during the morning by way of congratulations to Few, "but after hearing his inaugural address any man would have felt like congratulating the College." "It was," said Dean Frederick S. Jones of Yale, "the address of an idealist." Thus was begun the administration of William Preston Few as President of Trinity College, and Duke University, a service of almost thirty years, nearly equally divided between Trinity and Duke. One is reminded of the prediction of President E. B. Craighead of Tulane when he said at the inauguration: "As President Few is still a young man, we may reasonably expect the reign of Few to continue some twenty-five or thirty years at least."

xv

President Few was in fact a young man, only forty-two, and still clean shaven except for a moderately heavy mustache. In later years he grew a beard, which he kept neatly trimmed but which served to give a little more fullness to the face; it helped to make him a man of distinguished appearance. He was six feet tall lacking nearly one inch, and gave an impression of spareness, a certain gauntness, which made the term "Lincolnesque" appropriate. His eyes were brown, rather large, luminous, capable of a kindly twinkle, and yet not without a degree of sharpness on occasion. His dark brown hair, which he retained all his life, was luxuriant and very fine, and in later years it was tinged with gray. His complexion was slightly ruddy. He dressed simply and was without sartorial distinction. Once when he was in New York, and perhaps looking somewhat more than well traveled, a friend sent him to a tailor where he was measured, and thereafter he received two suits each year until the donor's death.

He was never an orator, and he had no voice for singing. He was a remarkably modest man and so seemed shy and diffident at times; an orator, he may have thought, attracted attention to himself rather than to the content of his thought, and this Few wished to avoid. He spoke with few gestures and no dramatics, no crescendo—only an even and thoughtfully phrased expression of his ideas, sometimes spoken so softly as to be barely audible. One wonders if he was ever completely at ease on the platform. He had to do a good deal of public speaking, and most of it he probably did not enjoy, yet it is remembered how in his short informal talks to college students he was very impressive and could bring them to an absorbing interest in what he said. If he lacked the power of a vibrant personality, he possessed a quiet charm which was especially effective in small gatherings, and he was always listened to with respect. He had a certain air of kindliness, of benevolence, which was as genuine as his quiet and pleasant voice. In short, he looked like what he was: a college president, shy, earnest, devoted to the causes of education and the church and anxious to do great good and little harm. He was a scholar; yet, all in all, he was a man of sound judgment, especially when viewing large matters of policy rather than the petty details of routine administration. He was a student by preference, a scholar by training, and an administrator only by force of circumstances. His abilities as an administrator were acquired rather than native.

XVI

In the summer of 1911 President Few journeyed to Martins-
ville, Virginia, accompanied by former President Kilgo and
Professor R. L. Flowers, and was there married to Miss Mary
Reamey Thomas. Bishop Kilgo performed the ceremony, and
Flowers served as best man. The bride was a strikingly handsome woman with a charm and personality all her own. She
was a graduate of Trinity, class of 1906, and as a student had
had an English course with Dean Few. Their friendship had
come about through a common acquaintance with the Dukes.
Miss Thomas's interest in literature was so stimulated that
she decided to continue her studies in English at Columbia
University after her graduation from Trinity. It so happened
that when Dean Few went abroad in the summer of 1908
Miss Thomas was on the same boat. There was nothing pre-
arranged about this, but old acquaintance was renewed with
the ultimate result mentioned above. It was a happy marriage.
President Few was a devoted family man. His sense of family
unity was strong, and he was devoted to his parents and to his
brothers and sisters. When his sister Sallie married while he
was away at Harvard, he wrote from Cambridge of his disap-
pointment that he could not be present, adding, "I know that
your duty is no longer first to us, but I hope that we may all
cling together as parents & children and brothers & sisters,
with as little interruption as varying interests & pursuits will
allow. Whatever may come to pass, see to it that yours is a
bright, happy home full of sunshine & smiles. . . ."

Five children, all sons, were born to the Fews: William,
Lyne Starling, Kendrick Sheffield, Randolph Reamey, and
Yancey Preston. Preston, the youngest, while still a child developed a serious physical illness, but his father said that he
had one of the clearest minds he ever knew. Theirs was a tender
and intimate relationship until young Preston died at the age of
sixteen, March 23, 1939. This was a great tragedy in President
Few's life. Once he wrote to his younger sister, Ellie, in April,

1936, to tell her that Preston was not well: "In fact we have practically no hope that he will ever be well & hardly a fifty-fifty chance to raise him. You can realize that for me this is a vast & abysmal sorrow. So staggering that it has required a long time for me to take it in. But I will meet it as I've met every other ordeal in my life with courage and patience. I give him all my spare time & expect to do this as long as I live. . . ." A year after Preston's death his bereaved father wrote, March 23, 1940: "Poor little Pres died a year ago today. I realize that he is better off as it is, but even this does not lessen my sense of loneliness and loss. He was so highly gifted, so noble, yet so hard beset by life! How can I ever get away from the poignancy of such memories. But tomorrow is Easter & we must look away from the past to the future."

Few as a father was not a disciplinarian, but he possessed a sympathy and understanding that enabled him to work indirectly toward the same ends. Something of his thoughtfulness for his sons' pleasure and welfare is illustrated by this letter to his sister Ellie, with a message for his brother Pierce, January 30, 1923: "Tell Pierce that I unfortunately told my boys that a dog was coming to them from Red Top. They, especially Kendrick, are on their heads about it. If perchance James did not want to part with the dog let me know at once so that I can check the great expectations of my boys; & if the dog is to come ask them to send it on as soon as convenient." Once he wrote to B. N. Duke: "My father and mother have never seen any of my little boys. Either the one or the other of them has been too young for travelling. I am laying my plans to carry them all over to South Carolina. . . ."

In December, 1921, he wrote his mother that they were planning a visit: "Mary & I with the three older boys are coming over for a visit just as soon as the winter weather begins to break. I wish so much that we could be there now.

We've tried to get to you all some little Christmas tokens; &
more than that we love you devotedly & are thinking of you.
Heaven's richest blessings on you now & always." His parents
enjoyed a ripe old age. In acknowledging a note of sympathy from Mr. and Mrs. B. N. Duke on the occasion of his
mother's death, Few wrote: "My mother was eighty-three.
She and my father would have been married sixty years if she
had lived until next April. He is ninety-three and is standing
up as well as could be expected under his extreme age and be-
reavement." The mother died in 1922; the father early the
next year.

Few's close association with his own children probably increased his sympathy for the students and their problems. As
he grew older he seemed to relish more his association with the
students, and he grew immensely in their esteem. At intervals
he was invited to dine with some of the students of the Woman's College, and they seemed delighted with his talk, which
was rich with literary allusions and beautifully phrased, and
yet informal and touched with humor. In 1939 he wrote for
the Wofford *Journal:* "I have lived intimately with students
since I was sixteen years of age. It has been one of the great
privileges of my life."

XVII

Perhaps Few was wise in casting his lot with Trinity; but
he needed also to be patient, for he was to spend sixteen years
as Professor and Dean and fourteen as President before the
creation of the Duke Endowment, an event that he considered
rather as a new beginning than as an end. It was a small college, to paraphrase Webster, but there were those who loved
it. It was also a good college. In his first report to the Trustees
President Few said that attendance during the year had reached
a total of 363 students, not including 182 in Trinity Park
School (the preparatory school which had been started in
1898) and 71 in the extension courses in secondary education.
Trinity had a good reputation in important places. Only a year

before Few's election the President of the Carnegie Foundation for the Advancement of Teaching had written to Kilgo: "You are one of the few college presidents of this country who are attempting to graduate each year an individualized group of men rather than a group which is merely more educated than when it came to you." And the General Education Board of the Rockefeller Foundation was to give continuing evidences of its faith in Trinity.

If Few was fortunate in his college, he was also fortunate in his associates. He had a small but strong faculty, now thirty-two in number instead of ten as in 1896 (although not yet as large as the Board of Trustees), and William I. Cranford, Professor of Philosophy, had succeeded Few as dean. The Chairman of the Board of Trustees was quoted as saying that Cranford had "more common sense than all the rest of the faculty combined," a remark intended as a tribute to Cranford rather than as a reflection on the faculty. Robert L. Flowers, Professor of Mathematics and "Secretary to the Corporation," was one of the two professors who had transferred from Old Trinity in Randolph County when the College was moved to Durham. In the "absence of the President" he was "responsible for the business administration of the College." "Bobby," as he was affectionately called, was three years younger than Few, a graduate of the United States Naval Academy and a man of warm human qualities which made him invaluable in difficult situations with either students or faculty. There was also on the campus as Professor of German a young man whom Few had known at Wofford and brought to Trinity as an assistant in English, William H. Wannamaker. He later transferred to German, studied at Harvard and in Germany, and in 1917 became Dean of the College. Last but not least there was Bishop Kilgo. The announcement at the 1910 Commencement that he would remain in touch with the College as Trustee and resident on the campus was greeted with a "burst of applause."

Few, Flowers, and Wannamaker were the triumvirate, providing each for the other a sort of system of checks and balances and finding each in his own sphere a way to make his own unique contribution. There was a workable harmony among these three, perhaps a striking fact when it is remembered that men of positive character and high devotion can scarcely fail to differ at times in their plans to build and strengthen the institution they love. Theirs was a jealousy of devotion, a rivalry in good works, never a struggle for power. President Few never had reason to doubt that he was head of the institution. He was by nature cautious, even slow, in forming judgments and, perhaps for that reason, careful to consult with advisers, but he had a lively sense of his own prerogative despite his quiet and unassuming ways. He was appreciative of the work of his colaborers. When Wannamaker was made Dean, Few wrote to B. N. Duke: "Wannamaker is a veritable wheel horse, and that part of our organization will move, I doubt not, under his administration." On the occasion of the celebration of Few's twenty-fifth year as President he said: "With me was also inaugurated, and at my request, Robert L. Flowers. We have lived together, worked together, planned together, thought together. So far as I know, there has been no slip between us in all these nearly forty years."

XVIII

President Few found himself to be a busy man. His last secretary remembered him as one who kept regular office hours, appearing promptly at nine o'clock; usually he had a heavy load of correspondence. He did a great deal of work in his office, and he seems to have been efficient in keeping up his work. Kilgo was reported to have intimated that he was a little too fond of his office rocking chair. Nevertheless, he had a fine reputation for doing his share of the work in educational organizations and committees and as a lay leader in the church. More than once he remarked that "this" had been the busiest year of his life.

His job was undoubtedly a strain on him physically, for he was never robust, and there were periods when he was under orders to spend very little time in the office. His greatest handicap in life was his health. He had been frail as a child, and a severe case of measles had left his eyes impaired. His eye trouble at Harvard was diagnosed as optic neuritis. His vision was 15/15; there was no astigmatism. He was afflicted with headaches until he was sixty. At the age of fifteen he had typhoid; a little later he was bothered by inflammatory rheumatism in one knee. He slept fairly well but was somewhat affected by worries and went to bed early to get the necessary sleep. A medical examiner reported in 1919 that his occupation was "without special bearing except that a heavy burden of strain" seemed to be carried. This must have been near his low point, for his weight was down to 120 pounds. It was remarked in 1930 that he "never takes a vacation." Some of his nervousness was probably due to an irritable skin, which itched spasmodically. He spent the summer of 1920 in a Baltimore hospital. In the autumn he reported that he had gained twenty pounds in weight and felt encouraged, though he was not living up to the orders to spend only one hour a day in his office. Not long afterwards he was writing Ben Duke that he was just recovering from the "flu." Once Duke sent him a bottle of medicine, contents not specified, and Few reported, "I thank you for the bottle of medicine which came yesterday morning. I began taking it at lunch yesterday." After the summer in Baltimore he wrote to his doctor: "The year following . . . . from a health standpoint was the most disastrous in my experience, culminating last March in double pneumonia which held me long and was followed by a long and tedious recuperation. . . ." It was probably during this illness that his family doctor and others called in for consultation despaired of his life, and when his doctor started to tell him that the end was near he is reliably reported to have said: "That won't work—you haven't done all you could do, and I haven't done all I could—let's get together on this." In a few days he was up. His health improved considerably in the late twenties, possibly due to a tonsillectomy, and it may be that his health in the last ten years was his best ever.

XIX

For the President there were a thousand problems, and no sooner was one disposed of than two more would rise to take its place. There was the matter of public relations, for example. Few, never forgetful of the power of public opinion, was much more fortunate in this respect than his predecessor. To a considerable extent he kept himself out of the public eye; with respect to the College, he was extremely modest. Understatement was his forte. He never liked to parade numbers or mere size. He wrote in 1915 to the editor of the *Christian Advocate:*

. . . college opens tomorrow morning. We are in better shape for the opening than I have ever known the College. . . . In due time we will give you a statement. . . . I hope, however, you will do all you can to discourage the undue interest on the part of our people in mere size and numbers. This emphasis is unwise and unchristian. We are going to have at least as many as we had last year and last year we had the largest attendance we have ever had . . . . we are in a position to resist strongly the craze for numbers and the pagan doctrine of mere bigness.

A few days later he wrote the editor:

If you care to you can say concerning the opening at Trinity, without quoting me of course, that according to authoritative information the enrollment this year in the College proper will reach five hundred and fifty as against five hundred and twelve last year. The numbers in the Trinity Park School and in the Department of Education will run the grand total beyond the eight hundred and twenty-six high water mark of last year.

You know my bias against parading numbers and size but perhaps as much information as is indicated above will be demanded by your reading public.

[61]

All of which is something to think about in this age of high-powered "public relations." But Few appreciated favorable notice of the College in the press. After his first Commencement as President he wrote to thank Josephus Daniels for the coverage given by the *News and Observer*. Mr. Daniels, who had had little praise for the Dukes, Kilgo, and Trinity replied: "I have yours of June 12th and thank you for it. I appreciate it very much. It is rather rare for a newspaper man to receive a note of thanks for any service he renders a public institution and your note is, therefore, all the more appreciated."

Few was a good citizen, lending his support to many worthy causes, but he was never active as a civic leader except in so far as his place at the head of the College made him so. He was not without convictions in political matters, but he avoided active participation in politics, and he never presumed to make political pronouncements. It is a fair guess that he voted for Theodore Roosevelt, Wilson (whose inauguration at Princeton he attended), and the Republican national ticket after 1928. Like many other independent voters in North Carolina, he was a registered Democrat. He did not care for political labels—inadequate always—but perhaps he came nearest to fitting the term "Jeffersonian liberal." He had little faith in what he considered the political and economic vagaries of the New Deal.

He was always active in the work of the Methodist Church and in educational organizations. "A few minutes after I was elected to my position," he said to a group in High Point, "Bishop Kilgo said, 'Your life will largely be in the hands of Methodist preachers and you will find them the noblest in the world.'" And so it was. He was for many years a steward in the Duke Memorial Methodist Church in Durham, and he was a regular attendant at the Sunday morning and evening services, "a twicester," he said. It was alleged by some critics that he became a shrewd ecclesiastical politician. At the time of his death he had been a member of the Educational Commission of the Methodist Church since 1898, a member of the General Sunday School Board since 1914, and he was usually a delegate to the General Conference. In 1938 it was reported that he was absent from the North Carolina Conference for the first time in thirty-nine years. For many years he was personally responsible for the distribution of funds provided by James B. Duke for retired Methodist ministers and their widows and orphans, and he took particular pleasure in forwarding to Mr. Duke the letters of appreciation from the recipients.

The year after his election to the presidency and Lowell's visit to Trinity, he was chosen a member of the Committee of the Board of Overseers of Harvard University to visit the Graduate School of Arts and Sciences, serving with Owen Wister and Henry Cabot Lodge among others. In 1913 he was President of the North Carolina Literary and Historical Association. In 1918 he became a Trustee of the Negro Rural School Fund which was supported by the Anna T. Jeanes Foundation, and the following year he was made a member of the executive committee. He was a delegate to the third annual meeting of the Southern Association of Colleges and Secondary Schools, Knoxville, 1897, and he was a delegate to many subsequent meetings; he was elected president of that organization in 1932, having been nominated from the floor in disregard of the nominating committee as the result of "a popular uprising of appreciation for him." It is an understatement to say that the influence he quietly exercised behind the scenes and in committees of the Southern Association was considerable; his colleagues became increasingly aware of the wisdom of his counsel.

XX

But there was much more for a college president than the mere performance of his public functions. There was much that was trivial, routine, perhaps unpleasant. The matter of disciplining a girl for carving her initials on the dormitory mantel could be a bit embarrassing (there being no dean of women), and it is little wonder that the President chose to write her a letter, to save her, he said, the embarrassment of coming to his office. He was more at home in giving advice to a young man, twenty-three years of age, who had to go to work early in life, but who was now able to raise five or six hundred dollars and wanted an education. The advice was to start to college; it was a "road which may seem long and hard but on which you will have to take only one step at a time. Only try to be sure to take every time the right next step." Then there was the woman whose son wanted to enter Trinity, but she was not sure he was qualified. "He is not up very well on his Latin," she wrote, but he was a member of the Methodist Church, had no bad habits, had been "raised to work on the farm[,] is large, has a strong body and is very fond of playing Base-ball." He was "considered one of the best players. . . . He wants to help pay his way, through college, by playing ball." For a college that had been de-emphasizing athletics since Crowell left, there was little to be done. Few replied, in part:

You will understand, of course, that I shall be glad for Trinity College to be of any possible service to your son. . . . As to his playing baseball, I think that is a good sport for boys. I do not think highly of it as a business, and I hope he will abandon the purpose of engaging in a professional athletics for money. No reputable college in the world pays students for that sort of thing. . . .

To a former student who was coming back, he was more encouraging:

I am sure that you ought, if possible, to complete your college course. I hope that you will not allow yourself to be influenced too much by quick lunch methods in your education. I want you to have a college degree but I particularly desire that you have what that ought to stand for. If you rush yourself too much you will not get out of your college career what it ought to give you.

I am volunteering this advice because I am interested in you and I am anxious for you to do that which in the long run will be best for you.

Then there were the two brothers who got homesick and returned home almost as soon as they had arrived at the College. President Few addressed his "Dear Friends":

Boys who come out of homes in which there is affection and tenderness often suffer in the same way when they go from home for the first time. Homesickness, however, is merely something that one has to fight down. I think that you will probably feel like returning to college after a few days, and the way will be open for you to do so. We shall all welcome you back and do our best to make your stay at the college full of success and happiness for you. I particularly want you to understand that I am interested in you and concerned about your welfare. I feel sure that it would be a mistake for you to stay out for a year unless it were absolutely necessary . . . .

The boys returned.

Always there was the problem of the poor student, and President Few never lost sight of the individual student and his obligations to his parents. For example, in 1915 he wrote a father that he enclosed his son's report:

It will not be satisfactory to you as it is not satisfactory to me. He has not done as well as he should have done. I am going to keep in close touch with him for the rest of the year. I have made some changes in his course of study, and he has a program now that he can follow. Unless he convinces me from time to time that he is doing his best, I will advise you promptly. I hope that you will urge him to all possible diligence and co-operate with us, especially at this time. . . . I do not believe he has any bad habits except the bad habit of wasting his time. . . . If you have any suggestions. . . .

The matter of discipline, which seems not to have been a serious problem, is illustrated by the rather general reply early in his administration to a letter from another educator in which specific questions were raised as to drinking, dancing, card-playing, and the punishments meted out therefor under various circumstances. Few's answer was:

Under the direction of the President the Dean has charge of student discipline. Drinking, card-playing, and dancing are forbidden at this College. We would perhaps hardly expel a man for a first offense, unless it was an aggravated case and he had a bad record in general. But the offender would be seen and given to understand the situation, and his father would be written to. Another offense would usually bring an expulsion. Matters of conduct are not placed before the faculty at all. If a man is brought up for failure to attend properly to his duties, that is a matter for the faculty. If he gets into trouble on account of cutting his recitations, that is in charge of a committee that keeps the records, and on recommendation of this committee the faculty acts in matters of discipline that grow out of non-attendance upon classes.

In all these college questions we have worked out a system of our own. I doubt if it will be of any value to you. Any system must be thus worked out with particular reference to the conditions which it is to deal with.

Few was well known in educational circles and was frequently turned to for advice. Once, in 1913, his kinsman, James E. Dickey, president of Emory College and later Bishop, wrote "Dear Cousin William" that Emory was building a new dormitory and that he would like to know "just what you furnish in each room," and the charge per room. He added, "Any information that you will give me concerning dormitory will be greatly appreciated, as this dormitory business is a new scheme with us." The reply, to "My dear Cousin James," explained:

In our new dormitories we have had for each room a set of drawers made to go inside the closets to use instead of bureaus. A mirror with a shelf under it is put outside near the electric light. The fixture in each room has one electric light that stands up so as to light the room, and a drop light over a table which is placed beneath it. There are two single beds, and chairs, and shades on the windows, and this is all that we furnish. The rent is eighty dollars a year or forty dollars for each occupant, when two men use one room; and sixty-eight dollars a year when the room is occupied by one man.

The quality of the faculty was necessarily a matter of concern, but this related primarily to its teaching ability and scholarship. Private matters remained private matters. This query came to Few in 1914:

Will you . . . . inform me whether all the members of your faculty are required to be members of the Methodist Church, and if not, how many you have who belong to other churches? Do you find your work embarrassed in any way by the presence of one or more members of other churches in your faculty?

The answer was:

It so happens that at the present time every full professor in our College Faculty is a member of the Methodist Church. This has not always been true. Several assistant professors and instructors are members of other churches. A college that has a rather large teaching staff can not enforce a requirement of membership in one church, and in fact I do not believe myself that this is desirable if it could be attained. . . .

Inevitably the question of faculty salaries arose. When the war-induced high cost of living reached the campus in 1917, President Few received this letter from a member of the staff:

Necessity demands that I write you to ask that you and the executive committee give me more salary this year. My expenses have been more than $300. over my salary and I have been just as saving as I could and have also denied myself of things that I needed.

During my seven years of housekeeping I have spent over $2,100. to live more than I have made salary, that is the truth and nothing but the truth.

No man can be happy who cannot meet his expenses and have to deny himself of the necessities that go to make up life. I hope that you will take this letter in the spirit in which it is written.

I have nothing but the best for you and your family and a most prosperous year.

Another member of the staff did not ask for a salary raise, but said that if he was getting all he was worth he would like to know it. Fortunately, the executive committee, less than two weeks later, voted "to send to each teacher and other officer of the College now in service a special check for an amount equal to ten per cent of the salary that was paid him for the year ending August 31, 1917." President Few added on his own behalf, in letters addressed to the faculty:

I only regret that the College cannot make this special check much larger. But even so, its value will be enhanced to you if you can fully realize the genuine appreciation for your work and the great good will which go with this check.

Let's covenant together to make this the best of all the years in the history of the old College in whose service we have the precious privilege to work.

The two complainants remained in the service of the institution. Few's friend, C. W. Toms, a member of the executive committee, in returning to Few a copy of his letter to the faculty remarked: "You always express yourself forcefully, but in this instance you have really surpassed yourself."

Few himself showed little concern for money in a personal way. He had some small investments, but at times his family expenses were high, and the obligations he felt to his parents were considerable. Yet toward money itself he seemed indifferent, even perhaps to the point of being careless. His salary in 1917 was $4,000, just twice that of President-emeritus Kilgo who served as Lecturer and who of course was receiving another salary as Bishop. It is probable that Few expected others to feel as he did, that the privilege of serving was itself a significant part of the compensation. He was genuinely appreciative of his faculty, however, and he realized he had some valuable men.

The following letter to his friend Frank C. Brown, head of the English department, may be worth quoting at length; it illustrates some of the problems existing as late as 1922:

I have received your interesting letter of Sunday. I appreciate deeply the need of an additional man in the English department. In fact it is hard to see how we can get along without one. But Mr. Duke is so anxious to have everything as nearly right as possible, and he has done so much for us that I am not willing even to mention this matter to him. If you feel that you have a mandate from him to put in an additional English teacher at a salary of $2500.00, I must leave the financial part of the transaction entirely between you and Mr. Duke, with one word of caution. Annual contributions of this kind are perfectly fine in so far as they help us for the time being to "stay where we are." But I have some doubt whether it is right to bring in an outside man unless the salary is permanently provided for by actual endowment funds. I am, however, entirely content to leave this phase of the question to you, to Mr. Duke, and the man who comes in if one does come in.

Please be assured that I carry on my heart the needs of your and all the other departments. Day and night I struggle with this problem. It is the great sorrow of my life that I am not able to provide adequately and promptly for the needs of all of you.

We are hard pressed every year, but we are especially pressed this year from several directions: repairs on our buildings, delayed by war and high prices and long overdue, must be carried on now. The Trinity Park School plant especially must be thoroughly overhauled to be used for college purposes. We have already too long delayed for similar reasons the putting in of additional shelves at the library; and this is now being done and also much-needed repairs and replenishings of the scientific laboratories. On account of the rate of exchange, now is the time of all times to purchase foreign books of which, as you well know, we have many needs. The time has come when we must pay for the street work in front of the college (all the other street work has been done without cost to us). We now sorely need additions to our central heating plant. There has been no increase there in twelve years, although most of our buildings have been put up within that period. Besides your additional man in English we greatly need a second man in Education; a second man in Physics; and a third full-time man in Law.

President Few was careful to send a copy of this letter to B. N. Duke in New York, and less than nine days later he was writing Angier B. Duke, Mr. Duke's son, who was a graduate of Trinity and who had been quite generous in helping to provide for a gymnasium and swimming pool:

We have at least ten or fifteen unusual men on our staff. They have been at the College for a long time, they are whole-heartedly devoted to it, they are a part of its best traditions, they are in close and sympathetic touch with its constituency and its public; and they are at the same time highly expert in their forms of service. This is a combination that will be hard ever to reproduce. And I am very anxious to get the College as far along as possible before these men pass off the scene; and also while your Father can get personal satisfactions out of seeing the steady development here.

A letter written to B. N. Duke not long after Few became President suggests that the plenitude of problems to which he was accustomed had existed from the beginning. Mr. Duke was abroad at the time.

We have been very busy at the College this summer. I have been here all the time except when I had to go away on business for the College. So have Professor Flowers, Professor Wannamaker, Mr. Newsom, and their corps of assistants. We have been busier than ever before, and interest in the College is constantly growing, and friends being raised up for it everywhere. Despite the fact that the new Dormitory gives us room for 120 more men than we had at the close of last year, still all our rooms in all the buildings are signed for, and there is already much demand for additional lodging.

The East Dormitory is about completed except finishing up the basement and painting the inside woodwork, and there is every reason to expect that it will be ready for occupance in due time. The walls of the administration building are almost up. Mr. W. A. Salmon has had a relapse, and is now desperately ill. His case is regarded as hopeless. It is sad in itself, and it has unfortunately delayed work somewhat. The dormitory which Mr. J. B. Duke has been so good as to offer to build has not yet been begun . . . . We have been delayed in these plans by the effort to get a dining room in the basement. In spite of our utmost endeavor this has had to be abandoned on account of the failure to get any sewage connection. This basement will be available for dormitories. I believe that we can rush this building through to completion by February 1.

We are repairing the quarters in the red brick dormitory which I have for seven years occupied, to be used this year as a first class boarding house. . . . I get a good deal of satisfaction out of this arrangement, because it will supply a need that has been long felt. The dining room in the Inn will be continued for another year, and will be conducted under the direction of a competent committee of the faculty, which is supposed to have towards the dining halls the same relation as the committee on athletics bears toward athletics,—that is, to have supervision of the management without taking any of the financial risk. I hope within a year or two we may be able to work out here a satisfactory system for feeding the students on a large scale.

We succeeded in getting the use of the city's rock crusher and a force of hands at actual cost. I think we are getting a good job of work, and I hope shall be able to save some money. The work, however, will be a little slow, and we may be delayed somewhat in completing it. I believe the best way to treat both the drives and the walks is to use macadam and put on a binder to hold and preserve it. The bulk of this work I hope will be completed by the opening of the College.

Christian's job of dirt moving goes on satisfactorily. Mr. Hibbard is also doing well with his force, except that he is hindered by a drought which has not been equalled in this region in my time. . . .

Our great new bell has arrived, and has been placed in the temporary tower. It is, I think, all that we hoped for.

Doctor Kilgo has moved into his new residence, and I am getting ready to use the President's house.

The plans for the gateway have not been settled on, and I suppose nothing will be done in this matter until your return to America.

I was at lunch yesterday with Toms and Will Flowers. Mrs. Toms and the children are at Hertford. He seems to be enjoying his "vacation," but I suppose he keeps you informed as to his movements. Perhaps I had better not set about telling on him.

President Few was not an emotional or excitable man, and he no doubt early learned to take the good without too much elation and the bad without too much depression (although there is the story that the unexpected death of Thomas Fortune Ryan put him in bed for a day, because Few had previously conferred with Ryan and had been encouraged to draw up more complete plans for a program to which Ryan might contribute). His philosophy toward his work was well stated to his friend and former associate, Plato Durham, a Trinity graduate who had gone to Atlanta in 1914 to become dean of the theological school of Emory University:

I hope you are beginning a venture which may prove of great and lasting benefit to the Church and the cause. You can count on me to serve you whenever it is in my power. You realize as well as I that it is a long hard task to build up a great educational institution of any kind. It takes time, energy, wisdom, and infinite patience. The vision is inspiring, but the routine is often dull and gray. I wish for you and all your co-laborers a heart and will for the great undertaking.

We may suppose that Few received encouragement from others less often than it was deserved, and he must have found satisfaction in the following letter from his friend Wallace Buttrick, who was soon to become President of the General Education Board and who on another occasion said to Few, "I have written thus fully and familiarly because I like you. . . ."

Let me follow the impulse of the moment & thank you for the South Atlantic Quarterly, the April number of which I have just been reading. It is a fine thing to have a part in putting forth such a fine magazine. The article by Mims on Prof. [C. Alphonso] Smith's O'Henry Biography, & the article by Prof. Bassett on Wm. Garrott Brown gave me an old fashioned spinal thrill.

Mine is a busy, all too matter of fact & hum-drum life for much reading & so a draught at your fine fountain is most refreshing. God bless you.

XXI

One episode which may be related pained President Few because it involved his good friend Bishop Kilgo. It was not a personal difficulty at all, but it was made to seem so at the time because it resulted in Kilgo's resignation from the Board of Trustees and as President-emeritus. The trouble arose out of a simple, and no doubt thoughtless, college prank. On Thanksgiving evening in 1914 a person or persons unknown raised the sophomore class flag and perhaps an undershirt, on which was said to be a skull and cross-bones, on the flagpole which had been erected in 1903 at the suggestion of Robert Lee Durham, '91, a veteran of the War with Spain. The ceremonies attached to the United States flag had become a tradition at Trinity, and President Few took special pride in the fact that Trinity was, as he thought, the first Southern non-military college to erect such a flagpole. The school was definitely nationalist in its sentiments and outlook, and Bishop Kilgo, who was a frequent speaker in the Chapel, took occasion to speak harshly of the sophomore class for this implied contempt, as he thought, for the American flag. As the *Chronicle* reported it, Kilgo gave them a "rather hot and spicy sermon in the nature of a Phillipiad against the man or men who raised a class flag on the college flag pole. He went so far, it is said, as to state that unless the culprit were discovered he would sever his connection with Trinity College." Kilgo, in short, took "a most serious view of the affair," and the persons responsible were "little less than traitors." He was said to have called the young men "sons of 'buffaloes,'" a term currently used to suggest a person who would give aid to the enemy in time of war. The sophomore class, in response, "rather indignant and grown rather more impulsive than necessary," held a protesting meeting, and later, in a public communication, accused the Bishop of "meddling."

Kilgo may have had reason to be sensitive to such accusations. After his elevation to the bishopric he had continued to live on the College campus, and he held a lectureship in the department of biblical literature. He was intimately concerned with all the doings of the College—it could not have been otherwise—and he was a member of the Executive Committee of the Board of Trustees. In 1915—the year he moved to

Charlotte—he was elected President-emeritus "in order that he may continue to have a specific relation to the administration of the college . . . ," and B. N. Duke's gift of a granite wall for the campus was announced by Kilgo. In 1916 he was awarded an LL.D. degree by Trinity College. The interest of both Few and Kilgo in every detail of the College is illustrated by Few's reply to Kilgo's suggestions about improving the College grounds:

All of it conforms with my own views, except that perhaps I ought to say that in trimming up some of the trees and front and planting all evergreen shrubbery I have tried to follow the specific ideas of Mr. Duke. While he deserves credit for whatever I have had done along this line, I have myself passed upon every detail, the planting of every shrub and the cutting of every limb; and I have used the best judgment I could command after having got all the free advice available.

Whether or not Kilgo was "meddling," the incident about the flagpole and Kilgo's remarks on the subject got in the newspapers. At this distance it is a little difficult to realize the stir created. One communication which Few received was from Stonewall Jackson Durham, a brother of the man at whose suggestion the flagpole had been erected. He wrote:

I am much annoyed by the article . . . . giving Bishop Kilgo's strictures on the class of 1917 . . . .

I do not relish the idea of John continuing in a class that has thus been characterized in gross by so eminent a man as Bishop Kilgo.

John was at home Thanksgiving day and on the road Wednesday night, and I presume was not involved in the offense. But these facts are not known abroad, and he must share in the reputation that the Bishop has given his class.

I would be glad if you would inform me just what was done that was dishonorable, and whether the Bishop's characterization is to stand as the judgment of the College.

To which President Few replied:

Last Thursday night, following the Thanksgiving holiday, while I and several others of us were away at Charlotte attending the Trinity alumni meeting and Teachers' Assembly, some man or men ran up the flag pole a sophomore banner which was found there Friday morning. I returned Saturday afternoon, and found that Dean Cranford was proceeding, as was proper, to see if he could find out who did this. Since it was a sophomore banner, he naturally supposed it was done by a member or members of that class. Of this, however, we are not now certain. We shall probably get at the truth of this sooner or later, although it is of course possible that we may never know.

Bishop Kilgo, in conducting chapel exercises Monday morning, made a speech on the subject. As I understand it, he did not mean to call these men ugly names, unless, or except in so far as, they were involved in the original act or in conspiracy to protect the offender. The newspaper notoriety I regret, but it seems to me a better policy for an institution like this to pay little attention to newspaper perversions, except in cases where the necessity becomes unmistakable.

I appreciate your letter, but I think you need feel on the score no uneasiness about John. And for that matter, he seems to me to be in every way a first-rate student and high minded youth.

Thus the matter stood for some time. The Bishop was incensed, the Class of 1917 outraged, and the culprit not found—in fact was never found. Nevertheless, the Bishop was deeply hurt at the umbrage taken by the sophomore class at his remarks and demanded from it an apology. The apology was not forthcoming. The Bishop was understood to have said that unless he got the apology demanded, he would oppose the authorization of diplomas for that class by the Trustees. Meanwhile the United States had entered World War I, and in May, 1917, President Few wrote Kilgo that practically all the seniors who could pass the physical examination were going into the service. He added: "The unrest and confusion that has been apt to attend the day preceding Christmas and commencement are with us in intensified form and will be with us until after commencement. This will give you some appreciation of the difficulties of our position. It takes a teacher to teach now and a student to study. And we haven't too many of either. . . . I see Mr. Duke right often." Was this a hint that there were enough troubles present?

Also in 1917 Mr. James H. Southgate, a devoted friend of Trinity and Chairman of the Board of Trustees for many years, had died, and it was necessary to elect a new Chairman. Prior to the meeting of the Board, C. W. Toms, one of the President's most intimate friends and a member of the Board, had suggested to Joseph G. Brown, another member, that Bishop Kilgo should be elected Chairman. This suggestion had general approval, and Kilgo was duly elected Chairman and Brown Vice-Chairman.

The honor accorded to the Bishop failed to put him in a proper frame of mind to sign, as Chairman of the Board, the diplomas of the graduating class. In fact he opposed the diplomas being signed at all, and when the rest of the Board did not concur in this drastic action, it was rumored that he wished to file a dissenting opinion. However, the diplomas were signed by the Vice-Chairman, and the class duly graduated.

Here the matter might have ended had not a newspaper reporter who was not at the Commencement, although invited, chosen to write an article in the Greensboro *Daily News,* which was not at all complimentary to the Bishop and which indicated, to the Bishop at least, that someone had supplied the reporter with private information which he could not possibly have had in his ordinary capacity as a reporter. The reporter, an acquaintance of President Few, had been doing some incidental publicity work for the College, for which he had received a small compensation. His article in the newspaper intimated that there had been an attempt on the part of Bishop "Jack" to have R. L. Flowers elected Vice-President of Trinity and that it was intended to put Flowers second in command at the expense of the new Dean, Wannamaker, who was Few's man. "Somehow," said the reporter, "this interesting thing did not get in the papers. That's where academic efficiency shines. The newspapers the following morning carried the very sober and harmless announcement that Professor Wannamaker had been elected dean. That of itself conveyed the impression of rank, and [that] Professor Wannamaker in the nature of things would be the next highest man." The article further revealed that the Bishop drew a salary of $2000 as President-emeritus and asserted that far fom being a "meddler," as the class of 1917 alleged, he was a power on the campus, "the ruling spirit of the executive committee which fixes salaries and isn't liable to make any mistakes in their apportionment." Among other disparaging remarks, the reporter alluded to the Bishop's prayer at the Commencement ceremonies: "They say it was sweeping, for the bishop is a powerful man on his knees. They could not segregate in the many recommendations to the throne of grace any petition for help for the boys of 1917. But they and the kaiser were the shining exceptions."

Immediately President Few wrote to the Bishop:

I did my best to keep the floating rumors about commencement affairs away from the newspapers, but it proved to be impossible. Some of these rumors have been served up in the worst kind of form. Lest you may not have seen it, I enclose an article that appeared in the Greensboro News of yesterday. I am preparing a statement to send to the newspapers. I hope you will approve of it and allow me to publish the same. Since it concerns you and in a way the Board of Trustees, I do not feel that I can publish it without your approval. . . . I am infinitely sorry that you have had to be harassed with all this. But I hope that you will allow it to trouble you just as little as possible; and I am going to do the same. I am sorry I could not have managed it better, but I have done my best; and I shall have to depend upon the good Lord as I have in other trying occasions.

I shall be very glad if you will allow us at this end of the line to handle all this matter for you so that you may be saved any personal contact with newspapers. We will do the best we can and will be glad to use any suggestions you see fit to make. I have not prepared the enclosed statement without close consultation with the wisest advisers in my reach. And we are doing our level best to get out of it with as little harm to anybody concerned as possible. At least please always remember that our intentions are good.

And as for me, whether or not I may be able at all times to keep step with the hard pace you set for me and the College, I believe in you with all my heart; I follow you gladly; and I expect to follow you to the end of the way.

The statement was not printed. The Bishop refused to express an opinion, saying,

I must now as I have continuously during all these years of this affair, decline to express my opinion on the course which you should take. . . . All that is personal I have no regard for. Only what concerns the moral standards of the college concern me. . . . I have never asked any man to defend me, as you will know.

Kilgo's letter was dated June 12, 1917; on the next day Few wrote:

You have had to undergo so much for the College and kindred causes that I am distressed beyond measure for you to have further harassment. Believe me, I am willing now, and have all the time been willing, to sacrifice myself in order to save you from any sort of suffering. . . .

Again, June 25, Few wrote to Kilgo:

The personal tone that I feel to underlie your last letter is very precious to me. The time will come when all this will appear to you in better light. It is inevitable that you should have disappointments in the College as in every human being and in every institution in the hands of human beings. But you are going to find that the College will always wear an appreciation of your services, your devotions, and your faiths, in its very heart of hearts. The complications will straighten out, and the devoted men who have worked here so long will do more rather than less for the dear old College and for the Church, and for the causes which they are both set to carry forward. The College will achieve not less but more even of your "cherished aims"; and your name will always stand out as that of the man who, under God, has done most for it.

The Bishop, nevertheless, had determined to resign. He quoted the reporter's item from the Greensboro newspaper and gave that as the "immediate cause" of his "withdrawal from official connection with Trinity College." The Board met in November; on motion of Mr. Toms, to whom Kilgo had written in June that he was tired of being "nagged at & misrepresented," the resignation was accepted. The difficulty, as is so often the case, arose out of a misunderstanding, not between Kilgo and Few so much as between Kilgo and the class of 1917. The class had denied knowledge of the flag affair. But somehow Kilgo got the impression, as Few wrote, that

two of our students confessed on promise of immunity & were given an easy penance. I don't feel it would be fair to you to leave you in what seems to me to be a misapprehension without offering to tell you the facts as I know them. I read with sorrow in your last letter to me that you will always feel you have received a raw deal at the hands of Trinity College. Would you permit me to write you on these two points in full & for your own use alone? And will you, please, continue to build on my friendship as a thing that no earthly event can ever shake.

In the same letter, written evidently before Kilgo's resignation had been accepted, Few said:

I take literally the first opportunity to write you; & there is not much to say now except to tell you that I'm sorry; that in the end I hope the Board may find it possible not to accept your resignation; that you must not desert us just because you think we have blundered; after all these years of work & sacrifice together in a great & inspiring cause; & that you must not be embittered & let your & our old newspapers & other enemies separate you & the truest of all the friends of your life. Believe in us & give us a chance, & it will all come out right in the end. And please count me the unchanged & unchanging friend & disciple of a lifetime. I don't know how to write more; & if you believe this, as surely you must, there's no need for more.

Kilgo's notion that two boys had confessed and had been let off lightly explains why Kilgo spoke harshly of the class when it denied any knowledge of the affair. The class denial was not withdrawn, as the Bishop demanded.

Stonewall Jackson Durham, who had protested Kilgo's remarks in 1914, had not forgotten, though his son John had been duly graduated. In August, 1917, he wrote President Few with reference to another son:

My son, Plato, who last year took special work at the A & E College at Raleigh, has decided that he wants to take a regular literary course, and I am considering where this shall be taken.

I was and am greatly annoyed at the injustice that Trinity permitted to be practiced upon the class of last year. And if the facts are as I have been informed I would be unwilling to send Plato to Trinity.

I wish you would let me know whether the College has done anything to vindicate the members of the class of '17 that were guiltless of any wrong, or, if not, whether any such course is projected.

I will appreciate your replying as promptly as convenient.

To which Few replied:

I am glad to know that your son Plato has decided to take a regular literary course, and I shall be glad to see him come here. Because of his name and by every other token he pre-eminently belongs here.

In regard to the other subject about which you write, I will speak with perfect frankness as fully as I may. I carried into the trustees the names of the members of the class of 1917 with my own endorsement and the endorsement of the faculty, and their degrees were voted and awarded in due form and have back of them the full authority of Trinity College. They are as valid and as untarnished as any degrees ever conferred by the College upon any of its graduates. . . .

Nevertheless, son John, President of the Class of 1917, appeared before the Trustees at the meeting at which Kilgo's resignation was accepted, and requested that the Trustees investigate Kilgo's charges and make public a statement. The Board ordered that a report of the matter be made to the Board in June, 1918, but here the record ends.

B. N. Duke, to the relief of President Few, was not alarmed at Kilgo's resignation. On June 25 Toms, who had just visited Duke in a Philadelphia hospital, wrote to Few that he had learned that Duke "was receiving the Durham papers and knew of Dr. Kilgo's resignation. He spoke of the matter rather incidentally, and I purposely refrained from comment, except to point out the great work that the College is doing and its great future." President Few, who tried to avoid writing anything that might disturb Duke during his illness, had nevertheless written him on the twenty-fifth, evidently before he had received Toms's letter:

I have got the impression that you have heard also about Bishop Kilgo's proposal to resign, and perhaps I ought to say a word about that. But there is not much to say now. The less said, the sooner mended. I understand from Mr. Joseph G. Brown, acting president of the Board, that the Board will not be called together at this time, and, therefore, everybody will have sufficient opportunity to give the whole subject the fullest consideration. Bishop Kilgo, I need not tell you, has acted out of conscientious motives; and whatever the outcome may be, there will be no lessening of appreciation for his services [or] of personal devotion to him that all of us here have felt for these twenty odd years.

In 1922 the General Conference retired Bishop Kilgo because of his health, but, through the aid of President Few, who was a delegate to the Conference, "his salary in full was continued for one year." To quote from a letter of Few to B. N. Duke:

He [Bishop Kilgo] made the trip to Hot Springs [where the Conference met] and seemed to stand the journey out rather well. But as we were returning with him on a special Pullman, he became ill near Memphis and was removed to a hospital there. I got off with him and made the best possible arrangements for him. He is in a good hospital, in charge of an excellent physician, and has Bishop Murrah, of Memphis, and other friends about him.

Bishop Kilgo later returned to his home but did not live long thereafter. In the fall of 1922 Few had a letter from his old friend Plato Durham, a brother of Stonewall Jackson Durham:

I was standing at Bishop Kilgo's grave a few days ago, thinking of many things. Among the memories that came to me there was one concerning the last words he ever said to me, just a few weeks before his death. They were these: "Few was good to me at Hot Springs and did all he could." He said this with a look of tenderness very plainly visible on his face.

I am writing you this because it is a very blessed thing for me to remember, and I have no doubt will be an agreeable thing for you to know; for if the sadness of the years of misunderstanding necessarily pained your heart, the knowledge that at last there was this changed attitude will be a comfort to you.

XXII

President Few seemed to be a quiet, reserved man, shy and somewhat drawn within himself, a man with a quiet smile rather than a boisterous cascade of laughter, with a dry wit and an occasional witticism rather than the volubility of the eternal raconteur. He was discriminating in his choice of friends. He had few intimates outside of his family and those with whom he was closely associated. But he was singularly fond of those whose affection he shared, and it is likely that this fondness was more easily expressed in correspondence than face-to-face.

Among his early friends was William Garrott Brown, a sensitive spirit, a good writer, a shrewd judge of men and events, and one whose time on earth was short. They had been roommates for a time at Harvard, and in his lingering illness Brown must have found consolation in the following letter from President Few, December 25, 1911:

I have ordered sent you some Christmas flowers. I can think of no more fitting way to express my love, my constant anxiety, and infinite yearning for your continued welfare. I hope the message may be duly conveyed. I wish you a very happy Christmas and a new year full of prosperity and peace. May you go gently all your days! And remember that I have always loved you with a womanlike tenderness and devotion. . . .

Another year Few wrote:

The year has been a busy & happy one for me. And while you may not have been actively busy in the same way I hope that you have found happiness within yourself. For the older I grow the more I am convinced that the conditions of happiness are largely internal. . . .

Aside from Washington Duke, whose acquaintance with Few lasted some eight or nine years previous to his death in 1905, the member of the Duke family with whom Few was most intimate was Benjamin Newton Duke. They were kindred spirits; their aims and hopes for Trinity were much the same, and there can be little doubt that Benjamin's influence on his brother James B. was the greatest single factor behind the creation of the Duke Endowment. Benjamin kept his home in Durham; his friends and relatives were here; his two children, Angier B. and Mary, were graduates of Trinity; he and Few worshipped at the same church, and their outlook on life was probably much the same. Benjamin was elected to the Board of Trustees in 1889, and it was he who provided the money for Few's salary after his first year's appointment. He took a keen personal interest in all the work of the College even to the most trivial matters, and he obviously had great confidence in Few's judgment. Few of course advised with him constantly when he was in town and kept in touch with him by mail when he was away. There is no hint that there was ever the slightest difference between them. There was, rather, a mutual confidence and understanding which never knew the least strain. Benjamin's benefactions were not as large as those of his brother, but they were more constant, and they came at critical times. Of all this Few was deeply appreciative, but the thought behind the gift and the feeling of loyal support in difficult times must have lightened Few's heart many a time. Again we quote from Few's letters. Writing Benjamin Duke when he was in the hospital in Philadelphia in the summer of 1917, Few said:

As you know, I am not much of a man to give expression to my personal feelings; but I want you to know how much I esteem and love you and that you have multitudes of friends here and elsewhere who feel the same way.

Again in 1922:

I am this morning taking the first opportunity on my return to put in writing some expression of my appreciation for your latest manifestation of life long generosity to Trinity College. To carry a great cause like this on one's heart all the time as I have to do is sometimes a trying experience. Your ready sympathy and continuing helpfulness have been and are to me like the shadow of a great rock in a weary land. I feel sure that you have some compensation in the feeling that you are thus doing a permanent good upon the earth. And I shall certainly never cease to be glad and grateful for the lovely way in which you treated me in New York recently as on so many other occasions.

Few had the fullest appreciation of what B. N. Duke meant to Trinity. In 1919 he wrote to Duke: "You have been the foremost influence in the making of Trinity College, and your place in its history will always abide." The next year he wrote, ". . . it is you who have been the inspirer and guide of Trinity's development for more than a quarter of a century."

Just a few months after Few's inauguration he had to write B. N. Duke about the destruction by fire in 1911 of the Washington Duke Building. Fortunately the building was insured, but "some things were burned that cannot be replaced." He did not intend to worry Mr. Duke about it:

We are now housed in the new academic building. It is spacious, comfortable and beautiful. Work has already begun on the new dormitory. Tearing down the old building will be a simple matter. As soon as the insurance has been adjusted the walls will be removed. The official records of the college, financial and academic, were saved from the fire, being either in our safe or in the library vault. The literary societies, the South Atlantic Quarterly, the alumni records, the admission records, and a good many other things suffered severely. Fortunately no other building was injured at all, and I think not a single tree was hurt. The students all escaped injury, though their personal belongings, books, clothes, etc., were nearly all lost. The fire involved us in many inconveniences and extraordinary tasks. We came through it with a loss of only one day, and I believe the College is running smoothly.

Three months later he wrote:

You must realize how much I appreciate your repeated kindnesses to us and the gifts that make possible the College as we know it. I am doing my best to keep the College worthy of such goodness, and to make it stand always, as you desire it to stand, for progress and the widest human service. I have never felt so hopeful for the future as I feel now, or so sure that it is destined to do a great, lasting, and beneficent work for mankind.

In 1913 he wrote:

Since Tuesday morning when you and your brother gave such a remarkable exhibition of beautiful generosity to Trinity College I have been constantly thinking of what you have now for so long meant to me and to a great cause in which I believe with the whole heart. During the past fifteen or twenty years I know that you have often felt the financial responsibility for the College to be very burdensome. I am glad to believe that it is at last in a position where you will not feel obliged periodically to come to the rescue, but where you and others of the family can give to it just as you feel inclined to give. Burdensome as I know this responsibility has sometimes been to you, I believe you will be more and more grateful for the good fortune that has brought you into the place of chief benefactor of this College. Most thoughtful men agree that despite all of its defects education is to be a main reliance of our civilization. You have the unique distinction of being in this region a pioneer builder of education on a vast scale, for it is already clear that Trinity is to rank among the very greatest colleges of our country.

President Few was correct in thinking that Duke sometimes felt the College to be a burden, for near this time Duke was writing his friend, George Foster Peabody, who was trying to interest him in some philanthropy: "As you probably know, I have been carrying Trinity College almost single handed and alone for many years. I feel that I am doing more than my share of work of this kind." This was an opportune time for one of the local pastors to write words of encouragement to Duke: "We have just closed our District Conference, which was one of rare power. Dr. Few delivered a great address on Christian Education at the eleven o'clock hour Friday."

Another of Few's intimate friends was C. W. Toms, a graduate of the University of North Carolina and for a time a member of the faculty, formerly Superintendent of the Durham Public Schools, a member of the Board of Trustees of Trinity College, and an associate of the Dukes in the tobacco industry. His background gave him a high appreciation of both President Few and the character of the work of Trinity College. He had frequent opportunity, either himself or through friends, to bring to the attention of the Dukes and others of their associates some of the more pressing needs of the College. He was a lifelong friend of Few and of Trinity, one whose devotion is less well known than it should be. He had known Few well when he was engaged in school work, and he perhaps had a nostalgic yearning for the academic life. Once in 1914 he wrote President Few, "I always enjoy a day with you and hearing you talk, and regret exceedingly that I was unable to see you on Saturday last. My time was so completely occupied at the factory that I was unable to get away." His appreciation of Few increased; in 1920 he wrote, "You are doing a great and good work for a great cause, and you grow stronger each year. You deserve good health and happiness, and I want you to have both at all times." Few, for his part, never ceased to realize his indebtedness to Toms. In 1922 he wrote: "You have meant much to me and to Trinity College through all these formative years."

When B. N. Duke was in the hospital in the summer of 1917 he was visited by Toms, who wrote to Few: "Your letters give Mr. Duke infinite pleasure, and I do not understand how you can tell him so many things that he really wishes to know and nothing to worry him. . . . I hope that you will write him often." Duke was interested in all the local news and the details of what was going on about the town and the College. President Few had the happy faculty of writing just such a letter, his letter of June 20, 1917, for example:

I have some good news for you which I hasten to communicate. We began on Monday to move the house Mr. Hunt has been living in, and the dismantling of the house is now well under way. Dr. Glasson informs me that he will get out of his house without delay. That part of the grounds will look better when you see it next. When you get back in the autumn and feel like it, you and I, with Mr. Hunt's help, can plant trees and shrubs there and elsewhere. The college grounds as a whole are good to look on now, probably more beautiful than they have ever been. Our truck farm, too, looks more promising now than it has. Mr. Hunt is an expert in his way.

I went day before yesterday down to your house. The peas on the land between Mrs. Stokes' and Mr. Mahler's look well, and the drains are taking care of the water perfectly. I think you will get a good crop. The grass in your front yard is flourishing. Every Darlington oak that I saw is living. We must have a good many of them for the college grounds next autumn. Salmon's force was cleaning out the garage, the work being practically complete except the tracks for the gates, which have not come. Mr. Shroyer was busy with his work. And so altogether the out-of-doors at your house as well as at the College are good to see.

The town began on Monday morning to complete the double ends of Milton Avenue between the railroad and Main Street. The College has signed a petition for the building anew of Main Street from the city limits on through our property, and to be continued on to Edgemont.

Mrs. Turner, a well-to-do Methodist woman of Oxford, is beginning to build a house on the lot adjoining the Buck Lyon place (built, you remember, by Mr. Yuille and now occupied by Mr. Carmichael). I am told that Mrs. Turner is coming here to educate her children and I am also told that she is building a very handsome house, something on the order of the Foushee house. I am told that Mr. E. J. Hill will build a house on the lot next to

Mrs. Turner which will be almost in front of the Memorial Parsonage.

It is impossible for us to estimate with any approach to accuracy what effects the war will have on the attendance of students at the College next year. It looks to me now better than I had supposed it would look. We shall certainly be short in the upper classes, and conditions may indirectly affect the entering class. In any case, we have this solid consolation—if the numbers are smaller, we can do better work. And I believe we will do better work next year than ever before.

In a characteristic letter, July 2, 1917, after discussing the building of sidewalks on Buchanan Road and the extension of Milton Avenue, Few continued:

The ivy which has been planted on the outside of the wall round the athletic field is doing well; as is also the privet which is planted by the wall on the inside. Mr. Hunt has his force of hands today on the truck farm. It is in fine condition and promises good returns. One of the Durham papers remarked the other day that it was the best garden in town and probably the best one in the state. We have planted for 1,000 bushels of sweet potatoes, and unless we have bad luck, we are apt to get that yield. Perishable stuff we shall have to can; because everybody has a garden this year, and the market now is overcrowded. We canned snaps last week. The peas and practically all the things we have planted are doing well.

Mr. Hibberd gave the College some banana trees which we last week planted in the ravine beyond the end of the West Duke Building. These plants grow to be tall, and I think they will make a good appearance, located as they are. . . .

Mr. R. L. Baldwin sold last week at auction the land which lies between Buchanan Road, fronting the John Harris place, and Watts Street. Mr. H. G. Hedrick, a member of our law faculty, who recently married Mary Sasser, bought one on Buchanan Road. Mr. Frank Fuller's place was also sold at auction last week and brought a good price. Mr. W. L. Foushee bought the residence for $2800. I do not know what he will do with it. I should think it is rather large to remove without tearing it down. . . .

I saw Mrs. Duke and Mrs. Stokes at Memorial Church last night. I found Mr. North trying an interesting experiment there.

He is holding the Sunday night services out-of-doors, on the lawn in the rear of the church, and the time has been moved up to seven o'clock. There was a good congregation on hand last night, and the experiment seems to be successful from the beginning. . . .

Dr. and Mrs. Brown left last week for Harrisonburg, Virginia, where they spend the summer. Professor Brooks is in Nashville at Bruce Payne's summer school, but he will be back in about ten days for the remainder of the summer. Dr. Boyd also teaches during the summer at Peabody College for Teachers at Nashville. Professor Flowers, Professor Wannamaker, Mr. Newsom, Mr. Markham, and other helpers remain here with me during the summer attending to summer business, which is always heavy. We are all rather busier than usual this summer, but we are well and entirely content to be busy about a cause in which we believe with the whole heart.

Take the best care of yourself and keep in good heart. You have done more good in the world than you realize, and I have no doubt you will do still more good in the years that lie ahead of you. Personally, I feel all the time the need of your sympathy and cooperation. . . .

Some idea of Mr. Duke's pleasure in receiving these letters may be gleaned from his reply, June 28, 1917, penciled to "My dear Few":

I have received your letters. . . . It was good of you to write me & I appreciate your doing so. Your letters were full of just what I wanted to hear especially the one written June 20th which told me so many things of interest.

I am glad the old faculty houses are to be moved, it will help the looks of the Campus & I am delighted to know work has been resumed on the north end of Milton Ave., hope they will complete it this time. The falling of the wall again & the Dr. Kilgo matter does not disturb me every thing will come out O. K. in the end. If the war does decrease your attendance you can do better work & will give you time to get your breath & catch up with things.

One thing you failed to tell me about & that is the progress being made with the side walk work on Buchanan road,—how is that coming on? Have they laid the walk on Trinity Ave between Col Flowers and Mr Wannamakers corner—at Buchanan road? You can tell me about this in your next. I am getting on slowly & the Doctor assures me I will ultimately get rid of this nervious affliction but it is tedious & tiresome. About all I have to break the monotony & serve me as past time is the few letters I receive & I certainly enjoy getting them. As long as none of them contain any thing disturbing or calculated to cause me any worry it is alright for me to get them & not one I have received yet has contained any thing that has worried me the least bit. Glorious work the Red Cross people are doing. We gave them $26,000 & I wish it had been more.

Write me when you can. With love to your family & some for your self.

XXIII

There is no thought of tracing in detail the development of the Duke Endowment, but since this and other financial matters concerned President Few during all his administration, it is appropriate to outline some of the situations faced. Despite the fact that Trinity College when Few became President had an endowment of about $450,000, said to be the largest of any private college in the South, there was continual need for funds. The College had growing pains, and it did not begin to serve adequately its existing clientele, to say nothing of the section to which it was committed. The first donation of "W. Duke and Sons" was $1000 in 1887. Washington Duke's benefactions, until his death in 1905, amounted to about $500,-000, despite the fact that he was reported to have said to Kilgo, whom he had driven to Trinity on his arrival in 1894: "Well, there it is. I never expect to give another dollar to it, and I wish I had never put a dollar into it." President Kilgo, in a memorial address on Washington Duke, said he gave "something like a million dollars." B. N. Duke gave regularly and liberally. He made gifts totaling $120,000 in the years 1898-1901. In 1901 he agreed to give $6,000 annually for the support of certain departments in the College. In 1904 he pledged himself with his brother James B. to give annually a sum sufficient to maintain the Law School—at least

$3,000 each—and in 1909 he increased his yearly contributions to $20,000. The year of Few's inauguration he gave $150,000 for buildings. James B. Duke gave liberally but less regularly (by 1903 he had given the Library, as well as $10,000 for books and $10,000 for furniture), but it was not until about 1916 that his notion of an endowment began to take form. Even then he was undecided as to its exact nature except that it should be in the region served by the Duke industrial developments, and he was by no means ready in 1910 or for some years thereafter to make any advance commitments.

One of the organizations to which Trinity and other worthy colleges turned was the General Education Board of the Rockefeller Foundation. No sooner was Few inaugurated than he was writing his friend, Wallace Buttrick, Secretary of the General Education Board, about some changes in the endowment campaign (already started by Kilgo), due to a reduction in the matching funds contributed by the Board. Said Few:

> Will you accept these terms? I have absolute confidence in our financial future, but just now you have an opportunity, rare even for your Board, to put us at once in a position which, without your aid, we will probably not reach in two or three years. Please consult with Mr. Gates and let me hear that you are going to strain a point to help us in an emergency when we need your help as we are not apt to ever again need it. . . .

Within two weeks the matter was agreed on the basis of Few's suggestions.

The next year, 1911, Few was saying to the Trustees: "The first need of the College today is an increased endowment. If the work as now projected is to be carried on successfully, the endowment must be at once increased by an addition of at least one million dollars." In 1914 he reported that the seven gifts announced at the last Commencement totalled $1,418,061.89. Even after the foundation of the Duke Endowment he was always aware that the Duke program would need additional funds. Ten years after the Endowment of 1924 he pointed out to the Trustees the need for buildings, library, scholarships, research funds, and added: "These are some of the immediate needs. . . . No financial goal has been set, and no intensive campaign for funds will be undertaken; but it is felt that here is an opportunity that ought to appeal to those who are concerned about endowed universities in the United States, particularly in parts of the country where such universities are most needed."

There were endowment campaigns from time to time, and contributions were made through the Methodist Episcopal Church, South, and related organizations, but naturally and inevitably the Dukes became the mainstay to which the College could turn. There was always financial pressure: operating deficits, carried on temporary loans from the bank, were common; and the matter of repairs to the buildings, a new steam boiler, and such like, to say nothing of professors' salaries, demanded judicious economy.

President Few was eager to win and hold the favor of the Dukes, but he was careful that both he and the College should deserve it; he was careful not to ask more than he had a right to expect or hope for; and he never made himself obnoxious by undue insistence or by uncalled-for extravagances. He did not know James B. Duke as intimately as he did B. N., and it was probably not until his later years that James B. came to appreciate him fully. James B.'s interest in tobacco, aluminum, power, and related enterprises consumed his time and energy, and even after he had seen the vision of the Endowment, he bent every effort to put his business affairs in shape to make the Endowment possible. President Few had need to be patient. It was fortunate that his good friend Toms was in close touch with the Dukes and with friends of the Dukes and was both willing and able to drop a suggestion at the proper time. This is not to imply that the Dukes did not know their own minds, but only to say that the form of their benefactions remained fluid, to some extent at least, and the Dukes were not given to indiscriminate charities. It may be noted in passing, however, that the Duke benefactions were not limited to Trinity College, nor was the later Endowment limited to Duke University; it included aid for other educational institutions as well as hospitals, orphans' homes, rural churches, and retired ministers. It was through Toms and B. N. Duke as well as those immediately connected with the College that James B. Duke came to appreciate the possibilities of Trinity. The notion of a university with all its ramifications, as distinguished from a college, and also the idea for an adequate plan for the administration of the Endowment came in part from President Few.

The Dukes were concerned that Trinity be careful of the quality of its work and that it should be administered in keeping with its financial condition. Their admonition was: "Don't let Trinity get a craze for numbers. Be careful to do sound and good work." In thanking James B. Duke for a donation, President Few wrote in 1914:

We want you to understand what we are doing and to approve of it. I do not want to feel that you have thrown us overboard. But I do want you to feel that we will live within our means; that we will incur no added financial responsibilities without the approval before hand of your Brother and yourself; and that any further contributions are to be free will offerings made because you feel like making them and not because they are expected of you. . . . I am particularly anxious that you shall get enduring personal satisfaction and happiness out of what you have done for Trinity College. . . .

A few years later, when thanking James B. Duke for a gift of $100,000, he said:

I sincerely believe that the work planted here by the Duke family will stand out in the long years of the future as an unequalled contribution in Southern civilization to liberalism, to right thinking, and to the great moral causes of mankind. To have a small part with you in this great undertaking is the glory of my life and the inspiration of all my labors.

It seems to have been in 1916 that James B. Duke first spoke to Few of some larger plan for Trinity. World War I intervened, and Duke found himself deeply immersed in many things; it was thus not until 1919 that Trinity affairs began to move forward. In February of that year President Few proposed to J. B. Duke a plan (which he had previously submitted to Toms) for the creation of a Duke Foundation to be interlinked with Trinity College through a self-perpetuating Board:

I have thought a good deal concerning the plan about which you were good enough to talk with me recently; and if I understand your ideas, it seems to me they may be carried out by some such scheme as I am indicating below. . . .

If you and your lawyer find that the property cannot be administered under the charter of Trinity College, I would suggest that you create a separate corporation, perhaps to be called the James B. Duke Foundation or Fund, as you might prefer. Let the trustees . . . be self-perpetuating . . . let these trustees be the seven members of the Executive Committee of Trinity College. There will be a vacancy in the Executive Committee of the College next June, and I hope you will consent to become a member of the Committee. . . .

If you are a member of the Executive Committee of the College (the body responsible for all finances of the College) and also a member of the board of trustees of the new Foundation, you could become intimately acquainted with the financial conditions and needs of the College, you could direct the business and manage the property of the new Foundation, and you could determine the allotments to be made each year. During your period of service you could determine all questions of policy, and then I am sure you could safely depend on the character of the men who survive and succeed you to carry on. . . .

Few then wrote to Toms about J. B. Duke:

I believe if you will give him a good opportunity, he will talk to you on the subject. We must do our level best now to impress

upon him the needs of the College. For instance, I cannot satisfactorily fill the vacant chairs in Education and Bible (the two
departments that make the widest popular appeal) at a salary of
$2500, and I cannot offer more without raising our entire salary
scale. If I am held to the present salary basis, I will lose within
the next two or three weeks the best prospects I have. The time
is upon us when we must go forward or take a second place.

J. B. Duke became a member of the Board of Trustees in
1919. Immediately after the June Commencement, Few was
writing to Toms:

Everything has gone off in fine shape. . . . I think it is probable
that if you could have been here we might have got some other
things done. The tides of life were running high, and it is at such
times that it is possible to do things. Mr. Duke attended most of
the occasions, entertained some of the guests, and seemed to be
happier than I have seen him in a long time.

Toms, in New York, was not forgetful of Trinity, for he
was soon writing Few that he had talked with certain close
associates of J. B. Duke, and they with each other, and he was
assured that "they will all endeavor to work together for the
good of Trinity College." A few weeks later Toms was writing Few that he had seen B. N. Duke, who was ill in Atlantic
City, and that B. N. had talked of giving Trinity some securi-
ties then, say $300,000, instead of providing for the College
in his will. "I talked to him," said Toms, "in the little time
that I had privately, in regard to the needs of the College.
He seemed disappointed at the conversation which he had with
his brother at Tate Springs, in that he could not interest him
especially in the present needs of the College, but he explained that his brother was very much interested in another
proposition at that time, which accounted for his apparent lack
of immediate interest. . . ."

President Few thought at this time that Trinity might get
$600,000 to $750,000 from the Educational Centenary Fund
of the Methodist Episcopal Church, South, and perhaps as

much as $300,000 from the General Education Board. As he wrote Toms: "Within the next few weeks I shall suggest to you that you bring all possible pressure to bear on President Alderman, of the University of Virginia, to go before the General Educational Board at its December meeting and help put across our proposition. I will do the same thing with some other men, and we ought to succeed. . . ." The following month, September, 1919, Few was quoting to Toms a paragraph from B. N. Duke's letter: "In speaking to my brother in reference to college matters last week, he agreed to contribute $1,000 a month for the running expenses of the institution. I am very sorry he did not make it at least double this amount. I shall, of course, contribute a like amount." All this added up to a pretty picture for President Few, and in October, 1919, he wrote B. N. Duke: "You will appreciate the satisfaction I have at knowing you think the urgent needs of the institution can be taken care of without too much delay. With this done, I am sure that we are now on the eve of developments almost beyond our dreams."

XXIV

One of President Few's major disappointments and also one which shows his co-operative spirit was the failure of the state and some of the denominational institutions within the state to accept his proposal for the establishment in Durham of a hospital and medical school as a joint enterprise. In December, 1922, it was announced in the press that Few had proposed that the University of North Carolina, which then had a two-year medical school and had under consideration a plan to build a full-fledged medical school, should join with Trinity to build a medical school. It was reported that Wake Forest College, which had a two-year medical school, and Davidson College, which had suspended its two-year school, would be welcomed into the joint venture if they wished. It was usually said that Dr. Few had a large sum of money at his command, to come, it was intimated, from the General Education Board and J. B. Duke. On that point Few himself made no statement beyond his opinion that if a suitable plan of cooperation could be worked out it would receive financial backing. The number of millions involved varied from time to time and from newspaper to newspaper, but the Durham *Herald* stated that Trinity and the University would each contribute four million, that there would be a joint building fund, and that there would be an endowment of three million contributed by Trinity, and the state would agree to appropriate annually a sum equivalent to the income from the endowment. It was explained that Dr. Few had been working toward the establishment of a medical school for seven or eight years, that the idea had originated with the late George W. Watts, of Durham, who had made the provision for the fine Watts Hospital, located in Durham, and that the establishment of a medical school "was one of the pieces of unfinished business left when he died last year."

The origin of this proposal went back at least two years, and is best explained in Few's own words:

In the beginning, that is from the early part of 1921, as my mind turned to possibilities of a medical school I was puzzled by the circumstance that North Carolina, according to opinions that had been so often expressed, did not have cities large enough to support a clinical medical school. The State Medical Society and medical authorities had taken the position that a clinical medical school must be located in a large city and that North Carolina had no such city. Therefore they maintained that North Carolina should content itself with the establishment of "preparatory" (pre-clinical) schools of medicine at convenient points in the state. So far as I knew then or can discover now that represented the best medical opinion available in North Carolina, in 1920. I secured from the United States Bureau of the Census in Washington population compilations within a radius of fifty miles, and within a radius of one hundred miles, and to my surprise I found that a hospital located in Durham would be accessible to as many people as if it were located almost anywhere else in the south-eastern states.

It seems that the Rockefeller Foundation, whose chief interest lay in the field of medicine, had been trying to locate a place in the South Atlantic states where it could assist medical training. It may have been more than a coincidence that President Few's mind began to turn in the same direction. By December, 1921, much progress had been made, as is revealed in a letter from Few to Toms:

Dr. Flexner and Dr. Buttrick said they thought a medical school here ought to start with $6,000,000 and that they would stand for $3,000,000 of that amount and believed that their Board would, provided we can get another $3,000,000. I told this to Mrs. Watts today, and she said if we could get $2,000,000 of this she thought $1,000,000 could be got here. All this looks pretty good.

I think you ought to talk to Mr. J. B. D. If he will say he will give us $1,000,000 within five years, I will undertake the task of raising the rest. If he will give us $2,000,000, success will be assured; and I of course wish he would give three or more.

You realize what success in this would mean. A great medical school here would put us on the map, for it would appeal to all classes, to all parties, to all denominations not only in the entire state but throughout all the Southeastern states. Within a radius of two hundred miles of Durham there are 6,000,000 people and not one first-class medical school. It is a wonderful tribute to us that a Board in New York City would invest $3,000,000 in us. Surely we ought to do our dead level best to meet the reasonable conditions they impose. Dr. Flexner said to me the Board once into a large amount like this would sooner or later, no doubt, do still more. I think the time has come when everybody who can put in a lick ought to put it in. I hate to trouble busy men like you, but if we can get this done, your acute troubles for us will be drawing to an end.

President Few continued to work on the idea and prepared the way for an interview between Buttrick and Flexner, of the Rockefeller Foundation, and Duke. He explained this to

Toms and said, "Unless this interview comes off without your assistance, I should think perhaps the best service you could render would be to help it along if you know ways by which you could do so." By early December, 1922, the matter had become more urgent, and Few was writing to B. N. Duke:

I wish you and your Brother would give just a few moments' thought to the Medical School matter about which I have spoken to you both. I consider it practically certain that if we do not get it, it will still be put in Durham, built partly by the Rockefeller money, and controlled by the University of North Carolina. If there is to be a medical school in Durham, Trinity ought to have its hand on it. With one of the most important departments in Durham and a hard-surface road making Chapel Hill almost a suburb of Durham the time might come when we might have to struggle for educational leadership in our own town. While there can be no rivalry in good works, we ought to look out for the causes we have on our hearts. I expect Trinity to become one of the great institutions of America. It may take years. That will largely depend on how far along we can put it in this generation. We must do our best to keep the road open.

I still believe if you and Mr. J. B. wish it we can get this medical school; or through the Rockefeller Board we can have some part in its control; and if we should completely fail I feel sure that we can handle the matter in such a way as to leave the College stronger in the eyes of the Rockefeller people and other such great foundations. If you and your Brother agree with this view of the matter, I will come to New York within the next ten days, and we will come to close grips with the proposition. Whatever is done must be done within the next few weeks. And this seems to me to be a matter of so great importance that I could never forgive myself if I had to feel through the years that I had left any stone unturned.

Ultimately a plan for a co-operative medical education program was proposed, and the announcement led to a tremendous amount of discussion throughout the state. It was universally agreed that such facilities were needed. The President of the University of North Carolina, Harry W. Chase, issued a statement favoring it if an acceptable plan of co-operation

could be found. "I am frank to say that there are such possibilities of doing a big thing for the state in a big way that it
is my earnest hope that the difficulties may be solved." Governor Cameron Morrison approved the idea and was active in
its behalf. The *News and Observer*, on the other hand, stated
that Few's "offer includes a proposal to take care of the greater
part of the State's expenditures for the first two years . . .
leaving the State to come in later when demands upon its
finances may be less stringent," but suggested, in the same
issue, "Dr. Few's proposal in all probability will be rejected."
The Durham *Herald*, however, remarked: "The plan is so
practical, so far reaching in its scope, so broad-minded, so unselfish that on first consideration it strikes a responsive chord
in the heart of every North Carolinian," and went on to say
that the medical profession, the University, and Trinity "have
been wrestling with the problem of a four year medical school,
trying to find the best solution. It remained for President Few
to find it."

Few kept B. N. Duke informed of developments. On December 20, 1922, he wrote:

I went to Raleigh yesterday to see Governor Morrison, President Chase of the University of North Carolina, and others concerning the possibility of a jointly operated medical school. . . .
The Governor and Dr. Chase seemed enthusiastic about it, and
every other thoughtful man I talked with. The News and Observer may oppose it, and there will probably be a good deal of
splashing of the waters; but it looks now as if the plan might be
approved all along the line. If it is approved, then I will do my
best to put it over. In any event I am sure it will do us good.
We have tried to help the State meet a great need, and we have
shown our willingness to cooperate. And we will be stronger than
ever before as we steadily seek to develop and preserve a sound
public opinion in the State, upon which everything depends.

I enclose herewith a clipping from the *News and Observer*.
Needless to say this reporter got no intimation from me of all
this rolling in money that he writes about. I mentioned no names
and no amounts. I said what a medical school ought to have, and

I declared my belief that we could succeed if we could agree upon a perfectly sound plan. Everything else is due to the reporter's fancies. . . .

The plan came under attack from several quarters, and in the end it failed, as the *News and Observer* had predicted. President Few's view of the matter is found in a statement which he prepared for the Committee which had been formed to consider the plan, but which the Committee did not make public:

I felt sure that the State needed one medical school but not two. And it occurred to me that it would be wise to see if one strong medical school might not be secured by uniting the two movements. . . . I have stated . . . that if a workable plan of cooperation . . . could be found I would undertake to raise half the amount needed for a complete medical school to be located in Durham and operated in connection with Watts Hospital.

Immediately it was requested that other colleges of the State be associated with the enterprise and I saw the wisdom of the suggestion. Then the point was made that this plan of cooperation might seem to be a violation of the American doctrine of the separation of church and state. While I was not personally concerned of [with] the validity of this objection I saw that there would be practical difficulties. . . .

I still believe this undertaking can be carried through to success by which we might build here in North Carolina one of the great medical schools of the country. I earnestly hope that public sentiment as represented in the General Assembly, and out of it, can be brought to support some big cooperative movement—just as big as the limitations of circumstances will allow, in which all the educational forces of the State may work together to do this really great thing.

Some one may ask suppose the State should undertake to establish this medical school and the undertaking at some stage of the program should fail. My answer would be that the State would be no worse off than it is now. As the proposer of the plan I would probably get my share of the blame. But I am used to taking risks and I willingly take this one. I should not feel disgraced by failure or even unduly cast down. I would probably just try some other way to help the State meet the need of a complete high-grade Medical School.

And suppose we succeed; and I believe the chances favor success to a united movement. Then we should have here in North Carolina a great medical and hospital centre for the use of our people for all time.

But let us all assure ourselves that this is not a big plum to be pulled down. It is rather a great task to be achieved.

The failure of his co-operative plan did not embitter President Few. Immediately, there was a movement on the part of Durham citizens to bring the proposed medical school of the University of North Carolina to Durham. Mr. John Sprunt Hill, a wealthy friend of the University of North Carolina, the son-in-law of the late George W. Watts, founder of Watts Hospital, of which Hill was President of the Board of Directors, was interested in the movement to locate the proposed University of North Carolina Medical School in Durham, which became known as the "Durham plan." Early in February, 1923, Few wrote to Mr. Hill:

. . . it may not seem to you to be wise to try to go on with the larger undertaking contemplated in the "Durham plan." I therefore hope that you, your committee, and your trustees will feel free to offer to the trustees of the University of North Carolina for their medical department the cooperation of the Watts Hospital and whatever else you may have to offer, if that seems to be the wise course to pursue.

While as of course you know, this is now purely a Durham plan and Trinity College has nothing whatever to do with it, I cannot let this occasion go by without telling you how deeply I appreciate your cooperation with me in all that I have tried to do for medical education. . . .

I am just as willing now as I have ever been to work for a first class medical school. And I will be completely loyal to the larger Durham plan until it succeeds or is finally thrown aside.

President Few's later comments may be of interest:

This whole movement fell through. The plan was not free from difficulties; and its failure may have been inevitable. The

State was not then ready for cooperation. On the other hand, there is here in North Carolina at the present time a widely recognized need of adjusting and co-ordinating all our educational institutions, whether supported by philanthropy or by the direct taxes of the people, so that they may be used to the best possible advantage. . . . The Medical School episode, aside from having an important perhaps an essential place in the history of medical education in North Carolina, has further significance in the fact that this sort of cooperation would have been easier if it had been begun in 1923 than it will ever be again. At any rate, it is a satisfaction to know that the forces which have made Duke University were then, as they are now, on the side of cooperation. . . . It incidentally, however, served two good purposes—it kept the road open for a first-rate School of Medicine later on, and it put Mr. James B. on his mettle.

XXV

It is entirely possible that J. B. Duke's observations led him to the conclusion that his benefactions would have to remain within the realm of private philanthropy and that the future of the privately endowed institution would have to be in strong hands. With time, and even with adversity, the bonds between the Dukes and Trinity became strong, the ultimate proof of the confidence in President Few and the causes which he and the institution sought to serve.

J. B. Duke wanted his philanthropy to take the most beneficent form, of course, and something of his insistence upon the quality of education at Trinity may be gleaned from President Few's letter of appreciation for a large gift written in October, 1922:

We will not assume one single new responsibility until we have adequate resources for the new undertaking. We will limit the number of students if that becomes necessary in order to do the best work. We will not seek numbers but make quality our watchword. And we will work hard to develop the right kind of character in our students and graduates. As I understand it, you and I are thoroughly agreed on these big fundamentals. I hope to have more and more opportunity to talk with you. I have learned much from you, and I expect to learn more. . . .

And now for myself, I thank you with both hands and all my heart. You have given us all new hope and new courage, and we will strive on to make the old College just what it ought to be.

During his later years President Few was working on a history of Duke University, and he had drafted chapters on the different divisions of the University, but unfortunately he did not live to complete the task. It would seem appropriate, however, to quote from his all too brief account of the creation of the Duke Endowment:

So far as I can discover James B. Duke made the largest gift ever made by one individual for the founding of a university in the history of the world. . . .

In the first place, it ought always to be remembered that Mr. Duke had long had it in mind to render some signal service to humanity. Indeed, I believe that he had carried through life a purpose of this kind. He probably acquired it in his early years from his father, Washington Duke, in many ways an extraordinary man. Furthermore, Mr. Duke, like his father, had a deep appreciation of organized Christianity and the Church, and their value to human society. . . . It is also probable that his interest in Trinity College was strengthened by the fact that the College rested upon moral and religious sanctions. He loved his native state, and—an experience common to men—this feeling grew much stronger as he drew toward the end of his life. Along with other members of his family, two of whom were graduates and others of whom were ardent supporters, he came to have a personal interest in Trinity College. . . .

It was in 1916 when Mr. Duke first spoke definitely to me concerning his purpose to give away during his lifetime a large part of his fortune. It is true that on two former occasions he had intimated to me such a purpose; and Mr. B. N. Duke had many years before told me that at some time his brother would be sure to become interested and would go far beyond what he and his father had been able to do. Mr. B. N. Duke once said to me, "when my brother does become interested he will do so much that he will eclipse what I have been able to do," declaring in effect: "he must increase, but I must decrease". . . .

. . . . Meanwhile I believe that Mr. Duke had had no thought of the establishment of a university. Our talks had been about strengthening Trinity College and other philanthropies. I had as yet laid before him no plan for building a university. I had found it difficult to work out a plan by which a new university could be built and in which Trinity College with its setting and constituency could be included. I continued to find this difficult in spite of the fact that I had given it a great deal of thought and talked with a good many others about it.

In March, 1921 I had a serious illness and during this illness I had a good deal of free time to reflect. The whole idea of the University became clear in my mind. I dictated it to my wife and requested her to see that it reached Mr. Duke whatever the outcome of my illness might be. Almost immediately I passed into unconsciousness from which I am told no one expected me ever to return. In the long days of convalescence I developed in my own mind the plan precisely as I later on laid it before Mr. Duke. The first day that I was able to leave my house I went to his office and explained the plan to Mr. B. N. Duke, who happened to be in Durham at that time. He said at once that he heartily favored it. As soon as I could go to New York I laid the whole plan before Mr. James B. Duke. Future developments made plain that the idea took strong hold on him, but he gave no evidence of it that day. This was the occasion on which I suggested that the new institution be called Duke University. There were both in North America and in Great Britain many colleges, some independent and some parts of universities, with the name Trinity; and it seemed to me therefore to have too little individuality to be attached to a great university. But I was, of course, heartily for keeping Trinity as the name of the College, just as there is a Trinity College at Oxford, one at Cambridge, and one at the University of Toronto. Mr. Duke has some times been blamed for insisting that the institution be named Duke University. It is for this reason that I am here going to some pains to make it plain that this was not his suggestion but mine.

While it was not until December 11, 1924 that Mr. Duke signed the Indenture by which Duke University and the Duke Endowment were created, he had been working definitely and hard toward that end for a good many years preceding. In 1921 he came to Durham and from his brother's residence sent for me. It was very cold weather, snow was on the ground, and I was in bed with influenza. But I immediately went to see him and spent some two days and nights going over with him and others details that in the end had to do with the founding of the University. As soon as I could do so I returned to my own home; and I had a recurrence of influenza which rapidly developed into pneumonia. It will be seen then that this desperate illness was caused by devotion to the movement of the launching of the University and out of that illness grew definite plans upon which within less than four years the University was launched. This personal incident is worthy of record here if it serves to illustrate again the moving spirit of the American College, its dedication to the causes of mankind, its unselfish service to youth, and all its beautiful idealisms of excellence that make it, as I think, the best loved institution among us.

. . . . I can never forget when in early December, 1924, Mr. Duke called some of us to his residence in Charlotte. There were present a good many of the men who have been most directly concerned about the development of the University. We spent there two days and nights engrossed in considerations of great importance. We tried to isolate ourselves completely but in spite of all we could do there was a leak and the full text of the Indenture had to be hurried to the press of the country . . . for two or three years prior to December, 1924 we had had great difficulty in keeping from the public premature information about our plans. Some of the experiences of this kind have been among the most difficult of my life. We felt fully compensated for all our discouragements and difficulties when we knew at last that the University was certain to be built.

In the spring of 1924 Mr. Duke authorized us to begin the purchase of land adjacent to the campus of Trinity College. He had in mind the purchase of a good deal of land; for, as I once heard him say, he never knew when to stop buying land. We proceeded at once to get options and to buy, first land that adjoined the College, and then on into contiguous territory. The land was not especially desirable and was not easy to get. It came more and more to look as if we had a difficult task before us. In the meantime, one afternoon I took a walk with three of my sons out into the woods west of the College, and that afternoon I accidentally rediscovered a beautiful woodland tract to the west of the campus through which I had often passed in other years when I was given to horseback riding. It was for me a thrilling moment when I stood on a hill, looked over this wooded tract, and realized that here at last is the land we have been looking for. . . . Purchase of the land north of the campus continued and at the same time there was lively buying to the west. This large acquisition of land by some then unknown persons created excitement in the community . . . the total acreage acquired amounted finally to 5,706.13, a large part of it in forest or in process of reforestation.

A good many of us were thrilled again when we became sure that we had found a local stone, easily available, durable, beautiful and in every way fitted for our building requirements. . . .

Just at the time we were beginning to build and organize the University Dr. Wallace Buttrick was resigning from the presidency of the General Education Board, a position in which he had rendered distinguished service to American education. During a tour of this part of the country he called to see me. This visit was most interesting and profitable to me. As he told me good-bye he said, "the Universities of the country will tell you that they are for you, but," he added slyly, "they won't be." I have found some truth in this. Academic people, some of whom knew better and others could have known, will have to bear a good deal of responsibility for confusing in the early years public opinion about Duke. I hasten to add that whenever we have needed friends there have been fair-minded and able educational administrators and teachers to come to our support. I am tempted to list some of these. If on second thought I do not I have the personal satisfaction of knowing that these names and these kindnesses will be forever borne in grateful memory. Some of these friends, if they ever read this, will recognize themselves, I hope.

The metamorphosis of a small college, with professional training restricted to law and engineering, into a University with its Hospital, Medical School, Divinity School, College of Engineering, School of Forestry, Graduate School, and a Liberal Arts College (including the co-ordinate Woman's College) greatly strengthened in all departments, and with new departments added, was a greater transformation, and in a shorter space of time, than had ever occurred in the South. Thus President Few found himself at the head of a vast and difficult undertaking. James B. Duke, who expected to give much of himself to the building phase of the program, died in 1925, and it was left to President Few and the officers of Trinity College, especially the Secretary and Treasurer, Robert L. Flowers, and the Dean, William H. Wannamaker, in association with the officers of the Duke Endowment and the Trustees, to see the enterprise through.

Inevitably there were those who questioned the ability of small-college men when thrust into situations calling for large administrative skill, educational foresight, and wise leadership. There were many who wondered if Few were a big enough man for the job, and there was at one time a more or less still-born movement to oust him, but it was found that he had a toughness and resilience which surprised even his friends. On all sides it was remarked that never had a man been seen to grow so much, that his latent capacities had blossomed forth in an unexpected manner, and that his genius had confounded his enemies and gratified his friends. The truth seems to be that Few's was no new-found inspiration from a secret source, that the touchstone of his educational statesmanship was to be found in a philosophy of life and a scheme of education which had been maturing within him for thirty years. All through life he had found that he had only to take one step ahead at a time, and he had tried always to make that next step the right step.

Those who thought the administrators of the University lacked sufficient confidence in themselves—a natural thought, for they were charged with an undertaking appalling in its immensity—found that Few was never a fighter by choice but that if trouble arose he could give as well as take. So long as he thought the principle sound he was undismayed. He marshaled his forces well, though their direction might purposely be obscured by tactical maneuvers. His great courage arose from the strength of his moral convictions, which were of long standing. It is doubtless true that Few grew as the University grew. Certainly, he was more in the public eye, and his increased stature may have been due in part to the new knowledge and appreciation of him. Few's modesty and his readiness to subordinate himself in the larger work of education always minimized his true worth. The improvement of his health about the time of the Endowment permitted increased vigor and strengthened him for the tasks ahead. But Few had always been alert, had looked to the future, and was anxious to succeed. He never rested on his laurels. In 1935, a decade after the creation of Duke, he wrote his sister Ellie:

In the year that has intervened since I sent you Christmas greetings one year ago I have a feeling that much has been accomplished here, especially in the inner development of the University; and I am sure I have learned lessons that will be useful to me the rest of the way. . . . You have helped me now through a long period of years, particularly in your enlightened and sympathetic understanding of the best that human life holds for us; and I am most grateful to you. . . .

XXVI

It is not appropriate here to trace the development of the various divisions of the University or to appraise the important contributions made by Few's associates (which he would have been the first to recognize), but we may look briefly at some aspects of his outlook on life and education. The thought is merely to suggest here what is more fully amplified in the following collected papers.

It was characteristic of President Few that he should speak calmly, deliberately, and after mature reflection; as he did not strain for effect in his public speeches, neither did he in his formal writings or in his reports to the Board of Trustees, where he undertook to discuss, appropriately enough, some of his educational concepts. He was never purely emotional, never sensational, but always sober and deliberate. He aimed always at fundamentals, and he chose to express himself in simple terms. The pungent phrase and biting sarcasm he avoided; his was the softly spoken word of hope and cheer. His approach was never controversial. His writing was never turgid or merely anecdotal, but philosophical. His was an effort to state general principles rather than their detailed application. Though he was aware of our national and sectional shortcomings, he was not an alarmist, and he was realistic in his knowledge that we make progress slowly. He was convinced that a balanced education offered the soundest hope of moral, intellectual, and spiritual progress. He was not interested in fads or panaceas, for they were fleeting and transitory, which is one reason why many of his writings have an enduring quality, undated and timeless, and are not without application to the contemporary scene.

He was not an extremist. One cannot imagine him waving his arms and shouting to the crowd in a crisis some such phrase as "we stand at the crossroads of destiny. . . ." He would more probably have thought that we stand always at the crossroads and should have with us constantly a strong faith and a steady courage—that never was the time for excitement. He tried to keep to the middle of the road. Without the stigma attached to the trimmer, he nevertheless thought it no mean happiness, as Shakespeare put it, to be seated in the mean. He was keenly aware of the inevitability of change, of the need for progress, and of the rising tide of industrialization in the South; but, on the other hand, he was aware of the debt to the past, the lessons of the ages, the need to conserve all that was good in society—and to avoid the undesirable effects of too sudden change. Thus during the Great Depression he thought the difficulties through which we were passing would "search out the weaknesses in the institutions of organized society," and enable us "to dicover our mistakes and get our bearings." But, he added, "I am not here falling in with the rather common assumption that we are in an entirely different world, that the former things have passed away and that all things have become new." "Time in its course," he said, "alters things; and it is as bad to be behind the time as to be ahead of the time.

In either case the time will be out of joint for the individual and the nation."

There is ample evidence that he was on the side of progress. More than a generation after President Crowell had departed from Trinity, he was paying a tribute to him as "the first college executive to bring from the outside into a postwar Southern state the real breath of progress. He achieved the difficult task of moving the College from a quiet village to a growing center of industry and population and placed it in the main currents of American life. He revived this College with new ideas and fresh aspirations and stirred awake this whole commonwealth. . . ." The willingness to go forward was a tradition at Trinity. "This trait," Few wrote in 1925, "has persisted through every period of its history and the true hallmark of all its spiritual sons is this sturdy refusal to get stuck in outworn traditions and this constant will to walk in the ways of progress. . . ." In his inaugural address he said that the College would "always throw itself unreservedly into the doing of the supreme duty of the hour." "A while ago," he said with reference to the threat to academic freedom in the Bassett case, this duty was "to break the shackles of politics and traditionalism." He was happy to feel that he and Trinity College had a small part in making North Carolina one of the most progressive states in the South. In speaking of three departed members of the Board of Trustees, Toms, Turner, and Peacock, he said: "I never knew any one of them to make a mistake. They were wise and courageous and on the right side of all questions. That is to say, they were always for progress and on the side of the future. . . ."

The message that James B. Duke gave to Walter Hines Page, when he came to dedicate the Trinity library, "Tell them to think for themselves," had fallen into a pattern already established. The pattern was broadened when in the Bassett case it became clear that one could not only think but could speak and write freely. There was an echo of the Bassett affair in the early depression years, and again the answer was the same. Mr. Norman Thomas, several times a presidential candidate on the ticket of the Socialist party, had spoken on the Duke campus at the invitation of a private group. Some friends of Duke had spoken to President Few in protest, thinking perhaps that this public appearance of Mr. Thomas at the University meant that the public would think the University had given its endorsement to Mr. Thomas. President Few replied in writing to the protest, without giving entire satisfaction, and then he suggested that he and the protestants

defer the effort to clear up these misunderstandings until we can have a talk together.

And when that time comes, I shall desire also to discuss with you three practical questions suggested to me by our correspondence: (1) Since the University had nothing to do with the invitation to Thomas and its officers knew nothing about it until his coming was announced, do you think that I, or in my absence some other officer representing me, should have refused to allow Thomas to speak in our buildings? (2) Is it the business of the University to protect its students from any except the orthodox views of economics and government, and particularly should students be forbidden to discuss those economic and governmental doctrines involved in what is known as Socialism? (3) Should I as President of the University be expected to know the ultimate truth in all the great fields of human knowledge and so at all times be ready to rule out questions that are not "fairly debatable," in economics and government, in psychology and philosophy, in zoology, in Biblical criticism and theology, and in all other subjects of university instruction?

These three questions seemed to put the matter at rest.

President Few would have a tolerant approach toward the problems of life. A reasoned, considered opinion, founded on facts and not bias, was, however, far removed from mere indifference. There was a need for men of positive convictions. But, unfortunately, there were some "who have strong and stubborn convictions, and convictions that are not always well founded. There are others . . . who have no convictions at

all. They live in a neutral world, a vapid and empty world
. . . without burning convictions none of us will be apt to go
far in the confused and uncertain world that we live in."

He recognized the fact that all history showed conflicts to
exist within society and that these conflicts could be best re-
solved or minimized by appeals to reason and by considerations
of mutual interest. "The selfish capitalist and the irresponsible
demagogue are two of our great national perils. The selfishness of the one intensifies the recklessness of the other. And
because of the extreme radicalism of the demagogue the conservative owner of property often fears legislation and resists
reforms that would be useful to himself and to society." His
hope for society was in the avoidance of extremes and the use
of "considerate public discussion" and the "conscientious use of
the franchise" to bring about "a spirit of perfect fairness and
honesty" in public life and "to create a moral necessity that
each man shall do his duty exactly as he sees it, free from any
sort of coercion. . . ."

He believed that a tolerant and reasonable public opinion
alone could form the basis of progress. An untutored electorate
was little better than a mob, subject to the chicanery of the
demagogue or the predatory interests of great wealth. The
tyranny of numbers he dreaded. He feared that the politicians
would "feel obliged to go with the multitude, to heed the loud
voice of the majority rather than the still, small voice of principle, of national honor and integrity. For while majorities
must rule in a democratic society, they are not always right,
and when they ride hard they lead to reaction and revolt."
Since we were destined in this country to have more rather than
less popular liberty, "the unwholesome restiveness of the present can only be permanently cured by the fitting of the masses
of men for enlightened self-government and by removing in
right and fair ways whatever of abuse may exist in the business, social, and political life of the American people." This

he recognized as a "stupendous task," to see that people were "strong enough to maintain their rights . . . and at the same time reasonable enough to give perfect respect to the rights of others . . . to make men too intelligent to be led by designing demagogues; in short to construct . . . a mighty tower of strength against blind ignorance as well as sordid materialism."

President Few was aware that improvements in society would have to rest on the support of public opinion. By public opinion he meant "the conscious and unconscious thinking of men about duty and conduct, and the embodiment of this thinking in prevalent ideals of life in such a way as to shape the collective and individual character of a whole people." Public opinion must be "intelligent, fearless, and free," and it could never be shaped by force, only through persuasion, which called for patience. "This patient waiting for the harvest often calls upon us to let the wheat and the tares grow together; it is perhaps in a sense a toleration of evil. . . . While error then must never be accepted as good, yet it may be, and often is, necessary to wait to strike it down, and we must be careful not to do good in such a way that evil will come of it." Above all, opinion must be free. "Any sort of constraint of opinion, whether it be tacit or overt, breeds an unhealthy intellectual atmosphere; and a sound and wholesome citizenship cannot be built up in miasmatic intellectual regions." Colleges and universities must also be free from governmental interference. "There is a tendency on the part of governments all over the world today to interfere with teaching. Even in America, and in some of the more enlightened states, we have teachers' oaths, and other threats to honest teaching . . . . colleges and universities must all the time be on their guard against the threat everywhere of government enlarging itself at the expense of liberty."

Co-operation brought about by persuasion and a genuine meeting of minds was seen by Few to be a major force in American, if not world, society. "Co-operation is undoubtedly an idea whose hour has come, and institutions of education ought to be the first to hail it. No one of our institutions can undertake everything." Co-operation in educational enterprises could bring "distinct benefits that might come to colleges and professional schools from their location on adjacent or neighboring campuses. . . . While I think a plan of this kind has great merit and disregard of it in the past has brought distress and relative failure to many educational enterprises . . . and while I believe the idea will be more and more considered, still it cannot be forced but must rely on a natural and slow growth. . . ." He instanced examples of co-operation between Duke and the University of North Carolina in the matter of libraries, training in medical social service, and other departments of study. This co-operative attitude extended outside the local area. Few was one of the three organizers of the Southern University Conference, which had for its prime object the maintenance of educational standards. He likewise initiated an informal conference of private or denominational institutions in the South. This group was useful in formulating standards and practices for the independent institutions, and President Few served as chairman as long as he lived. It was a matter for comment that during the expansion of Duke he continued active in the organizations concerned with the smaller and church-related institutions and that he sought to find ways to give them encouragement and support.

As an active Methodist layman, and yet with little concern for dogma, President Few was interested in the movement for Christian unity, especially within his own church. The split in the Methodist Church had its origin in the antecedents of the Civil War, and subsequent events had tended to strengthen the sectional antagonisms as well as the theological conflicts between liberals and fundamentalists. There were sharp internal divisions within the branches of the Methodist churches, so that a long and bitter struggle preceded actual unification. But Few always favored unification. As the issues were being discussed he was for "going into the matter fully and with patience, kindliness, and the utmost possible consideration for minorities." "I got my first bent toward unification of American Methodism," he said,

from impressive utterances of Dr. James H. Carlisle [who had come a long way since he signed the South Carolina Ordinance of Secession in 1860] while I was a student at Wofford College. . . .

I gave a good deal of thought to this question when my attention was focused upon it in 1906 by Dr. John C. Kilgo. . . . I have heard that Bishop Kilgo afterwards changed his opinion about unification. But I have seen no reason to change mine, developing as it did through a period of years and becoming pretty well fixed in 1906.

For the best part of my life I have tried at all times to stand for co-operation and friendliness in all directions; to emphasize essential things and to subordinate the unessential. I profoundly believe that this is the spirit that leads to usefulness and, for that matter, to success. . . .

He did not favor the elimination of religious denominations, but he did believe that "all denominations ought to work heartily together for the good of their fellows." He later became a member of the commission that prepared the way for the Uniting Conference which brought the principal Methodist churches together in 1939.

XXVII

President Few took pride in the fact that Trinity was national in its scope and outlook. His first report to the Board of Trustees suggested that the tribute paid by those who came to participate in his installation was "unmistakable evidence" that the College had "attained to a place of national importance." He thought the spirit of nationalism, as distinguished from sectionalism, should be fostered. "The first United States flag to float over a non-military college in the South, I think, was here. Here was originated the unique and beautiful ceremony about the flag that marks the opening and closing of every college year." This feeling of nationalism was genuine, yet it was compatible with the recognition that the institution, because of its location and because of special needs, owed particular obligations to the South and to North Carolina. When two new dormitories were named for former governors of North Carolina, Thomas J. Jarvis and Charles B. Aycock, President Few said, "Trinity College, although it rests upon a private foundation, is a state institution just as much as if it were supported by public taxation. The heroes of the State are its heroes; and it counts it a privilege to name two of its buildings after distinguished governors. . . ."

President Few was a child of the South. He loved its climate, its soil, its people with their neighborliness, charm, and essential goodness, but he did not love all the ways of the South. He was its constructive critic. "Why is it," he asked early in his career, "that a civilization which has produced such men as Washington, Jefferson, Madison, Marshall, and Lee is now without commanding leaders of national reputation; without constructive statesmen on a large scale; without ancient and famous institutions of learning; without literary journals and magazines of high merit and standing; without well established publishing houses, without artists and writers; without so many of the good things of life . . . ?" Where were the "men of strong convictions, of breadth, of large-mindness, of comprehensive view"? "We have had a long day of small things, of men of local, narrow, sectional outlook, who do not see from a national, widesweeping standpoint, to whom truth is not free and universal, but limited and of special application. We have too long regarded ourselves as a peculiar people, living under peculiar conditions, with peculiar problems to work out in peculiar ways."

Few's vision of the future was that of the cautious realist, not the vapid optimist, and it was this spirit that determined his outlook on education and his hope for the intellectual and spiritual regeneration of Southern society. He was aware that the South's poverty was in large part the result of the Civil War and Reconstruction, but he saw no virtue in poverty, for he recognized that the future of the South must rest upon an economic foundation. "One of our first tasks," he said in his inaugural address, "is the material uplifting of the section, the development of all kinds of business, the creation of wealth, and the building of vital forces of civilization." He welcomed the New South; he looked toward the future. "We are in the midst of a great industrial awakening; even in the old business of agriculture a new day has arrived." He recognized that the problems of the South, of long standing as they were, could not "be solved in a day or a generation," for they were "intricate and difficult of solution." And industrialization brought with it new problems in human relations. "The duty of the well-to-do towards the less well-to-do is a matter that has puzzled thoughtful and unselfish men from the beginning of civilization. . . . Much has been learned from the experience of the past. And I believe poor people in America today have a better chance than anywhere else in all time. Much still remains to be done, but this is not going to be done by crude, unfair or evil-minded agitators, or by well-meaning but ill-informed sentimentalists."

There was one aspect of Southern life which, a generation or two ago, was seldom touched at all unless in a negative way, namely the race issue. On the race matter President Few early expressed himself. He did not shout his views from the house-top, nor did he lead a crusade; he offered no quick and easy solution to the "so-called Negro problem"; he sought only to examine the coexistence of the black and white races in its fundamental aspects. It had been a mistake to give the Negro, "this hapless child of evil destiny," a status in society for which he was not prepared after the Civil War. "It is not liberty but sheer cruelty to throw upon a people responsibilities for which they are not ready, just as it would be a crime to give absolute freedom to an inexperienced child." The presence of the Negro had a "blighting influence" upon the whites, for the course of history since the Civil War had worked mightily to sharpen racial antagonisms and create bogus political, economic, and social issues which had driven the whites in the direction of "narrow-mindedness, intolerance, and injustice." It had come about, therefore, that the people had "little regard for the right in politics, in political parties, and in political methods. The necessity of preventing Negro political domination has led to unfairness at the polls until there is an unhealthy political condition among us. We have argued that the end justifies the means, and have lulled ourselves in the quieting delusion that we need not reap the fruit of our sowing. . . . Before we can prosper as we should we must free ourselves from every vestige of political dishonesty and unfairness and from all attempt through abuse, through social ostracism, or through any other means, to brow-beat others into our way of thinking." It was the essence of his thinking that one could do only what public opinion could be brought to sanction. The improvement of the status of the Negro might best be accomplished through the white race. "I am more and more convinced," he said, "that the surest and quickest way to settle this stupendous question is through the education of the white race through leading the masses of them into enlightened manhood, justice, and right."

For a number of years President Few was a trustee of the Jeanes Foundation, which had as its purpose the improvement of the Negro race, especially in the field of education. His faith in education as a means of bringing right attitudes to the people at large and his concern at injustice practiced upon the Negro are illustrated by his letter to a Trinity graduate in 1916:

I was out of the State when the Wayne County lynching occurred. When I read it in a northern city, I was deeply distressed. May I express the hope that you, and every other Trinity College man and every right minded citizen of Wayne County and North Carolina, shall do his duty to the utmost in keeping from the fair name of North Carolina the lasting shame that would be put upon it by the failure to bring to justice these notorious violators of the law? I sympathize with you and every other high minded man in the county because of the chagrin and sorrow that the tragedy in your county brought to all.

A similar letter went to the Governor of North Carolina. Few, like the Dukes, was a sincere friend of North Carolina College, a state college for Negroes located in Durham; he spoke many times on the campus, and he was a long-time friend of the founder, Dr. James E. Shepard.

Perhaps Few's most intimate colored friend was John Love. John attended him in his bachelor quarters before his marriage; later he was in charge of the mimeograph and stationery department of the University. He learned to imitate perfectly Few's rather plain and open signature and on occasion was authorized to use it. He was known about the campus as "Secretary" Love. There is a story, never officially denied, that once when Few was ill John was called in to affix the President's necessary signature to the College diplomas. (It is a curious fact that for some years around 1910 Trinity College was footnoted in the *World Almanac* as "without distinction as to race.")

XXVIII

For most of his long life President Few thought and wrote and spoke about the problems of education. One of the earliest of his schoolboy essays was entitled "Dangers and Disadvantages of Our System of Common School Education," in which he pointed out that everything depended on the teacher. On these, as on other matters, he expressed himself simply and clearly. He was probably not a profound student of educational theories, and he was not apt to be confused by trying to combine contradictory notions or impractical ideas with the realities faced by Trinity or Duke. He believed that an educational institution had to fit into its environment, as a native plant endowed with the characteristics necessary for survival rather than an exotic import without vitality or genuine substance. He admired Harvard; he took pains to see how Harvard developed into a real American university, and he did not hesitate to borrow ideas from Harvard, but he knew that Harvard's development had to be worked out according to its special circumstances. The Johns Hopkins, he thought, had been less successful, except for its medical school, for it had tried "to transplant to American soil a full grown German university." "An attempt in the South to imitate a university like Harvard would be equally foolish and prove equally unsuccessful. We cannot transplant. We must build for ourselves in the light, of course, of our own experience and in the light of what has been done elsewhere." And it must be a slow process, with patient experimentation, a truly indigenous growth.

A university, he said, must have at its center a good college which would struggle for "excellence rather than size; it will aim at quality rather than numbers,—quality of those who teach and quality of those who learn." This would require that admission be selective, with the result that some would not be admitted, which would seem hard until it was realized there was a place for them in society if they would fit themselves for it. Selective admission was required under terms of the Indenture of the Duke Endowment, which requested the utmost care to admit as students only those "whose previous record shows a character, determination, and application evincing a wholesome and real ambition for life." Education was expensive, and facilities were limited; Duke could take only the number for which it was prepared. "We are determined above all else to do well what we undertake to do." To select students wisely was difficult, of course, and mistakes would be made, for there was "considerable doubt as to the best ways to find students that are apt to do well in the University and afterwards in life." Whatever the methods devised, it would always remain "hard to pick the winner among colts that have not yet run a race." Especially in the democratic society of America there should exist the tradition of excellence. As Few said to a Trinity audience back in 1907:

> We place great stress on the dignity and importance of the average man, and we are very apt not to make enough of such a phenomenon as Shakespere in a nation's thought and life. We are too apt in all our acts, thoughts, and ideals to be content with the passably good, and not anxious enough in our search after the best.

He felt that the student ought to show by his own efforts and his own achievements that he had earned the right to an education.

> A sound civilization cannot be built by a generation that has had schooling without cost to themselves or their parents, without any effort on their own part, and without any sense of obligation to repay the debt they owe to society. . . . This is not the way to build a great civilization, but the certain way to build a race of half-educated, and sometimes half-respectable, panhandlers, who are not prepared to do honest work but rather seek short cuts that lead to false success. . . .
> There is no good reason now why every high-school graduate, even though he may have only been able to squeeze through an approved high school . . . should therefore be automatically admitted to college.

One aspect of American education which troubled President Few was intercollegiate athletics, and especially the abuses which attended them. President Crowell, before his resignation in 1894, had introduced intercollegiate sports with considerable satisfaction to the students, but the approval of the Methodist conferences and some influential laymen had been somewhat restrained. Early in Kilgo's time intercollegiate football had been abolished, and Professor Few had written an article for the *South Atlantic Quarterly* in which he had pointed to the abuses in that field, the failure of the colleges to remedy them, and the incompatibility of undue emphasis on sports with the highest intellectual endeavor. His second report to the Trustees in 1912 dwelt again on the subject. He referred to a tendency, then nearly twenty years old, "to use high pressure methods in recruiting students. . . ." The tendency had gone unchecked and had "a debilitating effect" on every college in the state. "This is, in my judgment, one cause that keeps North Carolina from being the most inviting field for higher education in the South." The tendency was "assuming the proportions of an organized and well-financed effort to raid the high schools of promising athletes. This is the most sinister manifestation of misdirected college loyalty. . . ." Nearly two decades later he expressed the hope that "a rising tide of intellectual interest might lift the whole level of undergraduate life and . . . sweep the centre of student activities away from irrelevant undergraduate absorptions and on to the main concerns of college education." In later years he came to accept the interest of the public in athletic games, but he felt that with a relatively small stadium and without a large center of population the University would not come to depend on income from football "so as to be conscious of the evils of gate receipts." It was a way, he granted, to finance the athletic program without adding the cost to student tuition and fees. Intercollegiate football at Trinity was prohibited in 1895, reinstated in 1920.

Just as he felt that intellect only was not a sufficient qualification for the benefits of college training, so in the case of professional schools he considered technical training alone not fully adequate to enable a graduate to render his fullest service to society. He thought that a school of law, for example, should "provide liberal training in law as one of the social sciences closely allied with government, economics, and business administration." More was required than the narrowly professional preparation. He spent much time trying to devise, with the assistance of the law faculty, a program which would broaden the training of both prospective businessmen and lawyers. It would include study under those expert in the fields of economics and political science as well as the law. He even thought of a separate school for the purpose, but closely co-ordinated with existing departments, offering a two-year course and perhaps a master's degree. The basic thought behind this was the great changes in society that had come about within recent years and the inability of present education to train men to cope with the new problems.

The central problem in the social and economic life of the nation (indeed, of all nations) is the relationship between government and economic enterprise. The intervention of the state in fields formerly left largely to private initiative has progressed for the past fifty years at an accelerating pace until virtually no significant field of business activity has been left unaffected. There is little reason to suppose that this trend will be reversed. . . . The situation created, especially within the past five years, is so pervasive that no persons in posts of business responsibility can escape contact with at least some of the problems raised. Yet few people are prepared by education to cope with these problems. Upon the legal profession has fallen the brunt of the task, but, by and large, the lawyer has been obliged to meet the new issues without either the benefit of a training which has been directed specifically toward them or the cooperation of business executives properly equipped to aid him in the development of policies adequate to the problems encountered. There has been blind opposition and perhaps still more blind acquiescence.

We need not here discuss the plan; it was still tentative at the time of Few's death. The point is that he already saw, before World War II, a need arising, and he was carefully preparing to meet that need when the opportunity came. His mind was not static; he was constantly groping for new insight into better ways for the institution to serve "the causes of humanity." There were other aspects of legal education which had his enthusiastic support, such as the Legal Aid Clinic, the Department of Legislative Research and Drafting, and the publication of *Law and Contemporary Problems*. The Law

School, like other departments of the institution before the Duke Endowment, was small, but there was a tradition of excellence of which President Few was quite proud. As he wrote in his proposed history of the University: "At that time (1924) a two-year law course was offered and the life of the school was the teaching power and radiant personality of one man, Dean Samuel F. Mordecai. Dean Mordecai's ideas on legal education were very advanced. . . ." It was a tradition which was to be followed, and President Few's progressive views on legal education were foreshadowed in his comprehensive report to the Trustees covering the years 1925-1931, when he said, "There is a widespread feeling that legal education will undergo changes comparable to the reforms in medical education a generation ago. Why should not this be the School to blaze the way? It would not have to fight its way against opposing traditions and could therefore be developed rapidly." There were times when he was accused of undue caution. The record would seem to suggest that it was the caution of wisdom rather than of indecision or timidity. Another example of his tendency to hold fast to tradition while at the same time working for necessary adjustments and improvements is seen in his suggestions about the Graduate School:

I think our Graduate School should follow the same general lines that are followed in the best American graduate schools; but as rapidly as we are ready for it we ought to separate more sharply between the college and the graduate school and give to the work of the graduate a more distinctly university character than has heretofore been the rule in this country. I advocate less of fixed routine and more flexibility than is common to American graduate schools, less instruction by courses and lectures and more individual effort on the part of the student under the guidance of the teacher.

Despite the fact that Few's name will forever be linked with the creation of the Duke Endowment, it should be remembered

[125]

that he was primarily a scholar and an educator, never simply a money-raiser, an administrator—his faith was in education that reached the individual, not in the cluttering machinery of an over-refined administrative system.

XXIX

One final example of President Few's interest in a broadening educational program sufficient to meet the needs of the time is to be seen in the development of the co-ordinate college for women. Here again there was a tradition to build on. The first women to receive a degree from Trinity College were the three Giles sisters, who graduated in 1878. Because of their interest in their brother's work at Trinity, they were allowed to take private instruction until, in their senior year, President Craven admitted them to his classes. Four girls, Fanny and Ida Carr, Mamie Jenkins, and Annie Pegram graduated from Trinity in 1896, the year of Professor Few's arrival, and thereafter "there was a slow increase in women students." In that same year Washington Duke made a gift of $100,000 to Trinity on condition that women be admitted to the full privileges of the College. This condition was later withdrawn by Duke, since none of his other gifts had conditions, but President Kilgo, and then his successor, continued to feel that more adequate plans should be made for women students. But after all it was a man's college, as is suggested by President Few's reply in 1911 to a woman applicant for a position on the faculty: "Your letter of the 4th has been received. We have no vacancy in Trinity College for which you are eligible. Our faculty is composed entirely of men."

As early as 1903 the Board of Trustees went on record as "favoring the extension of facilities for educating women and the establishment for them of a co-ordinate college." The earlier practice had been to give women the same "educational opportunities" as men, although, President Few reported in 1912, "we have never felt that this is precisely a co-educational college." He urged provision for the education of women, for then "the College's opportunity for usefulness and its influence will be doubled." But he wanted co-ordinate education after the plan followed at Harvard with Radcliffe or at Tulane with Sophie Newcomb rather than co-education as it had developed in America, especially in the Western universities. "I am convinced," he said in 1912, "that the time is near at hand when the College should establish a co-ordinate college for women rather than either reverse itself on the subject of education of women or further develop a system of co-education."

This would mean a separate college for women, but located near Trinity College and taught by the same faculty. The education of women should be equal with that of men. The superficial education to which women in the older type of institution had been subjected, with attention devoted to subjects having to do with the cultivation of manners and the refinement of tastes, was all very well so far as it went, but, wrote Few later:

In spite of such excellencies, the education furnished by most women's colleges has lacked substance; it has been devoid of ideas and has tended to go to seed. All thoughtful people are now convinced that the education of women should be put on an intellectual level with the education of men and that into the education of women complete intellectual sincerity should go. Colleges for men seem to a good many of us to be better fitted to provide this sort of education. It is easier for colleges for men to secure and keep great teachers, and after all teachers make colleges. There seems, too, to be no good reason why co-ordinate colleges or even co-educational colleges should not provide for the young women an adequate college life of their own.

In 1915 President Few proposed to increase the facilities "for a small number of women" by an investment of $300,000. Of this amount, $100,000 would be in land already given to the College, $100,000 in building and equipment, and $100,-000 in endowment. The endowment he hoped to secure from the General Education Board, and for Toms he drew up "a suggested letter which you can use or modify as you see fit.

I think it highly desirable to have Mr. W. W. F. bring his influence to bear on Dr. A." The references presumably were to Mr. W. W. Flowers, an associate of Toms and the Dukes in the tobacco business and a brother of Professor R. L. Flowers, and to Dr. Edwin A. Alderman, at that time president of the University of Virginia. With reference to the endowment asked of the General Education Board, the "suggested" letter said:

I realize that the proportion from your Board is rather larger than you usually allow; but you will understand that Trinity College has heavy burdens of its own to carry. It is just now endeavoring to build a gymnasium and two science buildings, in addition to other expensive improvements. Unless we can secure, then, some such proposition from the Board as we are asking for, we shall hardly be able at the present time to carry through our plan to provide adequate facilities for the education of women.

President Few did not originate the idea of co-ordinate education at Trinity; that had been done by President Kilgo, but he gave it active and thoughtful support. In 1921 Southgate Building, donated by the citizens of Durham as a tribute to the memory of James H. Southgate, a dearly beloved citizen and for many years Chairman of the Board of Trustees, was made available to the women. Thus the way had been prepared for a genuine co-ordinate college by the time of the Duke Endowment. Dr. Alice M. Baldwin, a native of New England and a distinguished historian trained at the University of Chicago, who had been appointed Dean of Women and Professor of History in 1923, was President Few's choice for the first Dean of the Woman's College when it opened in 1930. At the same time Trinity College, in order to maintain its continuity, became the undergraduate men's college of Duke University.

xxx

If there was one thing that concerned President Few more than another, it was the character of the faculty and the quality of its teaching. Whatever his interest in endowment and physical facilities, he never ceased to believe that "great men make great universities." It was a thought he reiterated often, and his constant theme in faculty meetings was better teaching. On that subject he almost had an obsession. As in so many other things, his hopes and aims matured early in his administration, and no better statement of his requirements for the ideal faculty can be found than in his 1912 report to the Trustees:

My chief ambition for this college is to keep among its teachers . . . really great men, who, though dedicated by the scholar's career to an unworldly and self-sacrificing life, are yet released from the anxieties of economic necessity; who have a gift for teaching and genuine interest in young men; who know their subjects enormously well and can gather about them a following of devoted disciples filled with the master's reverence for learning and fitted by the application of sound ideas to the conduct of private and public affairs, to bring into a society that pre-eminently needs them the clear head and the steady will of truly educated men.

Even earlier, just as he was beginning his own college teaching career, we get an expression of his ideal for the teacher in his remarks on Professor Francis James Child, his former Harvard instructor, who had just died. After referring to Child as a founder of a scientific study of Chaucer and to his monumental edition of the English and Scottish ballads in ten volumes, Few mentioned the impress he had left on a host of students, "whom he has taught to love honest work and to hate sham. He was an interesting and unique personality. The man was greater than the scholar. His interests were broad enough to include everything that has to do with the better life of men, and his human sympathies were extended to the humblest of his fellows."

President Few, unlike Kilgo, had the training of a scholar, and he understood the needs of scholarship. He worked for the establishment of a system of sabbatical leaves which would enable the teacher to devote more time to research and to fit himself better for his job; he favored a system of annuities, to which the college and the professor would contribute, to provide for old age and to compensate in some degree for the inadequate teacher salaries; and he encouraged the establishment of a University press to publish scholarly books and periodicals and to do a work which could not be left to the commercial press.

Whatever his encouragement to scholars, Few never forgot that the teacher should be greater than his subject. He had an instinctive distrust of the narrow specialist who, absorbed in some obscure and remote subject, permitted his own vision to narrow and who drew within himself to such an extent that he did not see the whole of life. Especially did he feel that the college, as distinguished from professional and graduate schools, should seek for its teachers "men of ideas and power rather than experts in the several branches of learning." "The almost exclusive use of scholarship tests in the selection of teachers," he remarked in his inaugural address, "is in my judgment, one of the gravest defects in American colleges and even in the greatest American universities. Scholarship enters essentially into the making of a good teacher, but so do also a genuine interest in young men and some gift for teaching." Something of his ideal may be seen in his remarks about Sidney Lanier, the Southern poet, who had the passion, if not the necessary training, of the scientific scholar, combined with "the reconstructive insight" of the poet: "For he steadfastly held before himself high ideals of both literature and life; but his ideals were not ethereal, impracticable, unapproachable, and they were not too fine to 'stand the strain of weaving into human stuff on the loom of the real.' "

Enough has been said to make clear that President Few, both early and late, clung to the ideal of a free teacher in a free university. In the mid-thirties he was saying, "Scholars worthy of the name must be kept free in their pursuit of knowledge and their setting forth of the truth as they have found it." That did not mean, of course, that a faculty could be irresponsible, forgetful of its trust to seek objective truth, or prone to take advantage of immature minds for self-gratification or to promote a pet theory. For the man of science, the thinker, the writer, the teacher, President Few had a place; for the head-line hunter, for the academic demagogue, and for the man without balance or perspective, he had no use. This idea was suggested in a more free-wheeling language than he was wont to use when he said: "A university does not need, and a great university will not have, an aggregation of free lances with their half-baked knowledge and, alas too often, with maggots in the brain." But he went on to emphasize that a university "must have scholars who are not too much influenced by the ferment of the time . . . patient searchers after the truth and recognized authorities in their several fields of knowledge. And such men must be protected from the interference of the ignorant and hysterical." Popular causes were not necessarily the right causes; but the cause of truth, popular or not, was always the right and duty of the university and its teachers.

It was not always easy for President Few personally to get close to members of the faculty, especially on short acquaint-ance, and it was not always that he was able to convey to them his full appreciation of their work, but Few's remarks about Professor William McDougall illustrate his support of un-popular causes and his appreciation of great men. Professor McDougall, an Englishman, had come to Duke from Har-vard; his field was the comparatively new one of psychology in which there were many conflicting views. Of all this President Few was aware when he said after McDougall's death:

The causes he contended for were not popular in his day and have not yet fully won their way. He was a great man, a great personality, and his death is a serious loss to the University and its prestige. . . . He has meant more to the University and more to me than I could possibly set down here in words. I am grate-ful beyond my powers of expression to him and to the many others like him who have made possible the rapid development of Duke University as a seat of learning. Great men make great universities.

XXXI

The reader of Few's published papers will find them clearly written, thoughtful, concerned with the fundamental aspects of education or moral endeavor. He need not look for the striking and arresting phrase which all men admire, but which, on analysis, is sometimes found empty and hollow, merely glittering. Nor will he find a new gospel or a new creed or any suggestion that the philosophy of the ages has been outmoded. Few was not strikingly original, nor did he try to be; he did not found a school of thought or pride himself on the novelty of his ideas. He lived in the South, and he loved the South. He was well aware of its weaknesses, but he did not set up as an iconoclast who would revolutionize Southern mores and bring the age of enlightenment full-grown to an unwilling section. Being thus, he built slowly, steadily, surely, and with the long view of the future. He was concerned with the training of men and women to know the good, to do the right, and to serve society as best they could; he was constantly striving to improve the means of doing this; and he was ever hopeful of the future without despairing of the present.

Perhaps his most lasting contribution, and the one in which he would have taken the greatest satisfaction had it ever occurred to him, was in promoting a union of education and religion. He had grown up in a Methodist home, he had attended a Methodist college, and he was a deeply religious man. He was also a man of high intellectual attainments and aware of the deep satisfactions and moral strength inherent in intellectual conquests. But, like many men of profound religious convictions, his faith rested upon no narrow creed; nor did his intellectual attainments rest upon "pure science" without regard for moral qualities. He was able to bring together the forces loyal to a comparatively small church school and the men and agencies necessary for the proper support and functioning of a university devoted to the search for truth both in the spiritual and in the intellectual realm. He was able to do this without disparaging either the spiritual or the material; he felt that, properly understood, as they would be in a wise educational scheme, they were complementary, the one adding strength to the other without impairing the validity of either. The plan of having the two North Carolina Methodist Conferences share in the election of twelve members each to the Board of Trustees and of having the Duke Endowment likewise represented on the Board was devised as a solution to the interrelated problems of legal requirements and effective control. This was a plan to which he had given much thought, for he wanted to avoid unfortunate difficulties which had been faced by other educational institutions in like circumstances.

Again we turn to President Few's inaugural address for a statement of the place of religion in education:

The southern college, if it be wise enough to understand its opportunity, will work in hearty co-operation with the churches. It will not seek to make friends with the churches for the purpose of using them as bill-boards on which to advertise its wares; it will not court their good-will in order to rally its constituency; but in all sincerity it will labor with them just to the end of strengthening and sweetening human life. The aim of Trinity College is stated by the words on its seal, "Religion and Education"; not two but one and inseparable: religion that comprehends the whole of life and education that seeks to liberate all the powers and develop all the capacities of our human nature.

Here was no reference to Methodism, to sectarian creed, or even to orthodoxy. Few was no doubt one of those sympathetic critics of whom he wrote elsewhere, who "might find it in his heart to say that less emphasis could well be placed upon empty profession and upon an indefinable and often meaningless orthodoxy." Judgment should be based less upon profession and more upon the amount of Christian service.

"This shifting of emphasis from formal profession and correctness of creed to one's actual work and the spirit in which one works would produce a more intelligent and Christian charity that would be glad to include those finest and most unselfish spirits who often in our day are spending themselves—in ways not quite the church's but in ways that are effective—for 'the glory of the Creator and the relief of man's estate.' "

A university worthy of the name should be free in the matter of religion. This did not mean, he said, "freedom from religion," nor any lessening of the obligation "to reassert a strong moral note." In short, it seemed to him "perfectly clear that information, training, learning, scientific research, intellectual culture—any or all of these alone" were not "sufficient to save the world of our troubled day. The world needs spiritual regeneration, and our University halls ought to echo with the voice of moral authority." He believed that this condition could exist in the South. "Serious-minded Southern people," he said, "are not hidebound and intolerant . . . but they are in earnest to see that the things of the mind and the spirit rather than stark materialism shall control. . . ." Religion and education President Few sought to fit together into a happy harmony better to serve the land he loved; he breathed a spirit of faith, hope, and charity which appealed to the nobler instincts of a warm-hearted and generous people.

President Few was interested in the appearance of the college grounds and the architecture of the buildings on the campus. "For the soul of the College," he said in 1912, "we would build a beautiful home." He loved the quiet and beauty of nature, and his letters to B. N. Duke contain such passages as this: "the grass and flowers are already beginning to take on something of the softened autumn look which to me makes the later part of August and September the most beautiful of all months in the year on the Trinity Campus." During the construction of the buildings of the University, President Few said, "Life for those of us most intimately concerned was

[134]

raised to its top capacity. The stateliness and calm of the buildings, the beautiful lights at night, and the enchantment of the place, particularly in its first years, who can ever forget?"

To him the Chapel was the center of the University. Something of his faith and aspiration may be seen in his description of that edifice. "Most of all," he said,

I have been thrilled by the noble Chapel, with its rare beauty, its organs, and its bells. I have been more and more deeply impressed with its meaning and its possibilities for good as I have gazed upon it by day and by night, as I have shown thousands of visitors through it, as I have listened to the music of the carillon and of the organ, as I have sat at week-day morning prayers, and at the perfectly beautiful Sunday morning services. The Chapel at the center of the University is intended to be symbolical of the truth that the spiritual is the central and dominant thing in the life of man. Can this idea be realized in our world and can religion and education in its highest forms ever engage successfully in a great formative, common undertaking to make this a better world than man has yet known? Duke University is founded in that faith and the Chapel is its perpetual witness.

XXXII

The most striking thing in President Few's career was his wholehearted devotion to Trinity College and to Duke University. For himself he asked nothing, for his institution everything. J. B. Duke was reported to have said when Few's arrival was announced, "Here comes the hundred-million-dollar man." In his restless urge and ambition for the University he risked being called an opportunist. As a man he was gentle and tender and singularly devoted to his family and friends, yet if the welfare of the institution required, he could be firm and hard and, some must have thought, even ruthless. Those who did not share his devotion or who conceived their duty differently were apt to find him stubborn and relentless in pushing for what he thought was right. He himself never had any doubt as to his motives, only of his judgment. With his love for peace and tolerance and harmony, he was apt to be called a master of indirection; and yet with his Christian tenderness and mystic faith he could be likened to a Quaker gentleman of the old school.

It was true that many found President Few not easy to know. There was a certain shyness and timidity about him that was sometimes misunderstood. It could perhaps be said that in the matter of personal relations his personality was not fully developed. There was a certain deficiency which at times made him seem awkward in dealing with individuals. As one who knew him well said, "He was exceedingly reserved and often plagued with a painful timidity, which, by many, was wrongly interpreted as coldness and rudeness." A conversation in his office might leave the impression that he was aloof or absent-minded. Occasionally he seemed uninterested, read the newspaper, or indulged in a low whistle that was more than a little disconcerting. In all likelihood he was totally unconscious of his mannerisms. It is possible that the very nature of his office and the frequent necessity of saying "No" seemed to put him in a defensive attitude. He was by nature somewhat nervous and fidgety, and he had a curious habit of reaching around his head to scratch it on the other side. One of his classroom mannerisms was the rather frequent removal of his breast-pocket handkerchief. He was said to have a terrific temper; if so, it was under careful control. As he grew older, and the burden of his cares and responsibilities in some respects diminished, he became more relaxed and jovial, and there can be no doubt that he genuinely enjoyed his opportunities to associate with young people. Perhaps he was in some ways a lonely man, too busy to enjoy fully his friends. His very position, to a degree, deprived him of those human relationships in which he found keen enjoyment. It is remembered that he liked to join old friends on festive occasions for an informal dinner and small talk, and, surprising as it may seem, engage in parlor games like "spin the plate." Those who came to know him were seldom aware of any seeming brusqueness; they found him to be a great gentleman, true and kind, and with an inner integrity beyond distrust.

Nothing gave him more concern than the quality of the faculty, and he agonized over the appointments for which he was responsible. He was sincerely interested in the welfare of the faculty, but he did not always succeed in making it aware of that interest. It may be said that in a degree he was inept in faculty meetings and in making the faculty want to work with him. This was, of course, directly contrary to his desire. He frequently urged the faculty, especially the younger members, to visit him in his office, but they seldom did. In the early days of Duke University and its speedy expansion, when the faculty was growing rapidly, there may have been an element of distrust between a President who seemed to some of his faculty to be too conservative, if not positively antiquated, and a youngish faculty, who seemed to the President to have plenty of brash confidence without the sobering years of experience. There was rarely any real hostility between President and faculty, but there was in some instances a lack of understanding and mutual acceptance. This was a matter corrected by time, and when a test came Few never failed to stand by the faculty. At the same time, he never failed to keep the reins of authority in his own hands. He was aware of his own ultimate responsibility, given to him by the Board of Trustees, though he had no thought of being a dictator, for he never forgot that education was a supremely co-operative enterprise. The faculty was seldom aware of his problems and burdens, since he kept his difficulties to himself. There can be no doubt that he had the courage to do the things that were difficult and the strength to make hard decisions, but there was at times a failure to draw from the faculty the help which would have eased his burden. He found it easier, and perhaps more feasible, in difficult matters to turn to a few trusted advisers. There was sometimes a lack of precision in administrative procedures, and informal understandings occasionally led to disagreements.

Those who had been on the faculty long came to know the President and to understand his apparent brusqueness. To them he could be direct and frank, even blunt, as when he wrote the Librarian in 1912: "I notice that there are lights that burn continuously in the Library. Please find out where this fault is and have it remedied at once." On another occasion, in 1916, it was necessary to call certain matters to the attention of the manager of the athletic field:

I observe that some of the students are running on the Circle in violation of our regulations adopted last year and concurred in by you. I have stopped a good many of them and find that they are usually Freshmen who have not been informed concerning the regulation. This would seem to be your fault. Please attend to this henceforth without fail. . . .

The protection of College property was felt by President Few to be a matter for serious personal attention. On one occasion some minor damage by young boys who lived near the campus brought this letter:

It seems that your little boys and perhaps one other boy in coming for the mail occasionally do damage to college property. They broke a glass in the post office the other day. If you will see that the glass is replaced and that the little boys do no further depredations to college property, I shall be willing to let the matter drop. I am sorry to have to call your attention to such a matter. . . .

A paragraph from a letter to B. N. Duke, 1916, read as follows:

I would not mention it, but you may see exaggerated accounts of it in the papers. Some students of Wake Forest College, after a game of basketball Tuesday night, painted the score—W. F. C. 28, T. C. 26—in various places on the campus. The damage was exaggerated in the papers, but the deed itself was a mean one. I have some detectives on the job and if I get sufficient evidence I am going to take the guilty men to court.

There were times, painful occasions they must have been, when the President was obliged to bring more serious matters to the attention of individuals on the faculty or staff. The following letter, carefully revised, is without date or address, and there is no evidence that it was sent:

Practically every job has a business side to it, and for any of us to succeed we must not only work hard, do our very best in fact, but it must all be so convincing as to satisfy the reasonable expectations of those for whom or with whom we work. In your years on the other campus frictions and some complaints have come to my attention from time to time. If on another campus and under wholly different conditions frictions should develop again, then it would begin to look as if the fault might be largely yours. I ask your serious attention to this consideration.

Treat all the boys alike whether they are socially attractive or whether they have poorly cultivated manners. Not only be sure of your own intention in this matter, but make it so plain and so sincere that no one can ever question it.

While your life and work are among undergraduates here make it clear to all of them and to everybody else that your first loyalty is under all circumstances with them rather than somewhere else. Surely you realize that without this you can accomplish nothing with college boys. I must believe it rests upon misunderstanding rather than fact, but it is just in this that I have heard most complaint about you. Remove at once and completely every possible ground of complaint against you at this point, or go immediately into something else in which you can hope to be of some use.

You know, I am sure, my personal friendship for you and the spirit in which I call these things earnestly to your attention. I want you to succeed; and if you fail in your new undertaking it will have to be in spite of all I can do for you. If I am mistaken in every one of them and you have no need for these warnings, then no harm has been done.

XXXIII

Though President Few was capable of great firmness and in individual instances exercised it, any really disagreeable friction over a period of thirty years was kept to the barest minimum. Mistakes occurred, as President Few knew they would in any human institution, but there was never an instance when it was necessary for the American Association of University Professors or other responsible persons to intervene in behalf of a professor. Few was consistent in his belief in the American freedom of speech, freedom of religion, and freedom of mind. This was appreciated by the faculty. He kept an open mind without surrendering his convictions, and those who dared to approach him directly found him willing to listen and patient under criticism. Some measure of the faculty's esteem for the President may be seen in brief statements made to him on the occasion of the celebration of the twenty-fifth anniversary of his presidency. These statements were prepared for a special occasion and may be subject to some discount, but there is no reason to question the sincerity of the writers. One professor said to President Few:

I like to remember the comment of one of your fellow graduate students at Harvard, made to me soon after we became Duke University—that he had great confidence in your leadership and in our future because he knew you would "innovate slowly" (Bacon's phrase, of course . . .). This I have admired, along with many other characteristics: not only your caution, but your shrewdness and carefulness, and your wisdom on many points in which I did not at first agree. . . .

Another, quoting from Gilbert and Sullivan's *Iolanthe,* with apologies that it was not from Virgil or Shakespeare, but with the hope that it had enough aptness to make up for its lack of exalted origin, wrote:

"On fire that glows with heat intense,
He turns the hose of common sense."

Another said,

I take pleasure in the reflection that amidst this material expansion you have not lost sight of the essentially human values; that those values, which were an intrinsic part of Trinity College, have been maintained . . . ; and especially that it is your purpose still further to forward in the years to come a truly humanistic education. . . .

One who had known him during all his years of service as President affirmed:

> ... to me the main characteristic of your administration has been one that has really made this success possible. It is best symbolized by an Open Door, an unguarded threshold that can be crossed at will by every member of the institution. Beyond it sits a President with a mind receptive to any ideas that may be presented. . . . Here lies the clue to the cooperative effort which has given our University stability, and I believe you can leave us no greater heritage. . . .

The head of a major division of the University wrote:

> In my reply to your telegram of appointment nine years ago, I stated that working with you would be a pleasure. It has been. You have helped and facilitated in every conceivable way. . . . I have never gone to you with any problem without receiving a wise and just solution. Your integrity, patience and cooperation always have been helpful. You have never issued orders, but whenever asked, you have given the soundest and friendliest of advice. Although many times we have deserved criticism, you always have aided by kindly encouragement.

President Few was a man of deep feeling and emotion and profound sympathy—one is reminded of Lincoln here—and yet he had a shrewd and realistic political sense (though somewhat lacking in the more obvious arts of the politician), and the hard courage never to falter in the course ahead. He may not have been a great executive in the sense of dynamic leadership and superlative efficiency—rather his greatness was in an inspired vision of the future and the quiet and patient determination to bring that vision into reality. The wisdom of the far-stretching future will surely show him to have been cautious when caution was in order, bold and courageous in time of decision, and a selfless dreamer who never lost the radiant vision of a better world. In all good truth we must say of him, as he said of so many who went before, "He lived in the beautiful hope of doing some permanent good upon the earth."

ROBERT H. WOODY

[141]

THE PAPERS AND ADDRESSES OF

WILLIAM PRESTON FEW

ALFRED IN RELATION TO ENGLISH
LITERATURE AND CULTURE*

FREEMAN, THE VERY COMPETENT and discriminating historian
of older England, has given this simple, comprehensive estimate of Alfred the Great. "Alfred is the most perfect character in history. No other man on record has ever so thoroughly
united all the virtues, both of the ruler and of the private man.
A saint without superstition, a scholar without ostentation, a
warrior all whose wars were fought in defense of his country,
a conqueror whose laurels were never stained with cruelty, a
prince never cast down by adversity, never lifted up to inso-
lence in the hour of triumph—there is no other name in
history to compare with his." This may seem to be excessive
praise, but it is perhaps no extravagance to call Alfred the
most perfect man of action of whom we know. Epitaphs are
proverbially optimistic, but of hardly any other could be written even in an epitaph the inscription on the base of the statue
erected to Alfred in 1877, at Wantage, his birthplace: "Alfred

* *The South Atlantic Quarterly*, I (January, 1902), 44-56. This paper was
written to be read at Trinity College on the occasion of the thousandth anniversary of the death of King Alfred the Great.

found Learning dead, and he restored it; Education neglected, and he revived it; the laws powerless, and he gave them force; the Church debased, and he raised it; the Land ravaged by a fearful Enemy, from which he delivered it. Alfred's name will live as long as mankind shall respect the Past."

It is easy to speak with enthusiasm of the many virtues of the many-sided Alfred. He was a brave and successful warrior. He was a great state-builder. He was a disinterested patriot and self-sacrificing lover and servant of his fellows. He was a wise man and knew how to deal with men. He was a manly man, full of energy and effort, a rough and ready toiler in the world's work, an olden time exemplar of the strenuous life. He was a gentle man and had all of a woman's tenderness, affection, and capacity for high and unselfish devotion. He was a saint, who lived untouched with fanaticism in an age of superstition, who was free from bitterness and narrowness, whose sympathies and ideals included the whole of human life and rested upon a wide, sane view of things. He was a scholar without ostentation and pedantry; "his noble nature implanted in him from his cradle a love of wisdom above all things"; like all fine spirits of the earth he had a delicate susceptibility to the beautiful things in the outward world, in the inner character of men and in literature; the noblest form of literature known to him, the old English song, he loved passionately, for the very good reason that

> It is old and plain;
> The spinsters and the knitters in the sun
> And the free maids that weave their thread with bones
> Do use to chant it: it is the simple truth,
> And dallies with the innocence of life,
> Like the old age;

he loved learning because he recognized in it the surest means for sweetening, strengthening, and sustaining his own life and for uplifting and enlarging the lives of his countrymen.

I shall not speak of the varied manifestations of Alfred's

practical genius; but I shall speak of him only in his relations to English literature and learning and of his influence in the general uplifting of the English race.

Aside from the wars in which Alfred was forced so often to engage in the defense of his country, we know little of the details of his life. Our most trustworthy source of information is the life of Alfred by Asser, a Welsh monk and scholar, who at the earnest solicitation of the king consented to live in the royal household six months of each year. The biography covers the years from Alfred's birth in 849 to the year 887. Asser speaks of Alfred always with affection and reverence, but, so far as we know, with justice and moderation.

I quote Asser's words on Alfred's youth. "He was loved by his father and mother, and even by all the people, above all his brothers, and was educated altogether at the court of the king. As he advanced through the years of infancy and youth, his form appeared more comely than that of his brothers; in look, in speech, and in manners he was more graceful than they. His whole nature implanted in him from his cradle a love of wisdom above all things, but, with shame be it spoken, by the unworthy neglect of his parents and nurses, he remained illiterate even till he was twelve years old or more; but he listened with serious attention to the Saxon poems which he often heard recited, and easily retained them in his docile memory. He was a zealous practiser of hunting in all branches, and hunted with great assiduity and success; for skill and good fortune in this art, as in all others, are among the gifts of God, as we also have often witnessed."

Asser also relates how that Alfred's mother (perhaps his stepmother) on a certain day showed Alfred and his brothers a Saxon book of poetry, which she held in her hand, and said, "Whichever of you shall the sooner learn this volume shall have it for his own." Stimulated by these words, or rather by the Divine inspiration (as Asser says), and allured by the beautifully illuminated letter at the beginning of the volume, he spoke before all his brothers, who though his seniors in age were not so in grace, and answered, "Will you really give that book to one of us, that is to say, to him who can first understand and repeat it to you?" His mother assured him she would. Thereupon Alfred took the book from her hand, went with it to his master, and in due time brought it to his mother and recited it. Professor Albert S. Cook, of Yale, has indulged himself in a pretty fancy that this same book has come down to us in the Anglo-Saxon fragmentary poem, *Judith*. It is all but certain that it was not Alfred's mother, Osburgha, who first interested him in the poetry of England, but his stepmother, Judith, the great granddaughter of Charlemagne, who in 856, when Alfred was six years old, became the wife of Ethelwolf, Alfred's father. Mr. Cook thinks it possible that the Anglo-Saxon poem *Judith* was written in honor of the brilliant young queen, and that this very book may have been offered by her as a reward to that one of her stepsons who might be the first to understand and repeat it.

This is a pleasing theory of Mr. Cook's, and in the absence of definite knowledge, we may as well accept it as another. And at all events it is pleasant to be told that Alfred, like Charlemagne, in early youth was inspired with a love of the national poetry; and he continued through life to recite the Saxon books, and especially to learn by heart the Saxon poems. He likewise early learned some of the psalms and several prayers, contained in a book he kept day and night in his bosom, and carried about with him to assist his prayers.

It is clear then that young Alfred was not wholly lacking in opportunities for self-culture, physical, mental, and spiritual. But like all men of delicate sensibilities and high ideals, Alfred, with better reason than most, chafed under the galling chains of destiny, and complained bitterly of his limitations. His friend and biographer tells us: "This he confessed, with many lamentations and sighs, to have been one of his greatest difficulties and impediments in this life, namely, that when he was

RACHEL KENDRICK FEW (1840-1922),
MOTHER OF PRESIDENT FEW

young and had the capacity for learning, he could not find teachers; but, when he was more advanced in life, he was harassed by so many diseases unknown to all the physicians of this island, as well as by internal and external anxieties of sovereignty . . . that there was no time for reading. But yet among the impediments of this present life, from infancy up to the present time, and, as I believe, even until his death, he continued to feel the same insatiable desire of knowledge, and still aspires after it."

Of Alfred's bodily affliction Asser elsewhere says that "from the twentieth year of his age to the present year, which is his fortieth, he has been constantly afflicted with most severe attacks of an unknown complaint, so that he has not a moment's ease either from suffering the pain which it causes, or from the gloom which is thrown over him by the apprehension of its coming." We are further told that this calamity was brought upon Alfred because in his youth he would not listen to petitions which his subjects made to him for help in their necessities. Asser quaintly remarks, "wherefore, seeing that a man's sins must be corrected either in this world or the next, the true and righteous Judge was willing that his sin should not go unpunished in this world, to the end that he might spare him in the world to come."

But in spite of all limitations of circumstances and bodily infirmities young Alfred quietly continued to give himself to the getting of those things that have to do with a manly life. He was an assiduous and successful hunter, he was an enthusiastic lover of poetry, he was consumed with an insatiable desire for knowledge, and with all humility and sincerity of heart he applied himself to religious devotions after the manner of so many of the finest spirits of the Middle Ages. While he was an exemplary disciple of the medieval religion of contemplation, it is his glory that he did not withhold his hand from the sterner services of the active life. Asser tells us that at the battle of Ashdown Ethelred, Alfred's older brother, then king, for a long time remained praying in his tent, while Alfred and his followers went forth like a wild boar against the hounds. During these youthful years Alfred, unlike his older brother Ethelbold, entered into no conspiracy against the king his father; he sought by no indirection to get for himself position and power. Like sincere and strong men in every age he did the duty of the hour, and did not enter into the mad rush after conspicuous position, which brings to serious men a weighing sense of responsibility. He no doubt realized early in life what he afterwards finely said, that "you need not be solicitous about power nor strive after it. If you be wise and good it will follow you, though you should not wish it."

It was such a youth as this who in the twenty-third year of his life became King of the West Saxons. Alfred's reign (871-901) may be divided into four periods. The first, the period of Danish invasion, extends from 871 to 881; the second, the period of comparative quiet, from 881 to 893; the third, the period of renewed strife, from 893 to 897; the fourth, the period of peace, from 897 to 901. His literary work probably belongs to the second period, the period of comparative quiet, from 881 to 893.

Alfred was all his life one of the busiest of men. He set himself the stupendous task of delivering his country from the ravages of fearful enemies, of giving force to the laws, of restoring learning, of reviving education, of raising the church. He was by no means a professional and leisured man of letters. He was a worker and reformer. He used literature as a means to the accomplishment of his work for his countrymen. What seems to be the beginning of Alfred's efforts at bookmaking is interestingly told by Asser and I may be excused if I quote his words somewhat at length.

On a certain day we were both of us sitting in the king's chamber, talking on all kinds of subjects, as usual, and it happened that I read to him a quotation out of a certain book. He heard it attentively with both his ears, and addressed me with a thoughtful

DR. BENJAMIN FRANKLIN FEW (1830-1923),
FATHER OF PRESIDENT FEW

mind, showing me at the same moment a book which he carried in his bosom, wherein the daily courses and psalms and prayers which he had read in his youth, were written, and he commanded me to write the same quotation in that book. Hearing this, and perceiving his ingenuous benevolence, and devout desire of studying the words of divine wisdom, I gave, though in secret, boundless thanks to Almighty God, who had implanted such a love of wisdom in the king's heart. But I could not find an empty space in that book wherein to write the quotation, for it was already full of various matters; wherefore I made a little delay, principally that I might stir up the bright intellect of the king to a higher acquaintance with the divine testimonies. Upon his urging me to make haste and write it quickly, I said to him, "Are you willing that I should write that quotation on some leaf apart? For it is not certain whether we shall find one or more other such extracts which will please you; and if that should happen, we shall be glad that we have kept them apart." "Your plan is good," said he, and I gladly made haste to get ready a sheet, in the beginning of which I wrote what he bade me; and on that same day, I wrote therein, as I had anticipated, no less than three other quotations which pleased him; and from that time we daily talked together, and found out other quotations which pleased him, so that the sheet became full, and deservedly so. He continued to learn the flowers collected by certain masters, and to reduce them into the form of one book, as he was then able, although mixed one with another, until it became almost as large as a psalter. This book he called his Enchiridion or Manual, because he carefully kept it at hand day and night, and found, as he told me, no small consolation therein.

This book which its royal owner prized so highly has been lost to us, but it is just possible that there may be some connection between Alfred's Handbook and the Middle English poem known as the *Proverbs of Alfred*, which contains many plain and wise sayings for the conduct of the everyday life of our ancestors. Some of these sayings may well have come from the mouth of the great West-Saxon king, and many of them are still found among the commonest proverbs of today. But whether the Middle English poem has any connection with the Handbook of Alfred or not, it at any rate shows clearly the high place Alfred held in English popular tradition of the thirteenth century. It was the memory of a ruler who loved his subjects as had no other, a man of gentleness and power, a king who was at once the father and teacher of his people.

The opening of the poem shows King Alfred surrounded by his *Witenagemot* ("the wise men of the realm"). "At Seaford," runs the opening line of the poem,

sat many thegns, many bishops, and many book-learned men, proud earls, warlike knights. There was the eorl Alfrich, who was very learned in the law, and also Alfred, the shepherd of the Angles, the Angles' darling, in England he was king. Them he began to teach, as ye may hear, how they their life should lead. Alfred was a very strong king in England. He was king and he was clerk, well he loved God's work. He was wise in word and prudent in works. He was the wisest man in England.

"Shepherd of the Angles," "England's Darling," these are popular names for Alfred in the Middle Ages.

Asser's account of how Alfred became interested in making books and the image of Alfred that has persisted in English popular tradition help us on the way to an understanding of the real impulses that lay behind his literary efforts. He conceived learning and literature to be but tools in the hands of wise and good men to be used, as Bacon has said, "for the glory of the Creator and the relief of man's estate." Alfred became in a sense a literary man not, I think, primarily, if at all, from an artistic impulse, but from what Asser calls "ingenious benevolence." He was, it is true, a fine-souled man, and had a poet's feeling for the high and beautiful; but the writings he has left us give us no reason to believe that he had the gift of supreme literary genius—what Keats has named "the gift of fine things said unintentionally." If this great old king did not have the supreme gift of genius, he had the most useful gift vouchsafed to men on earth—the gift of unerring wisdom; wisdom that is not the product of intellect alone, but comes out of a full, harmonious character, and at its highest becomes a sort of moral instinct that almost compels a man to live his life wisely,

"BILLIE" AT ABOUT THE AGE OF THIRTEEN

just as the natural instinct compels the bird to sing its song.
And yet however useful this gift of wisdom may be and however much it may deserve to be praised it can never produce a
Hamlet or the *Divina Commedia*. But one star differeth from
another star in glory, and we may be just as grateful to Alfred
for his work as we are to Dante and Shakspere for theirs.

Alfred was by temperament as well as by force of circumstances primarily not a man of letters, but a reformer, and his
interest extended to every sphere of life in the England of the
ninth century. During the first ten or twelve years of his reign
he was abundantly occupied with the defense of his kingdom
against Danish invaders. As soon as there came a period of
comparative quiet he began to apply himself to the betterment
of the condition of his people. This period of quiet lasted little
more than a dozen years, and it is remarkable how much Alfred
accomplished during these brief years. In the Preface to the
Pastoral Care Alfred speaks of the sad condition of his country.
War had devastated the land, knowledge had fallen away, the
people had lapsed into ignorance and savagery, the clergy had
become worldly and inefficient, many of the monasteries had
been destroyed, and with them the schools. The educational
as well as the religious life of the people depended wholly on
the church; for the church alone cared for the education of
children, and previous to Alfred's reign the church cared only
for the education of those who were specially dedicated to her
service. The clergy had become worldly in mind and manners,
and the church lacked absolutely a moral and intellectual basis.
Ignorance became widespread. Alfred himself says of the condition of things when he came to the throne: "So entirely had
knowledge escaped from the English people, that there were
very few on this side of the Humber who could understand
their rituals in English, or translate a letter from Latin into
English, and I believe that there were not many beyond the
Humber. There were so few of them that I cannot remember
a single one south of the Thames when I came to the throne."

Alfred found ignorance everywhere, the church worldly and inefficient, and the great bulk of his people living in misery. The cause of the poor was languishing. "For in the whole kingdom the poor, besides him, had few or no protectors; for all the powerful and noble of that country had turned their thoughts rather to secular than to heavenly things. Each was more bent on secular matters, to his own profit, than on the public good."

Alfred took measures to restore Christian culture in the church, to improve the character of the clergy, and to advance the cause of popular education. Old monasteries were rebuilt, new ones, majestic and goodly, beyond all the precedents of his ancestors, were erected, foreign monks were brought in from Mercia, from Wales, and from the Continent. One of these was the Welsh monk and scholar Asser, who during Alfred's lifetime began but never finished a biography of the king, a work that has come down to us, though not in its original form. Learned and pious men were put into places of authority. Schools were established in connection with the monasteries, and they were for the education of those not destined for the church as well as for the clergy. Alfred's wish was that all freeborn youths, who did not lack the means, should learn to read English. His charity began at home; he gave his own children that complete education, the lack of which he had himself felt so keenly, and his children became an honor to him. The conduct of his own household and the kind of men and women that came from it constitute one of the chiefest tributes to Alfred's character and help to confirm the claim that Alfred is the most perfect man of history.

One of Alfred's first internal improvements may have been in the direction of giving his people a better system and administration of law. "He was a minute investigator of the truth in his judgments, especially for the sake of the poor," and he also became a law-giver. The oldest monuments of English prose are compilations of laws. There was one compilation as early as the seventh century, and there were others in the eighth century. Alfred's code was based upon the laws already in force, and he was wisely conservative in modifying existing laws; but new statutes were added, and these indicate an increased power of the kingdom and a growing influence of the church. In the introduction and narrative passages the writer shows an easy mastery of Anglo-Saxon prose.

One of Alfred's ideals for his people was that all freeborn youths, who had the means, should learn to read English. And then his effort was to translate from Latin, the world language of that day, into English, for the use of all, the most useful books known to him. As Freeman has said, Alfred "writes, just as he fights and legislates, with a single eye to the good of his people." In his famous Preface to the *Pastoral Care,* writing to his bishops, Alfred says: "Therefore it seems to me better that we turn into the language that we all may understand, certain books that are most needful for all men to know, and so we may easily do with God's help, if we the stillness (tranquillity) have." "If we the stillness have." Infinitely touching are these words of the noble king, in view of all that he had it in his heart to do for the enlightening of his people and in view of the wars, the struggles of every kind, the shortness and tempestuousness of his life, that prevented him from accomplishing so much that he might have done.

In order that they might be used by every freeborn youth in his kingdom Alfred translated into the national language four great books current in that age: *A Compendious History of the World,* by a Spaniard named Orosius; the *Ecclesiastical History of the English,* by the Venerable Bede, a priest who spent most of his life in the monastery at Jarrow; the *Consolation of Philosophy,* by Boethius, a Roman in the days of Theodric the Great, who was a good part of his life confined in prison; the *Pastoral Care,* by Pope Gregory the Great.

The History of the World was written at the suggestion of St. Augustine and was the first universal history ever written.

In his translation Alfred omits, abbreviates, and adds at will. There are important additions. One of these is a complete description of all the countries in which the Teutonic tongue was spoken in Alfred's time. In spite of its defects this translation served as a manual of history and geography from which Alfred's countrymen might learn much. Bede's *Ecclesiastical History* was written in England and dealt with English history (and legend). It was then and, in a way, is still a book of great value. *The Consolation of Philosophy*, the famous work of "the last of the Romans," as Boethius used to be called, was one of those rare, germinal books that inspired productive thinking throughout the Middle Ages. It influenced Dante greatly, and the esteem in which England has held it is evidenced by the fact that translations have been made by King Alfred, Chaucer, and Queen Elizabeth. Through these translations many generations of Englishmen have been "edified and practised in philosophical thinking." It was perhaps an inner need as much as a regard for the wants of his people that impelled Alfred to translate this work. As Ten Brink says: "We can imagine with what feelings, in the evening of his eventful life, the manly heart of the great Saxon king absorbed those noble teachings of antiquity on the worthlessness of earthly happiness, on the supreme good, on the wise man's duty of composure in the struggle of life; and how he felt impelled to reveal this treasure to his people." So far as we know Alfred's last literary work was the translation of Gregory's *Pastoral Care*, which contains instruction in conduct and doctrine for all bishops. Of all his translations this follows the original most closely and is most carefully done. For it he wrote a long Preface, the historical value of which is inestimable.

Most of Alfred's translation was merely paraphrase. He omitted, abbreviated, and added to serve his own ends. He had great difficulty in understanding the Latin texts, and he certainly made use of the monks and scholars whom he col-

lected about him, in his efforts to get at the meaning of his
original. Not bound by the slavish purpose to translate literally, his style especially in the larger additions to his originals,
became free and characteristic, and these works of Alfred are
the best representative we have of early Anglo-Saxon prose.
While crude prose had been written before his day, he may
well be called "The Father of English Prose." His deeds as
well as these literary efforts helped to establish and develop
the language, and prepared the way for the nervous, vigorous
style of the English chronicle at its best, and the conspicuous
clearness and graceful finish of Aelfric's homilies.

While Alfred's writings are historically of the first importance, intrinsically they do not have high literary value. Alfred
has, of course, written nothing that has become an English
classic. He was not to any considerable extent even what Mr.
John Morley has somewhere called "a contributor to the universal stock of enduring wisdom." But we revere the name of
Alfred because he was one of the finest spirits, one of the most
perfect characters, and one of the most useful men, who have
yet appeared in our world.

The thousandth anniversary of the close of the distinguished
career of King Alfred the Great is being marked in one way
or another throughout the English-speaking world. This celebration is not intended to be a mere empty memorial. May I
not in conclusion, with perfect sincerity and without a tinge of
cant, remind you, young men of the English race, inheritors of
English institutions, thought, and literature, of which Alfred
was a mighty founder and builder, that you have in this great
English king a "model as well as a memory"? Let me draw
attention to some of the principles that seem to have governed
Alfred's life.

(1) Power is never good unless he be good that has it. No
man is better for his power; but if he be good it is from his virtues that he is good. From his virtues he becomes worthy of
power, if he be worthy of it at all. You need not be solicitous
about power nor strive after it at all. If you be wise and good,

it will follow you, though you should not wish it. Ah, Wise One! thou knowest that greed and the possession of this earthly power never were pleasing to me, nor did I ever earnestly desire this earthly kingdom—save that I desired tools and materials to do the work that it was commanded me to do. This was that I might guide and wield wisely the authority committed to me.

(2) Ah, my soul, one evil is stoutly to be shunned—the desire of false glory and of unrighteous power, and of immoderate fame of good deeds above all other people. Glory of this world! Why do foolish men with a false voice call thee glory? Thou art not so.

(3) This I can now truly say, that I have willed to live worthily the while I have lived, and after my life to leave to the men that come after me a remembering of me in good works.

We live in a part of the English-speaking world where Alfred's ancient ideals of civilization have not yet been realized; where many freeborn youths cannot read the English language; where our laws are not always in force; where the battle for right political, religious, and educational ideals demands of high-minded men the same moral earnestness and enthusiasm for humanity that made of Alfred a willing and untiring worker. Amid all the cross-purposes and warring voices about us, amid the heartsoreness that comes from seeing sham, pretense, and demagoguery of many kinds prosper among us for a season, amid the heartsickness that arises out of the widespread failure to covet the best things, yea, amid all "the impediments of this present life," let you and me learn from the example of Alfred that he is greatest who serves greatest, that he is most useful who does the most needed work, that we had best not desire the immoderate fame even of good deeds, that we need not be solicitous about power nor strive after it, for if we be wise and good it will follow us, though we should not wish it, that the only conscious ambition worthy of a wise and good man is just the ambition Alfred described when he said: "I have willed to live worthily the while I have lived, and after my life to leave to the men that come after me a remembering of me in good works."

SIDNEY LANIER AS A STUDENT
OF ENGLISH LITERATURE*

THERE HAS RECENTLY come from the press of Doubleday, Page & Co. a work by Sidney Lanier, in two octavo volumes and copiously illustrated, with the title, *Shakspere and His Forerunners*. The general scope of the work is indicated by the subtitle, *Studies in Elizabethan Poetry and Its Development from Early English*. The volumes embody two sets of lectures given by Lanier in Baltimore, one at Johns Hopkins University and the other to a class of women at Peabody Institute, during the winter of 1879-80.

The lectures—originally sketchy and hastily written—are here printed as they were delivered, the editor, Mr. Henry Wysham Lanier, confining his editorial duties entirely to selecting and arranging the lectures of his father. These lectures were prepared under great stress of circumstances, at a time when Lanier was bravely battling against the fatal disease that had already begun to close in on his life and against the hamperings of grinding poverty, while in the thick of his life-

* *The South Atlantic Quarterly*, II (April, 1903), 157-168.

long "threefold struggle for health, for bread, and for a literary career." The lecturer during his troubled life had had scant opportunity to study English literature, which, however, he loved so passionately.

It is not then to be expected that the book should make any addition to knowledge or even any serious contribution to the now large body of Shakspere criticism. From this point of view the book is perhaps worse than useless; these lectures might better have not been given to the public at all, or at least without having first been rigorously edited. The competent student of our older literature will not feel the need of the book and to the untrained it will prove but an unsafe guide. But the volumes have an undoubted value in the material they furnish for a study of Lanier himself and for an understanding of the method with which he approached the great subject of English literature; and the publication of the lectures may be justified because of the light they throw upon the beautiful character of this gifted, ill-starred poet, whose life and works become increasingly interesting and valued as time goes on. And, besides, the criticism by one genuine poet of another always has an interest, even if, as in the present case, the criticism is hurried and slipshod.

It would be easy to find fault with the book, for it abounds in faults; but fault-finding would be ungenerous in a critic of such a work as this and under the circumstances would be gratuitous. It would not be fair to estimate this last published work of Lanier in the light of present-day scholarship and critical opinion; but it will be more profitable to value these studies as material for that definitive biography of this foremost Southern poet, which is yet to be written, and to pay heed to the ways in which a true man of letters has here approached the greatest period in English literature. To inquire into Lanier's attitude towards literature is, I think, especially worth while at a time when there is much uncertainty abroad as to the right way to study literature, because his attitude seems to me to have been almost the ideal attitude. For he had the temper of a poet and the methods of a scientist.

Literature is not a science but an art, and the most human of all arts. This most human of all arts should not be approached in the spirit with which one would approach the investigation of facts. Literature does not, like the study of mere things, make its appeal solely to the mind, but to the imagination and to the feelings. The student of literature should not be simply a student, he needs something of the nature of a lover. That Lanier approached his favorite poets in the mood of a lover there can be no doubt. His friendship with the great dead poets came to acquire, as he himself tells us, something of the quality of worship.

He had the enthusiasm of all fine-souled men for good and beautiful things, whether in art, in nature or in human conduct. This gift of fineness of character is perhaps always necessary to a real appreciation of literature. There is needed a docile mind that is willing to lend itself to the mood of the book, and meekly and almost blindly to be led wherever the author wishes. Landor's pretty saying is not true here, if indeed it is anywhere, that

> Ignorance
> Never hurt devotion;

yet the spirit that makes possible any real appreciation of true literature is something like the spirit of the devotee, who in mere abandon of joy gives himself blindly to the worship of his idol. Your real lover of books will, like Whitman, find in art a place to loaf and invite his soul; and this sort of reader alone will get out of books the pleasure and power which they can give to those who use them aright.

But unless this pleasure is to degenerate into emotional dissipation, and unless this power that comes from great books is to be missed entirely, to this spiritual equipment of the poet —and to some extent at least this equipment is possessed by every real lover of books—must be added the mild reasonableness and rugged good sense—the product of knowledge and wisdom—that are not always a part of the equipment of poets. It cannot be doubted that Lanier was endowed with poetic temperament; but he also possessed the endowment—rarer among modern poets—of patient, intelligent sympathy with things as they actually exist in a world of men. This intimate sympathy with the established order of things—apparently as native to Lanier as his spiritual endowment—contrasts strangely with the romantic poet's insistent seeking after some far-off sweet golden clime and relates Lanier more closely to the modern scholar than to the typical nineteenth-century poet. By reason of his reverence for fact, the passion of the scientific scholar, and by reason of his reconstructive insight, always the possession of the poet, Lanier is, considering his limited opportunities, almost a perfect representative of the student and critic of literature and life. For he steadfastly held before himself high ideals of both literature and life; but his ideals were not ethereal, impracticable, unapproachable, and they were not too fine to "stand the strain of weaving into human stuff on the loom of the real."

To reconcile "soul and sense," and to give each a fair show is the problem in the individual life and in human history. "A soul and a sense linked together in order to fight each other more conveniently, compose a man," wrote Lanier in "Retrospects and Prospects," an essay written when he was a young man and in its attempt at philosophical statement and its theatrical style resembling Burke's youthful *Inquiry into the Sublime and Beautiful*. The value of the scholar as well as of the poet was early and clearly recognized by Lanier. These, if rightly taken, should help each other, and not hinder each other, as many men with a narrower point of view than Lanier's nowadays believe. In one of his Shakspere lectures Lanier makes a characteristic statement of his belief. "The poet puts the universe together, while the scientist pulls it to pieces, the

poet being a synthetic workman, the scientist an analytic workman; and while the scientist plucks apart the petals of faith,
it is the business of the modern poet to set them together again
and so keep the rose of religion whole."

An English poet delivered a course of lectures early in the
last century on Shakspere and other dramatists; and the difference in point of view between a critic like Lanier with the
modern educated man's respect for knowledge and the critic
who deals entirely in aesthetics may be illustrated by comparing the lectures given by Coleridge with the lectures of Lanier.
Coleridge lectured on such topics as "Definition of Poetry,"
"Greek Drama," "Progress of the Drama," "The Drama
Generally and Public Taste," "Shakspere a Poet Generally,"
"Shakspere's Judgment Equal to His Genius." Coleridge's
object appears to have been nothing more than to lead his
hearers toward an aesthetic and, apparently so far as he cared,
indiscriminating enjoyment of poetry. With Coleridge reading
poetry would appear to have been a purely emotional exercise,
making its appeal entirely to the feelings and the effects of it
being not far removed from the effects produced in him by
his fatal practice of taking opium.

Lanier, on the other hand, chose such topics as "The Eliza-
bethan Writers—The Formal Side of Poetry," "Shakspere's
Forerunners in Old English and Middle English Periods,"
"The Pronunciation of Shakspere's Time," "The Music of
Shakspere's Time," "The Domestic Life of Shakspere's Time,"
"The Doctors of Shakspere's Time," "The Metrical Tests."
Many of Lanier's topics concern what may be called Elizabethan antiquities. He was seeking to give his hearers some
adequate idea of Shakspere's time, of the characteristics of the
age, of the conditions of human life then, and to bring them
into contact with contemporary and older English literature,
in order that they might be able to estimate Shakspere at his
real worth and to know what is really Shaksperean from what
belonged to other poets of the age and other ages as well as to

Shakspere. This was not done for pure love of lore, but because it was believed to be necessary to one who wishes to study Shakspere for his essential value, who wishes to know just what his message to mankind is, who wishes to see him steady and to see him whole.

The object of this kind of study of poetry may perhaps be regarded as the same object Coleridge had in view, to understand it, to appreciate it, to feel it, to enjoy it, to attain that higher insight that enables one to see through the eye, not with it, adapting the phrase of the poet Blake. But for the average reader the object is more likely to be attained through Lanier's than through Coleridge's method, and the process is more apt to make men strong and sound of heart and mind.

The traits that characterize the literary criticism of these two men show themselves also in their personal characters and in their poetry. In the matter of character Lanier is unquestionably far saner and stronger. Upon their poetic achievement one cannot, whatever one's individual opinion may be, so safely pass judgment, if one must pass upon the finished product. "Christabel," "Kubla Khan," and the "Ancient Mariner" may in their kind stand higher than the "Marshes of Glynn," "Corn," and "Clover"; but Lanier did not have the opportunity to give adequate expression of himself in poetry. It is impossible to tell what his poetic achievements might have been had his life been cast amid favoring circumstances. In the case of a poet like Lanier shut in all his life by cramping limitations—limitations, too, of circumstance not of character, as in the case of Coleridge—it is juster to judge him by the general tendency rather than by the actual performance, by his reach rather than by his grasp.

It is time that I indicated with something more of definiteness Lanier's point of view in the study of English literature as it shows itself in the two courses of lectures which constitute the two volumes lately published.

Lanier appreciated as few English poets and aesthetic critics
have appreciated the value of the historic sense to the student
of literature, and especially the incomparable worth of a
thorough knowledge of the origin and growth of English civilization and English literature in all periods. Again and again
he deprecates the ignorance of our literary origins so widespread in England and America, and the deplorable and all
but universal lack of interest in the earlier stages of the native
literature. In one of the introductory lectures on Shakspere
and his forerunners we find him giving expression to his opinion on this subject in words that would carry joy to the heart
of the most mousing and exacting scholar of English:

No person can be said to have a fairly philosophical idea,
either of the English language or of English poetry, who is un-
acquainted with the beautiful literature of our Anglo-Saxon
ancestors. I marvel day by day at the state into which the study
of the English language has fallen, both in England and America.
We peruse Greek, Latin, French, German, and all other tongues,
dead or living, except English. How many are there among us
that know the true glory of the Anglo-Saxon tongue? You will
find ten thousand men in the United States who can read Homer's
poems to one who can read Beowulf; and yet one is an epic of a
people on the other side of the world, while Beowulf is our own
English epic. You will find ten thousand men in the United
States who have some fair idea of the first five hundred years of
classic poetry to one who has any idea of the first five hundred
years of English poetry; for, you remember, I had occasion to
remark in another lecture that while Chaucer seems very old to
our century, there was an English poetry which was as old to
Chaucer as Chaucer's poetry is to us, and this poetry, I complain,
is to all intents and purposes absolutely unknown to the English-
speaking people. In our schools provision is made to study every
language except Old English; and yet without Old English no
man can clearly grasp the genuis of modern English.

Of *Beowulf*, the English epic, in another lecture, he says:

Strange to say, this poem, though the oldest heroic poem in any
Germanic tongue—though substantially the oldest poem of any

[165]

sort—though probably a genuine English epic recording the adventures of a true, noble, valiant, and generous English-hero—strange to say, it is almost unknown to the mass even of cultivated English readers in either England or America, and I doubt if a copy of it is in twenty houses in the United States outside of the great libraries.

This last statement may have been true in 1880, but it is of course not true now, though ignorance of Old English literature is still common enough among so-called educated Americans to give point to Lanier's remark. In view of this, to him, lamentable ignorance of Old English literature Lanier, in his lectures, undertook to give his hearers some idea of the relations of Shakspere to the first thousand years of our poetry. He began with some account of Anglo-Saxon poetry, set forth Chaucer and the fourteenth century, discussed the Scotch poets of the fifteenth century, and finally in order to show Shakspere's relations to his own time passed in review the poetry of the sixteenth century. A large plan like this carried the lecturer far afield, with the result that all the first volume and a considerable portion of the second are taken up with discussions of Shakspere's forerunners and a general survey of English literature. Some readers may think that he gave too much time to these subjects and too little to Shakspere himself; but Lanier proceeded upon the theory that "without Old English no man can clearly grasp the genius of modern English," and I for one am not sure that his theory was wrong.

There was nothing of the dilettante about Lanier. He had the methods and spirit of a genuine scholar, and he approached the study of English, somewhat late in life and without special training to be sure, and yet with the scientific spirit and laborious methods of a modern philologist. He acquired an easy reading knowledge of English in all its stages, and he was even fascinated by technical linguistic questions, such as the discussion of "words and their ways in English speech." In one of his lectures to a class of women he is discussing the origin of the English words *lord* and *lady*. Failing for lack of facts to make clear every stage in the development of the second of these words he offers a suggestion to his class. "Why," he asks, "should not some of the intelligent ladies of this class go to work and arrange the facts—as I have called them—so that scholars might have before them a comprehensive view of all the word changes which have occurred since the earliest Anglo-Saxon works were written?" Speaking in the same lecture of the ambitions of women to do something useful he carries on his suggestion. "Of the numerous plans which I can imagine for women to pursue, I have just suggested to you one which would combine pleasure with profitable work in a most charming manner. Suppose that some lady—or better a club of ladies—should set out to note down the changes in spelling —and, if possible, pronunciation—which have occurred in every word now remaining to us from the Anglo-Saxon tongue." Consider that this is a poet making a serious suggestion to a class of American women, and it will at once appear how far the poet is removed from the dilettante. It may be worth remark in passing that just this method has been followed in the making of the monumental new English dictionary now appearing in instalments under the editorship of Dr. Murray. Readers have been found in all parts of the English-speaking world and many of them have been women.

The scientific bent of Lanier's mind is further shown by the emphasis he put upon the importance of method, of form in literature. In these lectures he went at length into the discussion of the scientific basis of music and poetry. As the editor tells us in the Preface, much of this material was left out of the published work because it had been elaborated in *The Science of English Verse*. "On all sides it is forgotten that inspiration, while it is certainly necessary in art, is yet worthless unless it descends into a soul prepared by toil and study and practice to give it the forms which burn forever before men's eyes." There is never any question in true art between technic

and inspiration. The artist must have both." With these views
on the importance of a knowledge of the technic of poetry and a
knowledge of English literature and civilization in all ages,
Lanier became the most thorough and scientific student, among
English poets, of the forms of verse and the language of
literature.

Lanier not only insists on the importance of "Old English"
to an understanding of the genius of modern English, but he
emphasizes the educative value of "Old English." In a paper
on the death of Byrhtnoth, in *Music and Poetry,* a volume of
essays, published in 1899, he speaks emphatically on this point.

One will go into few moderately appointed houses in this country without finding a Homer in some form or other, but it is
probably far within the truth to say that there are not fifty
copies of Beowulf in the United States. Or again, every boy,
though far less learned than the erudite young person of Macaulay's, can give some account of the death of Hector; but how
many boys—or, not to mince matters, how many men—in America, could do more than stare, if asked to relate the death of
Byrhtnoth? Yet Byrhtnoth was a hero of our own England in
the tenth century, whose manful fall is recorded in English words
that ring on the soul like arrows on armor. Why do we not draw
in this poem—and its like—with our mother's milk? Why have
we no nursery songs of Beowulf and Grendel? Why does not
the serious education of every English speaking boy commence,
as a matter of course, with the Anglo-Saxon grammar?

"For," he says further on in the same essay, "the absence
of this primal Anglicism from our modern system goes—as
was said—to the very root of culture. The eternal and im-
measurable significance of that individuality in thought, which
flows into idiom in speech, becomes notably less recognized
among us. We do not bring with us out of our childhood the
fibre of idiomatic English which our fathers bequeathed to us."
No one since King Alfred wrote, has spoken more intelligently
or stoutly than Lanier for the study of the mother tongue and
for the value of a genuine English education. Referring to

Professor Few in 1897

an old story of the deposition by Normans in the eleventh century of an English bishop on the ground that he was "a superannuated English idiot who could not speak French," Lanier remarks that we have ever since been trying to prevent our children from being called "idiots who cannot speak French," regardless of any possibility that they might actually become idiots who cannot speak English.

Lanier goes further in his plea for a study of "Old English." He maintained that our modern literature sadly needs Anglo-Saxon iron. "There is," he says, in a paper already quoted, "no ruddiness in his cheeks, and everywhere a clear lack of the red corpuscles. Current English prose, on both sides of the water, reveals an ideal of prose writing, most like the leaden sky of a November day, that overspreads the earth with dreariness, no rift in its tissue, nor fleck in its tint." "We lack a primal bone and substance; we have not the stalwart Anglicism of style." In a letter written in 1878 to Mr. Gibson Peacock, Lanier speaks much in the same vein of some of the latter-day poetry. "This is the kind of poetry that is called culture poetry; yet it is in reality the product of a want of culture. If these gentlemen and ladies would read the old English poetry—I mean the poetry before Chaucer, the genuine English utterance, from Caedmon, in the seventh century, to Langland, in the fourteenth—they could never be content to put forth these little diffuse prettinesses and dandy kickshaws of verse."

Thus it is that Lanier emphasizes the importance of older English literature to an understanding of modern English; thus he stresses its value in the education of the individual; and thus he contends that it may serve, as the study of early vernacular poetry has served more than once and in more than one country, to recall literature from false and artificial courses to nature and truth. It is therefore no wonder that he prized and sought to lead others to prize, the rich literary inheritance of English-speaking people, for he felt that this inheritance belonged to all English-speaking people. He had an unusually keen sense of the continuity of English, including American, literature and civilization; a sense that we Americans "are sprung of earth's first blood," that we

> Speak the tongue
> That Shakspere spoke; the faith and morals hold
> Which Milton held.

In his aims and ideals Lanier was, in spite of his poet's enthusiasm and fineness of soul, closely akin to the modern historical and comparative student of literature. Lanier's interest in the past was not mere enthusiasm. He valued the past and the literature of the past. An interest in the Middle Ages has been felt by other literary men, who may be roughly represented by Scott and Hugo in literature, and Ruskin in art; but none of these men understood or cared to understand the material which they used. They loved the literature and art of the Middle Ages for its romantic quality and for its unlikeness to the cold clear light and common sense of the eighteenth century. These men overestimated the beauty of mediaeval civilization and looked back with longing from the hard world of Voltaire and Pope to the gorgeous child-like Middle Ages. Lanier did not turn to early English literature in this spirit of adoration for the past because it is weird and unlike the hard present; but he turned to the past because he would understand the present. And again in this particular he is in striking contrast with the romanticists. While the past did not cast a glamour over Lanier as over Scott and Ruskin, whose feeling for the Middle Ages was due to ignorance of the actual conditions and to an overestimate of the beauty of mediaeval civilization, yet it held him with something of the spell of enthusiasm, and in his appreciation of early English literature there is a dash of that youthful ardor that is born of novelty. In 1880 Old English literature was a new subject of study in America and Lanier had only lately become acquainted with it. He was always without special training and never knew the subject really well. He perforce spoke as an amateur, and not with the compelling power that comes out of a fulness of knowledge. It is the amateur in him that exclaims: "Why does not the serious education of every English-speaking boy commence, as a matter of course, with the Anglo-Saxon grammar?" But perhaps this overvaluation of Anglo-Saxon grammar should not be charged up entirely to lack of knowledge when an American scholar of standing has recently taken practically the same position and has attributed most of the ills of modern education to ignorance of what he calls historical English grammar.

There are other evidences of Lanier's amateurishness, besides this tendency to emphasize what was novel to him and novel to American scholars of a quarter of a century ago. His whole attitude towards life as seen, for example, in his letters to Bayard Taylor, his enthusiasm for music, his enthusiasm for poetry, his enthusiasm for his friends, thoroughly fine and beautiful as they are, all speak the man from the provinces, rather than the man who is sure of himself, who is at the center of things, who has enjoyed, as Lanier bitterly complains he has not enjoyed, intimate relations with "men of letters, with travelers, with persons who have either seen, or written, or done large things." Better training and early opportunities for culture would have given him a larger knowledge and a sounder point of view. In the lectures on Shakspere and his forerunners a large part of his attention is given to pleasant discourses on his best beloved poets from Cynewulf to Habington, in whom it is evident he had but lately become interested. Although his account of Shakspere's forerunners occupies a considerable portion of the two volumes, there is no real grasp and thorough comprehension of the forces at work in English literature before Shakspere. There is too little clear-cut criticism, too little mastery of the subject, and too much of the mere rubbish of learning. And in these volumes, as in all Lanier's writings, much is said about his favorite theories of verse, involving as they do the interrelations of physics, music, and poetry. These theories appear never to have been sufficiently mastered to become workable, and they were in his way, both in his literary criticism and in the writing of poetry. His poems too often have the appearance of being experiments in verse forms rather than spontaneous creations of the imagination.

We may well feel infinite regret for the hard fate of this gifted poet, that denied him fit educational advantages, that burdened him with a frail, dying body, that led him by precarious ways, and that sent him to an untimely grave. If a kinder fate had given him a youth full of sunshine and opportunity for growth, if fortune had afforded him leisure for the development of his talents, we should have had in Lanier, as I think, almost an ideal student and critic of literature, and it would be highly interesting to know what might have been the poetic achievement, in his maturity, of a man who possessed at once the spiritual equipment of a poet and the mental furnishings of a scientific scholar.

SOME EDUCATIONAL NEEDS OF THE SOUTH*

FROM TIME TO TIME IN THE HISTORY of the world there have come epochs when the ordinary processes of national development have been superseded by more rapid methods and when civilization has gone forward at a bound. Such epochs were seen in England in the last half of the sixteenth century and in New England in the middle and later decades of the nineteenth century. Such an epoch, I believe, is dawning upon us here in the South. I thing I can see signs of it in the splendid industrial development of recent years, in our widely extended material prosperity, in a manifest tendency towards the break-up of the old sectional isolation and political segregation of the last half century, in the slow, but nonetheless sure, growth in vigor and independence of thinking, in a wide educational awakening, as yet vague and even till now ill-directed, but full of the promise of intellectual development and genuine human betterment. These tendencies are sufficient to make us hopeful of the future in spite of many discouraging features of our Southern civilization.

* The South Atlantic Quarterly, III (July, 1904), 201-211.

The life of the people of the Southern states after the Civil War had to be almost wholly reconstructed and readjusted to new conditions. This process of rebuilding was in every way difficult, and while under the circumstances the progress that has been made is remarkable, yet the rebuilding has not been completed, and the work of improvement and the study of perfection must ever continue to go on. But our tasks are unusually difficult, for there has been a most pathetic backwardness in the Southern states for fifty years. It is a chief business of all intelligent Southern men to seek to find a way out of this condition of things, and to lead our beloved Southland back to the proud place it once held in the sisterhood of states. Every civilization must be largely judged by the kind of men and women it produces and by the ideals of excellence for which it stands. To keep these standards true and high is a task hard enough to call out the best in us all.

I lay particular stress on the value of educational ideals because of the supreme place that education holds in the thought and hope of our time. Education is the one thing as to the value of which all men everywhere, at present, are agreed. The problems of our day are therefore largely problems of education. And I do not mean to minimize the importance of other mighty agencies at work for the uplifting of the race; for such agencies include the church, the home, the press, to name only some of the most significant. To make effective in this country all the influences for which these various agencies stand, they must be reinforced by a right system of education that can be applied to the large body of American youth. By this means many of the reforms for which earnest men have long toiled might be carried through to success.

To solve the educational problems that confront us today then becomes a matter of the utmost importance, and to keep before the thoughtful people and especially the youth of the country right educational ideals is a condition upon which depends the very permanence of our democratic society. All civilized nations are making efforts to solve these problems now more than ever before. Much progress has been made; but there is yet a great deal to be done, especially in the lower grades of education. What have we done, in the Southern states, what are we doing, and what do we propose to do? There are two foolish attitudes of mind that may disable the judgment of a critic of local conditions. The first is the disposition to despise everything that is familiar. The second is an almost selfish local patriotism that praises exorbitantly the things of one's own community, state, or section of country. It is the business of sensible people to avoid both these extremes and to speak of things just as they are.

The South has always had some beautiful ideals of life; of these it would be a pleasure to speak if they came within the range of this subject. But in educational matters, as in business methods, the South is only beginning to set before itself the tasks and undertakings that have engaged other parts of the country for generations. It is only a beginning, but it is a splendid beginning and full of promise. We are accustomed to lay all the blame for our educational deficiencies on the poverty that followed the Civil War. But this will not account for the facts. It was not the policy of the people of the Southern states to place a school house and a public library by the side of the church in every community, as the people of New England have done. In 1860 there were almost no first-rate colleges in the entire South. There were some that had distinguished teachers and social prestige unequaled by our colleges today, but they were not so organized as to become true seats of learning and large centers of culture.

Uncontrollable circumstances set us in the wrong way, but we are at last catching step with the modern world in the use we are making of the greatest agency of civilization; for education in the true sense of the word is now everywhere regarded as the surest and quickest method of promoting human progress, intelligence, and happiness. The power of genuine educational leadership has lately been exemplified anew in the movement which a very few men, led by General Armstrong at Hampton, Virginia, have set on foot for the industrial education of the Negro and Indian races. This work, begun by General Armstrong in a camp of refugees, has become so valuable and so impressive that there is a widespread tendency among educators of white youth to imitate it and to give undue emphasis to the same sort of education for the whites; hence the rapid rise and growth of technological schools, and agricultural and mechanical, and normal and industrial colleges all over the South. That would be an easy, if adequate, way to settle our educational question; but it is more difficult and far-reaching than that easy-going settlement of it would imply. We have a different race to deal with, with a different inheritance and an entirely different set of problems to handle. One of the first tasks that confront the South is, to be sure, the material uplifting of the section, the development of all kinds of business, the creation of wealth, and the building of real forces of civilization. One of the most useful lessons to teach our people is the lesson of work—hard, steady, unremitting labor. The object of education here should not be merely to give cultivation—cultivation of the mind, of the manners, of the morals of youth; it is not the part of any college that would contribute to the life of the people to stress education in a narrow or technical sense. Our model should be the English, rather than the German, university. Ours is a vital kind of work and we ought not to put the emphasis of our efforts on matters of organization, schedules of study, requirements for admission and graduation, proper correlation of schools and colleges, technical scholarship, original research and contribution to knowledge, important as are all these. These should not be sought first, but the first aim should be to create vital forces, to make hard workers for Southern progress, to produce men of ideas and power and women of refinement and genuine human helpfulness. These other things are more likely to come as a sort of unearned increment, than if they are sought directly and primarily. To make men of full, harmonious nature, rather than to create skilled workmen or specialists of any kind, should be our object, to make men of character rather than mere money-getters, if we must choose between the two. The Southern people are poor and ought to be encouraged by every right method to get more of the good things of this world; but to educate a race of mere money-makers would be to hurry in an era of sordid materialism that would be a more deadening blight to high and worthy living than ignorance and poverty have been. For the shiftless, homeless Negro or Indian race the first need is practical education; but our race should be supplied not alone with trained hands that will bring to us the material prosperity that we so much need, but also with trained minds that will bring to us the intellectual honesty and vigor ever more sorely needed in our life, and that will promulgate widely among the people right views on the so-called Southern question, on politics, on religion, on education, on scholarship, on literature, on journalism, and on all other human concerns. Our most pressing need is a body of rightly educated men in all walks of life who can inculcate in our people, and through their own deeds illustrate, the supreme value in Southern society today of plain, blunt intellectual honesty, of straight, clear thinking, and of downright freedom of speech.

Education is the great remedy, but it must be the kind of education that fits men and women for the actual life they are to live; otherwise it is not preparation for their tasks but it leads to failure and unhappiness. In our conditions what are our chief educational needs?

1. We need the primary education of all the people. I think the life of the well-to-do in the best estate of the South was the sweetest, though I doubt if it was the fullest and strongest, life that has been lived on this continent. But for the less fortunate there was almost as small opportunity as

there was for the poor in ancient Athens or under the feudal system of the Middle Ages. From the earliest days of our history down till now there has been a gross neglect of the lower classes of the whites. There has been a failure to develop much of the talent that has lain latent through all these generations. This has been the most ruinous waste in our civilization, for it has been a waste of human life.

And this neglect of the masses has been an economic waste. The stupendous cost of ignorance was long ago pointed out by General Francis Marion, the revolutionary hero of South Carolina. He said if the masses of the people of South Carolina had been enlightened they would have been united, and if they had been united the British after the drubbing they got at Fort Moultrie, in 1776, would as soon have attacked the devil as have attacked Carolina again. But the British heard of the large number who through ignorance were disaffected to the cause of liberty and they were therefore led to protract the war.

Marion then goes on to show that, owing to the foothold the British gained in South Carolina, the war was protracted two years; and he makes a curious estimate of the loss to South Carolina in those two years, at $15,000,000. "As a proof," he continues, "that such hellish tragedies would never have been acted, had our State been enlightened, only let us look at the people of New England: Religion had taught them that God created men to be happy; that to be happy, they must have virtue; that virtue is not to be attained without knowledge; nor knowledge without instruction; nor public instruction without free schools; nor free schools without legislative order." Here General Marion laid his finger on a fundamental defect in our old Southern civilization. A mere reference to all that this defect has cost our civilization is enough to fill every Southern man with infinite regret and sorrow. The public school system of the South may be said to date from 1870. The exhaustion that followed the Civil War, the night-

mare of Reconstruction, and the double system of public education made necessary by the presence of the Negro have
rendered progress slow; but there is at least a widespread interest in universal education, and all thoughtful men, even if
they do not always approve, should by sober counsel and wise
action help to direct and advance this popular movement for
the training of all the people and do everything in their power
to keep it out of the hands of educational quacks and men
who have an axe to grind. The movement as yet has manifested itself too much in idle talk, and I have less confidence
than the average man in the efficiency of mere talk; yet I believe it augurs well that the subject is everywhere in the air
and is constantly being brought to the minds of all.

The great need is more money for public schools. Public
sentiment should demand of our legislatures every possible
saving in other directions so that more money may be available for this use. Local taxation should be encouraged.
Teachers must be better paid. There is now no other way to
attract to the profession and hold permanently the right sort
of men.

There has been organized at the North the General Education Board, the declared object of which is the promotion of
popular education in the United States. Because the South
offers the best field for this kind of investment, the efforts of
this Board at present are put forth mainly here. In connection with this Board works the Southern Education Board,
which exists for the propaganda of popular education in the
South. As this movement is conceived by Northern men it is,
in my opinion, a large, constructive, statesmanlike piece of national philanthropy, and ought to do good and only good. It
is to be hoped that Southern men may co-operate, as far as
they have occasion to co-operate at all, in the same disinterested
and dignified way. If people on the outside wish to give money
to help forward popular education, or any other good work
among us, I can see no reason why we should not take it,

provided of course, it is offered in a perfectly proper spirit. But any truckling or posing in a receptive attitude on the part of Southern men would be a lasting humiliation to a right thinking, self-respecting people. Some of our most clear-headed men have seemed to see a taint of such truckling and straightway they have spoken out against the whole movement. The dread of the very appearance of evil has kept still others aloof from it, and whether the movement will finally succeed does not yet appear. It has already been useful in bringing about a better understanding between intelligent men of the North and the South, and since it is an effort to help us in our arduous tasks I could find it in my heart to wish that this undertaking, nobly conceived as I believe it has been, may be so managed as to bring large good to our people.

2. We need in its place and without undue exaggeration industrial education and manual training. In my opinion this ought to come before the child is sixteen years old, and I am not concerned with it because of its supposed utilitarian value, but for its value as training and support for youthful character. The minds and the characters of children are helped by accurate work. This result may be got from manual training and is most valuable early in the child's life. The doing of a definite piece of work and the coming into close contact with external nature tend to produce accuracy and practical ability. For country children this might best be got from the household duties, the garden, the stable, the farm. These last have the added worth of being actual service-work, not playing at work. For city children a good substitute is manual training. In most cases this should come before the child is sixteen, to be prolonged at technological schools by those who specially care for it and who will naturally be helped by it in their life work.

It is now popular for young men to go to technological, scientific, mechanical, and industrial schools rather than to the regular college. This tendency will do good in some ways, but unless checked it is sure to do great harm to the cause of education and civilization. It is for every reason desirable to keep our most promising youth in college, where the chief object is not to turn out skilled workmen, but to make men of high character and power. Many of these best youth desire a scientific education. The only way for the college to hold this class of students is to build up strong scientific departments, and allow such students to elect, during the later years of their course, most of their work in science, and thus get a thorough scientific education that will fit them in part or fully for the various scientific and technological professions, or prepare them for entering the best professional schools. And the programs of study in our colleges for women should be directed towards the development of the graces of character and conduct in keeping with the best traditions of Southern womanhood, and should supply the solid material for a liberal education that will fit our young women for the largest service to society.

3. We need high grade colleges. For the reason that all educational reform must begin at the top and work downward, I believe that the supreme need in Southern education is a small number of well-equipped and well-endowed colleges for men and women, so organized and so controlled as to become true seats of learning and large centers of influence. I have the utmost sympathy for the humblest college that is striving to give its students the highest it can give in character and in education. Nothing is to be condemned that helps to lick a cub of a boy into the lion of manhood or that tends to create a gentle atmosphere in which the bud of girlhood may bloom into the flower of womanhood. While the humblest college may be useful in a more or less local way in making men and women, yet it is to the well-equipped and well-endowed college that we must look for all educational reforms. Other colleges must be content to give students more or less what they and their parents desire, because their existence depends on tuition year by year. They cannot have the independ-

ence that is needed to lead in any reform, and they cannot carry influence enough to make the reform effective. "Everything great is formative," Goethe said, and hardly anything else is formative. If there is any hope of educational reform in the Southern states, and I believe there is, we must look to the leadership of a few of the best-equipped and best-endowed colleges. The work I have in mind to be done by the college cannot even be approximated except by colleges that have larger facilities and larger prospects than most of our colleges in the past have had.

Such colleges must stand fast for truth and freedom. There is much in the life of every people that tends to put undue emphasis on the local and the temporary and to obscure the universal and permanent. A great college must be free to seek this universal truth and free to teach it. The four years of the college course ought to be given, not to confirming picked youth in their inherited or acquired prejudices and preconceptions, but to the liberating and ennobling search for truth. This fight for freedom in which to live and grow will at times call for all the power and heroism of the strongest. But it is the same battle for liberty in which our forefathers fought, and we too must be free. We need not be discouraged if this freedom is sometimes abused; for every human privilege is liable to abuse, and it is peculiarly true, as Macaulay said, that the remedy for the abuse of liberty is not less of it but more.

It appears to some people that higher education is an exclusive thing, that its benefits are confined to a small number. As a matter of fact its blessings are as permeating and as widespread as the air which we all breathe. We often hear the officials of Southern colleges claim that their institutions are for the poor boy or girl and therefore no one is ever turned away. This claim is usually insincere and always fallacious. Our ideal ought to be put in reach of every youth the best opportunities. The aim should be, not to lower college standards so that anybody can enter, but rather, by building up higher and secondary education, to make a way for every youth to develop himself to the fullest and thus bring it to pass among us that every career shall be open to talent.

The college may help secondary education by creating interest in the subject, by diffusing better ideas about education, and by pointing the way to better educational methods and truer educational aims. The schools are furthermore absolutely dependent on the colleges for teachers who are competent to give instruction and who have themselves been so guided and inspired as they in turn may guide and inspire the youth committed to their hands into the higher fields of learning or to enter as earnest and efficient toilers into the work of the world. There is great need for competent young men in the preparatory schools; but for a well-trained man with high aims and hopes to become a school teacher in most parts of the South today demands the same moral earnestness and enthusiasm for humanity that carries a missionary to the jungles of Africa. Yet to the right men this kind of work offers a rare opportunity to serve men greatly; and I have the faith to believe there are those worthy who will hear this call to noble service and will receive the reward of success that may always be expected by those who do useful work.

One other thing that can be best done by first-class higher institutions of learning is to set before the youth of the South right and true and high ideals of scholarship, literature, citizenship, and real greatness of every kind. The majority of our newspapers, our Fourth-of-July orators (which category unfortunately includes too many of our public speakers), our political conditions, and, sad to say, many of our schools and colleges, and even some of our preachers and moral teachers are throwing the bulk of their influence against right ideals in many departments of life, or at any rate in favor of wholly inadequate ideals. I am not accustomed to paint for myself or for others the darker side of things. I only wish to emphasize the magnitude of the work that lies before the right-minded and right-educated men and women of this generation.

It is the duty of the college to seek after the most improved methods, the most modern organization, to maintain high educational ideals. It is the part of wisdom to utilize all the best results of modern educational progress, to make use of the most improved means for the attainment of the finest ends. But in paying attention to educational machinery, there must be no losing sight of the vital things in education. Important as are teachers and scholars, adequate material equipment, modern organization and standards, traditions of fine ideals and high achievement, not these are the glory of a college, but the generations of college students who here grow into men and women of intelligence and character and are sent forth into the world to spread truth and righteousness. For we do not educate men for the pleasure they are to get out of it. It is not the business of colleges to produce an educated cult whose chief end of existence is a sort of Epicurean refinement of tastes, to be enjoyed in isolation. Education is for service. Educated men of the South today should not spend their lives in easeful, kid-glove seclusion from their fellows, but in the stream of the world. They ought to be gallant and thoroughly disciplined soldiers in the long warfare for the emancipation of humanity out of darkness and ignorance into light and truth. The duty of service to one's fellows must be held high in all our colleges; for only thus may we observe the great commandment of Plato, "Let those who have lamps pass them on to others."

It will have been observed that I have an exalted conception of the function of a great college. I believe that from the revival of letters five hundred years ago until now every advance in civilization has been dependent on influences which have proceeded from seats of learning. These have kept alive the fires that have lighted every nation in Christendom on the way that leads to material prosperity and to the intellectual and moral worth upon which depends all individual and national greatness.

It will also have been observed that I do not take a too optimistic view of educational conditions in the South. There is a great deal to be done, but not more than we can do, when we cease to be overanxious to defend what we are and have been, look our conditions squarely in the face, study them dispassionately in connection with what has been done elsewhere in the world, hold to what is best in our own civilization, and have no fear to adopt from others what is better than our own. No strong man and no strong people ever slavishly imitated others. But the fear of following others in the things that are better than one's own is as weak and foolish as is slavish imitation. We are justly proud of many things in Southern civilization and of the peculiar type of Southern character, and it is to be hoped that these best things may be always kept.

I have urged with all the emphasis I could command that every educated man should do his full stint of work and should give his highest service to society. I would not close without drawing attention to the gentler side of Southern civilization. For it was the graciousness, the hospitality, and the beauty and purity of the social life that was the best characteristic of the old order. And education should help to keep and transmit undiminished the old grace, generosity, and magnanimity of our elders, and should contribute to the cultivation of mind and taste and the refinement of manners that make living with each other sweet and wholesome. For, after birth and breeding, great books stand first in their "eligibility to free, to arouse, to dilate," and loving and living in the beautiful charm of books is the securest nourishment of the poise and fineness of temper that form an essential part of the spiritual constitution of every gentle man and woman.

SOUTHERN PUBLIC OPINION*

BY PUBLIC OPINION I mean the conscious and unconscious thinking of men about duty and conduct and the embodiment of this thinking in prevalent ideals of life in such a way as to shape the collective and individual character of a whole people. To be effective for good this public opinion must be intelligent, fearless, and free. We Southerners are particularly sensitive to local and—though we are not apt to admit it—to outside public sentiment, and it is therefore important for us to enquire into our relations to our own Southern public opinion.

As Southerners we ought to be proud of our people as well as proud of our common country. I believe that the mighty founders and builders of this republic were largely Southern men. George Washington, himself our greatest American, was also our greatest Southerner, and while his great gifts of mind and character were a part of his inheritance from our

it. *The South Atlantic Quarterly,* IV (January, 1905), 1-12.
* One of three addresses given before the Trinity College Association of Charlotte, N. C., on the subject of Southern progress and some of the ways to advance

common English race, the peculiar type of the man was due to his membership in a Southern community and was characteristic of the best in Southern life. Jefferson, another Southerner, was the author of the Declaration of Independence; and Madison was the father of the Constitution; while Marshall left an enduring stamp upon the federal judiciary.

Why is it that a civilization which has produced such men as Washington, Jefferson, Madison, Marshall, and Lee is now without commanding leaders of national reputation, without constructive statesmen on a large scale, without ancient and famous institutions of learning, without literary journals and magazines of high merit and standing, without well-established publishing houses, without artists and writers, without so many of the good things of life that make civilization strong and great and beautiful? To these questions I know no satisfactory answer. But to ignore facts that anyone may observe from the car windows in passing from here to New York is not patriotic. Our patriotic duty is to look the facts squarely in the face, and see if there may not be a way out of this condition of things and into a better order of life for our people.

It is sometimes asserted that there is no healthy public opinion here in the South. that, in fact, the minds of men are not free. Of course strong men here are independent and fearless as of their very natures they must forever be. We have freedom of mind. I believe we have more of it today than we have had in seventy-five years; but we need still more of it, and I believe we are going to have more of it than we have now. We have today some independent and fearless newspapers in the South that dare to speak out at any cost. We have leaders of public opinion—men and women—editors, teachers, preachers, businessmen—who are liberal and broadminded, uncompromising and unafraid. We have schools and colleges that stand like bulwarks against which the surging passions of the hour dash themselves in vain.

This vigor and independence of thought is valuable because through it better ideas pass into the community and improvement becomes possible; but it is most valuable as an example and object lesson. As a people we have been exceedingly conservative in our thinking and too sensitive to criticism, which, wherever it exists in healthy condition, is apt to stimulate the minds of men and set them in the way to improvement. This sensitiveness to criticism has been developed mainly by our peculiar conditions. For half a century we were defending the institution of slavery, which was being condemned by the whole civilized world; and now for almost another half century we have had to deal with conditions and problems just as little understood by the rest of the country. Being thus for so long on the defensive, we have been too much shut in to ourselves and have lived apart from the general movement of contemporary life, cut off from the liberalizing and nationalizing tendencies that have been so strong for a hundred years; and there has thus been developed in us as a people a dogged determination to defend ourselves and a sensitiveness to criticism, especially criticism from the outside. This has produced a hampered and timid cast of mind; and the result has been a serious lack of robust thought. This manifests itself in many forms of Southern life. It manifests itself in Southern literature which has lacked ideas, which has, to be sure, been produced by fine-souled men, but men who were great in fineness of character rather than in gifts of virility and strength. It manifests itself in a disposition to turn away from the hard facts of the present back to the past, to the past glorified as it is in the glamour of our Southern imaginations, in exaggerated traditions, in memories that irradiate the scenes and days when life was fresh and young. It manifests itself in a disposition to accept existing conditions as ideally good and to look upon things as we might wish them to be rather than as they actually are.

There has resulted from this mental drift a lack of first-hand thinking and a consequent failure to produce inventive minds, to produce men who forge onward into new ways of doing things, into the solution of industrial, political, and educational problems. We have been without inventors, without constructive statesmen, without genuine educational leaders, without men of strong conviction, of breadth, of large-mindedness, of comprehensive view. We have had a long day of small things, of men of local, narrow, sectional outlook, who do not see from a national, widesweeping standpoint, to whom truth is not free and universal, but limited and of special application. We have too long regarded ourselves as a peculiar people, living under peculiar conditions, with peculiar problems to work out in peculiar ways. In a sense we are truly a peculiar people, working out our destiny under entirely unique conditions. There is nothing else just like it in all the world. But this does not, as one might easily infer from much of our speech and action, free us from the operation of ordinary laws of nature and human progress. Whatever *we* sow, that must *we* also reap. If we abrogate our laws through mob violence we must expect lawlessness and anarchy; even for us there can be no thought except free thought; even among us ignorance cannot cure anything; even we cannot learn to see by closing our eyes; even in a peculiar civilization like ours unhealthy political conditions must bring civic inefficiency and decay.

It is high time for us to open wide our eyes and look about us and beyond us to what others have done. Our problem is to learn the best that has been thought and said and done elsewhere, to become familiar with the results of experiments in civilization made in other parts of the world, to find out how others have successfully done their tasks in education, in politics, and in other human concerns, and to apply these results to our own conditions. This ought not to be an effort to take over bodily their institutions or any of the peculiar features of other civilizations, but merely to learn how others have solved their problems and to get lessons for the solution of our own. To learn valuable lessons from others is the best part of wisdom, but servile imitation is an unfailing sign of weakness. Here is the supreme opportunity of the Southern newspaper, the Southern college, and Southern criticism of today, to learn from the records of the past the essentials of human progress and to bring these lessons of life to bear on the solution of our own particular problems. This does not mean that we should try to be like England, or New England, but better than either. We must grow in our own way; but it is the part of wisdom to take whatever is good wherever we may find it, just as our Southern cotton mills furnished with the newest and most improved machinery are becoming the very best in the world.

This prevalent lack of first-hand thinking and of courage to speak out has brought about an unfortunate scarcity of plain, common, intellectual honesty. This shows itself in many ways. It is often seen where it might be least expected, in connection with educational institutions and educational discussions. Our whole educational nomenclature has become inflated and absurd. Every teacher is a professor and every professor is a distinguished scholar. Small schools are called colleges and poorly equipped colleges are called universities. In fact, most of the stronger colleges in the Southern states call themselves universities, though few of them ought to have the name. I have read the descriptions of a $10,000 school building "which will be, when finished, the finest university in the South." This is an exaggerated case, but it is an illustration of the pretense seen in too many forms of Southern life. We are apt to be devoid of perspective and at times to overrate our own men and our own institutions and our own selves. The practice of whistling to keep one's courage up or of shouting lest one be not heard may easily become a fixed habit; but however natural it may be, it is not so ennobling as to be strong without emphasis and brave without assertion. Such failure to grasp facts, such lack of perspective, such intellectual dishonesty, usually unconscious, would almost seem to shut the very doors of hope, obscuring as it does the true ends of our striving and leaving us in a bewildering confusion without a worthy goal in view. Perhaps after all is said the greatest menace to our Southern civilization is the failure on the part of those who ought to be our leaders—our schools and colleges, our newspapers and preachers—to hold up high and right standards of life. For civilizations, like men, must be judged by their ideals—the aims they set themselves—and their efforts to attain these. By these tests the character of a civilization can be determined as well as what its future achievement is to be.

We Southern people are most sensitive and least apt to be perfectly candid when we are dealing with certain subjects connected with our past and present as they are related to the Negro, with all that is involved in the so-called Southern question. Here there has been too much failure to look facts squarely in the face, too much assumption that we are dealing with a peculiar problem and so need not observe great principles of right and justice. We have at times forgotten that we must do justly and love mercy, or else we shall be more injured than are those we oppress; for as Emerson says the slave is forever owner and the victim is forever victor. This is a phase of the question that is not pondered as it should be. It is one of the great and inevitable wrongs that the presence here of the Negro is doing the dominant race. The problem is not so much what to do to elevate the inferior race as it is to save the whites from the blighting influences of narrow-mindedness, intolerance, and injustice. Through no special fault of ours and through no fault of his own this hapless child of evil destiny has planted in the heart of our young republic what Mr. William Garrott Brown has called the ancient curse he bears. Turn where we may, we see it; go where we will, we cannot escape it. And yet I have here nothing to say directly about this so-called Negro problem, because I am more and more convinced that the surest and quickest way to settle this stupendous question is through the education of the white race, through leading the great masses of them into enlightened manhood, justice, and right.

The same conditions have produced among us just as little regard for the right in politics, in political parties and in political methods. The necessity of preventing Negro political domination has led to unfairness at the polls until there is an unhealthy political condition among us. We have argued that the end justifies the means and have lulled ourselves in the quieting delusion that we need not reap the fruit of our sowing. However necessary wrong may sometimes seem to be, it produces its legitimate effect in the life and character of the people who perpetrate it. Before we can prosper as we should, we must free ourselves from every vestige of political dishonesty and unfairness and from all attempt through abuse, through social ostracism, or through any other means, to browbeat others into our way of thinking. We must come to vote as we think, without regard to the opinions of others and without regard to any consequences that may come to us through registering at the polls our real convictions on local and national questions.

The same disregard of actual facts and the same aloofness from the present have produced a type of religion somewhat different from the prevailing type now found elsewhere among men of English blood—a religion that is emotional, given to profession, and sometimes froward in its retention of outworn forms, rather than conservative of the simple, essential spirit of Christianity. From this kind of conservatism has come insistence upon regularity of experience and profession that has seemed to some to make religion a clog on Southern progress. Without authority to speak at all on the subject, I speak with the utmost diffidence and with the fullest recognition of all that the many generations of preachers have done and suffered

here in order to keep alive among us the feeling after God
and unearthly things that has saved us from materialism and
flat despair, and yet the most sympathetic critic might find it
in his heart to say that less emphasis could well be placed upon
empty profession and upon an indefinable and often meaningless orthodoxy. Men would then be more certainly judged not
by what they profess to be and believe, but by the amount of
Christian service they give and by the spirit in which they
give it. This shifting of emphasis from formal profession and
correctness of creed to one's actual work and the spirit in which
one works would produce a more intelligent and Christian
charity that would be glad to include those finest and most
unselfish spirits who often in our day are spending themselves
—in ways not quite the church's, but in ways that are effective—for "the glory of the Creator and the relief of man's
estate."

In modern times the most effective method for the
expression of public opinion is through literature—newspapers,
magazines, and books. Much has been said in attempted explanation of the bareness of Southern literature. Doubtless
other causes must be called to our aid in accounting for the
strange, sad fact that there has been heard no commanding
voice of these three silent centuries, immortalizing the story
of their marvelous achievement or singing their "mystic un-
fathomable song." But of one cause I feel sure; there is some
relation between our lack of education and our lack of literature. As a rule in the old days only men of the aristocratic
class were educated and their education was inadequate and
often vicious. The aristocratic class has not been the mainstay
of literature anywhere in this country and it has perhaps not
been the chief reliance for literature anywhere in modern times.
The neglect of the poorer whites—an inevitable consequence
of the institution of slavery and feudal society, and the most
ruinous social and economic waste in our old civilization—
made impossible the growth of a strong, intelligent middle

class, which has for two hundred years been the principal dependence for literature in English-speaking countries. This passive neglect of the common people easily passed into indifference to them. In such an atmosphere there prevailed an utter disregard of anything contemporary and American in literature, and in such an atmosphere there was no room for a native literature to live and grow.

An English critic has said that the essence of good criticism is the ability to praise what one dislikes, and, he might have added, the ability to speak soberly and judiciously of what one likes. Always one of the great weaknesses of a gentle, generous, and noble-hearted people like the people of the South is just the inability to do these two things. We have been too apt to see feelingly, as poor blind Gloucester says in King Lear, to see with our feelings, not with our eyes; to allow our sympathies, our affections, and even our prejudices to rule in our judgments, rather than reason and intellect. We have not made enough of the value of mind, of the discipline of hard and constructive thinking, and the practice of separating the operations of the intellect from those of the emotions.

Especially is this judicial point of view necessary when we approach the consideration of literature in any of its forms. Literature is too great and too universal to be permanently affected by any kind of boasting, overpraise, or mere passing sentiment. It can finally stand only on its intrinsic merit. The one honest, useful thing any critic can do for any author—or for anybody else so far as that is concerned—is to speak of him as he is; nothing extenuate nor aught set down in malice. For us of the South to do this in the case of poets like Timrod and Lanier, for example, and a novelist like Simms, is exceedingly difficult. They were all so "lovely and pleasant in their lives," made such heroic efforts against tremendous odds to lead the higher life, but were so cramped, cabined, and confined in their surroundings and so pitiable in their lot, that we can with great difficulty look upon them in any other light

than as martyrs to a lost cause. And yet they can all afford to
stand on their merits. Each one holds perhaps not a high but
a secure place in American literary annals. We may not place
Timrod or Lanier among the few great English poets. We
must not thus confuse or lower our ideals. For a high ideal
of excellence is the most sacred and valuable thing to a race.
We in democratic America constantly need to be reminded that
excellence dwells high among the rocks and to attain it we
must wear out our very souls. The man who in any of the
higher fields of effort, by honest endeavor wins some measure
of success, should receive the simple, sincere praise of all wise
and good men. To succeed in a humble way, to hold but a
small niche in the everlasting temple of fame, is worth all
that even Lanier or Timrod ever suffered.

We can claim that some of our poets were endowed with
the rare gift of writing beautiful verse. But I think no poets
in any time ever had a less favorable opportunity to sing their
songs. They were in most cases not widely educated, they had
few associations that could help them on the road they longed
to travel. They had small market for their wares, they had
no body of critical readers to keep them struggling for the
best, they lived in a section of the United States where native
literature was neglected, and in the midst of our Southern
civilization—a civilization in many ways beautiful, but entirely
devoid of intellectual ideals. This old Southern civilization
was so picturesque, life for the well-to-do was so sweet, rich,
and beautiful that we are apt to wonder why this civilization
did not produce literature. It seems to me that there are two
fundamental causes that made all kinds of high intellectual
attainment impossible. One was a belated survival at the South
of the spirit of English feudalism. The second was the institution of slavery. These two things strengthened each other
and had a baleful influence on Southern character. Feudalism
had a fine side to it and it did in its day great service to the
English race. But the chivalric ideals were entirely aristo-

cratic, and too much was thought of appearances. The old sense of personal honor, for example, at its best a fine thing, might easily degenerate into a regard for reputation and little concern for character. And just as chivalry cared only for the knights and ladies, so our older civilization was almost exclusively for the benefit of the well-to-do classes, and there was no chance to build up a great middle class, the mainstay of all modern civilizations. There was not enough value placed upon man as an individual. None but favored sons of fortune had a chance in the race of life, and their gaze was too much on the past. They were too well satisfied with things as they were. As men of the eighteenth century thought, so the people of the old South thought of their civilization, whatever is, is right. Then if it was "right" it must be let alone. With this point of view no thought is possible. All thought must be free, and to be free it must have a free hearing. But when thought must run in certain fixed, conventional grooves, there can be no free hearing.

Then the institution of slavery reinforced these tendencies in Southern civilization. Slavery was against the civilization of the nineteenth century, and the civilization of the nineteenth century was against slavery. We were at war with the rest of the civilized world, and we felt bound to defend ourselves. Our thinking, therefore, political, social, and religious, was not directed towards a search after the truth which makes us free; but it was concentrated on the defense of a civil and political order of things.

These conditions made impossible a vigorous intellectual life. There was a dearth of original thought and ideas. This lack of ideas is noticeable in all of our older literary men. They were as a rule noble men, finely constituted, well endowed, but there is a lack of vigor and maturity in their productions. They promise more than they fulfil. They are greater for what they are than for what they do. Over them all might be placed a broken shaft, as Simms requested should

PRESIDENT FEW AT THE TIME OF HIS
INAUGURATION, 1910

be placed over his grave, and on the broken shaft might be carved the epitaph which he composed for himself: "Here lies one who, after a reasonably long life, distinguished chiefly by unceasing labors, has left all his better works undone." We have this feeling about them all. They left all their better works undone. They did not give a full expression of themselves. This was partly due to the unfortunate circumstances of the individual lives, and partly due to the fact that these men were a part of the old Southern civilization, where a vigorous mental life was well nigh impossible. They have no great message for us, they have no body of truth. But there are poets who are almost great and yet whose poetry has slight substance; such is Shelley or our own Poe. They were both great artists and their verse at its best has the perfection of form and the essence of beauty that is everywhere found in poetry of a high order. Poe, dowered with more of the gifts that enter into the make-up of a great poet than perhaps any other American, was, as it seems to me, saved from being one of the foremost poets of the world by just this lack of ideas and by a corresponding lack of moral earnestness and power.

While few men of the old South gave themselves to literature as a profession, many of them had leisure and bountiful provision for the future and habitual mental refinement, and as a matter of course they amused themselves with literature, the arts, and abstract science. Virginia and South Carolina especially boasted their men of learning and belle-lettres scholars, but they were learned in older English and modern literature, the classics and abstract science. These were to them little more than the refined amusement of cultivated men. Few of them followed a literary or scientific profession or interested themselves in the experimental sciences or creative work in the field of literature or art. They did little, therefore, for the advancement of learning, science, literature, or art. They were masters in the law and in politics. But even in these fields as time went on and as men gave their minds more and more to the defense of our peculiar civil and political order of things, the conditions of our civilization ceased to produce great minds like Washington, Jefferson, and Marshall.

Even today it is not possible to make an extensive literary reputation in the South. Our Southern authors write for Northern publishers and a Northern public. Their reputations are made in the North and from there are reflected back to us. But we have living Southern writers of distinguished attainment and high promise, most of whom live in the North or will go there as soon as they can. I look to see their tribe rapidly increase. In epochs of activity and hopefulness literature has always flourished. I believe our changing conditions will produce unprecedented intellectual and literary activity. But after all, great literature cannot be made to order. For literature is a sort of flowering of the tree of life, and it can appear only when this body of life is sound and growing. It comes to a civilization that is strong and healthy and not in the miasmatic intellectual regions where we have lived for three quarters of a century. We must purify the air; we must give truth and freedom their old ascendant place in our life; we must recognize merit wherever it appears and we must exalt worth in whomsoever it may be found; we must promote intelligence and happiness among all classes of people; we must cease to stand apart from the currents of modern life, with our local sympathies and interests; and we must hold aloft in our democratic Southern society high, national, universal standards of excellence in all human concerns. Then, and not till then, shall we have a social, civic, and spiritual climature in which real literature may take root and flourish. As intelligent and right-minded men and women it will be our privilege to labor for the bringing in of that glad day. Whether our great man shall come even then is, as I believe a Frenchman once said, a secret safely locked up in the keeping of the immortal gods.

But whether these changed conditions would lead to the production of a genuine Southern literature or not, they would certainly create a healthier public opinion and make this a better place in which for us worthily to live our human lives. Our ancestors even where they failed, failed bravely, and left us a magnificent heritage of heroism, fine self-sacrifice, and high devotion to the right as they saw it. We ourselves have fallen upon times rich in promise and full of hope. With a past like theirs and a future like ours, right thinking and patriotic Southern men ought to remain here and work here even if sometimes at considerable cost of opportunity and ambition. The happiest men have always been those who have worked under a great inspiration, and it is a happy privilege to spend oneself in the service of an undying cause in which one believes with the whole heart.

Mr. John Morley concludes his life of Gladstone with these words: "Let us rather leave off with thoughts and memories of one who was a vivid example of public duty and of private faithfulness; of a long career that with every circumstance of splendor, amid all the mire and all the poisons of the world, lighted up in practice even for those who have none of his genius and none of his power his own precept, 'Be inspired with the belief that life is a great and noble calling; not a mean and grovelling thing, that we are to shuffle through as we can, but an elevated and lofty destiny.' "

We of this generation of Southern men and women ought to feel that for us "life is a great and noble calling; not a mean and grovelling thing, that we are to shuffle through as we can, but an elevated and lofty destiny."

WASHINGTON DUKE[*]

THE DEATH OF MR. WASHINGTON DUKE, in Durham, North
Carolina, on May 8 closed a most remarkable career. He was
born in 1820 in Orange, now Durham, County, North Carolina. His father was a respected man in the rural community
in which he lived; but he had a large family and to his son
came no inheritance at all. The son began life as a small
farmer on rented land. Under the old regime in the South
the small farmer had slight opportunity to rise. But this was
an uncommon man and no untoward circumstances could bind
him down. Ability, energy, and industry had their reward,
and each year leaving him better off than the preceding, by
1860 he had bought and well stocked a farm of three hundred
acres.

He raised one crop of cotton and it brought but five cents
a pound. Living in the bright tobacco belt of North Carolina,
he early turned to the cultivation of tobacco. Before the out-
break of the Civil War he had made up his mind to become

* *The South Atlantic Quarterly*, IV (July, 1905), 203-208.

a manufacturer of tobacco, and in a small way was actually launched in this enterprise when the war came. He entered the Confederate Army. After the fall of Richmond he was captured and sent to prison. A few weeks later when the war was over the government sent him to New Bern, North Carolina, and from thence he walked 135 miles to his old home. Arrived there, he found himself the possessor of a neglected farm, two blind army mules, and fifty cents in money. But he realized, as few others realized until long afterwards, that there was a new day in the South; and with his four motherless children he at once set about rebuilding his ruined home. In 1865 he was forty-five years old and was at this advanced age beginning life anew with practically nothing, and in a country stricken with poverty and devastated by war. From small beginnings many marvelous careers have been worked out in America, but not in America have I ever heard of a successful life begun under such unpromising circumstances; yet he became a wealthy man and laid the secure foundation upon which has been built up by himself and two sons a very great fortune. From the beginning their manufacturing enterprise was successful and from year to year it has grown until now it has encircled the world, and the sun never sets on their factories and warehouses.

These brief facts will be sufficient to indicate the extraordinarily successful business career of Mr. Duke. But marvelous as has been this accumulation of wealth under circumstances unparalleled even in America, where the self-made man is almost the rule and where fortunes have been achieved with magic swiftness and in gigantic proportions that stagger the imagination, still more marvelous is the spirit that controlled this wealth and the disposition that was made of it. For Mr. Duke became not only the builder of the largest fortune ever amassed in the South, but he became the South's foremost philanthropist. His helpfulness knew no bounds. He had come out of grinding poverty, he had lived through a period of intense sectionalism and bitterness, but his character came out untouched by these fires of adversity that had tried it. He helped churches, and hospitals, schools and colleges, men and women, Democrats and Republicans, Negroes and whites. In these miscellaneous gifts he perhaps distributed more money than any other one man who ever lived in the state.

But the largest recipient of his wealth was Trinity College, which will stand as a monument to his philanthropy. Before he began giving money to it this was a poor, struggling college in Randolph County. He brought it to Durham and became the founder of the New Trinity. Finding it wholly inadequate to the needs of modern education, he left it strong enough to rank in equipment and standards of work with the better colleges of New England and other parts of this country.

But, after all, the amount of his giving is not so significant and characteristic of the man as the spirit in which he gave his money and in which he sought to develop this institution. It might well happen that the will of a living college should be curbed by the will of a living or dead founder. It has happened that the founder or benefactor of a college has hung his own personality about the college like a body of death. The personality of Mr. Duke has indeed left an enduring stamp on Trinity College; but his influence has ever been liberating and inspiring rather than narrowing and deadening. His voice was always raised in behalf of truth and right and always against bitterness and narrowness, whatever forms they might assume. The qualities which dominated his character— liberality, broad-mindedness, and genuine goodness—are just the qualities which having entered into this college, must make it great in its mission of service to the state and nation.

It was for Trinity College perhaps a fortunate circumstance that after the Civil War Mr. Duke became a Republican. He was a Republican from careful thought and serious conviction, largely because, as he said, he believed in the Republican policy of public improvements. He never sought office and had no relations to politics other than those of an intelligent and interested citizen. But, joining the Republican party in the early years after the Civil War, he became one of a weak and despised minority. This might well have developed in him a spirit of bitterness and resentfulness, but it had the opposite effect of developing a catholicity in his feelings and judgments. Living through a period of civil war, disunion and dissension, he early saw the wisdom of putting aside all partisan heat and sectional hatred. While he had his own convictions which he maintained stoutly, yet he did not seek by force to impose them upon others. Many of his close friends and most of his employees were of a different political faith; but in his friends he looked only for sincerity and genuine excellence, and in business he applied no tests other than availability and efficiency.

So in religion he became a liberal. He was a man of strong religious nature. But his devout intensity did not breed in him any tinge of bigotry or intolerance. He combined the amiability of a genuinely pious and gentle soul with the wideness and generous forbearance of men who do things on a large scale.

Still more noteworthy and representative of the character of Mr. Duke was his quick determination, after the war, to turn at once from the dead past, to live in the present and face towards the future. The war ended, he at once felt himself a loyal citizen of a reunited country and became wholly national in his feelings, his political and civic thinking, and his business operations.

But these are in a sense negative qualities and might almost spring out of indifference to others and to their welfare. Mr. Duke was a man of action. With him gifts must prove their uses. He did not care for things that yielded no dividends. His very goodness was progressive and creative. A spirit of genuine helpfulness animated him from early life. When quite a boy he seems to have dedicated himself to the service of men. He once said: "Since I was twelve years old I have been trying to make the world better for having lived in it." When his first factory had grown to considerable size and he had begun to employ a large number of people, he organized a Sunday school in one room of the factory, and out of that Sunday school grew the church to which he belonged at the time of his death—the church built for factory operatives and until now attended by many of them, as well as by most of the teachers and students of Trinity College. And it has been the policy of his company, wherever they have put down a manufacturing plant to build also a church.

Mr. Duke never placed upon the College a hampering restriction of any kind and never embarrassed it by a personal wish or preference. His interest in it, however, was always active, and always made for progress and improvement.

The College having thus been made strong in its search for the truth which makes men free and thus fortified by the spirit and the example of its founder, developed a power that enabled it something more than a year ago to promulgate under most trying circumstances a declaration of principles on the subject of academic freedom that was not only a new thing in the South but was so clear-cut and fearless in its pronouncement as to startle the entire country.

This brilliant victory in the ancient cause of free speech was saved from being an empty achievement by the working, undoctrinaire character of the College, which had been so firmly established in the principles of truth-seeking and truth-speaking, to which Mr. Duke's triumphant example had lured and led the way. The College was not fighting for a mere academic privilege, but for the elementary and vital right to live unhampered and to work without restraint for the promotion of freedom, liberality, catholicity, national integration, and all the causes most precious to our Southern people, and for keeping alive here the fires that have lighted every nation

in Christendom on the way that leads to material prosperity
and to the intellectual and moral worth upon which depends
all individual and national greatness.

Mr. Duke's philanthrophy did not rest upon a weak senti-
mentality, but it was based upon a sound principle. This may
be illustrated by a saying of his, set, as was much of his talk,
in imagery somewhat homely but shrewdly just and impressive in its very homeliness, a saying to which he on more than
one occasion gave utterance "Some people say that I ought
to give my money to the poor. I don't think so. They would
soon eat it up. I want to give my money to help people who
are able to feed themselves."

The benevolent and genuinely Christian character of Mr.
Duke is illustrated in his attitude towards the Negroes, an
attitude assumed early in life and kept to the end. He was
always interested in them and sought by all possible means to
assist them. He was in 1890 invited by the Negroes of Durham to give an educational address. He could not do this, but
sent them a letter which was full of good sense and concern
for the Negroes' welfare. He built and equipped a hospital
for them in Durham, and all his life was liberal in his gifts
to Negro schools and churches. His charity to Negroes was
abundant, but even more wise and benevolent was his treatment of them as an employer. It is largely due to him that
the relations between the Negroes and whites are better in
Durham and the Negroes more industrious, prosperous, and
contented than I have known elsewhere. There is no Negro
problem in this community. It is quite certain that no other
man who has lived in this state was so loved by the Negroes.
Hundreds of them viewed his face the last night on which his
body lay in his Durham home, and thousands of them lined
the streets as his body was carried to its last resting place.

These qualities all go to show Mr. Duke a most remarkable
and withal very wise man. In the eight years I have known
him he has often reminded me of Abraham Lincoln. He had

an unequaled sense of proportion and instinctive recognition of
the eternal fitness of things, and intuitive knowledge of what
is right and proper. And these make up the most useful gift
vouchsafed to men on earth—the gift of unerring wisdom—
wisdom that is not the product of intellect alone, but comes
out of a full, harmonious character, and at its highest becomes
a sort of moral instinct that almost compels a man to live his
life wisely, just as the natural instinct compels the bird to sing
its song. This unerring wisdom seems to me to have been
the supreme gift of nature to Lincoln and likewise to Mr.
Duke. The two were alike again in the sure command of a
homely but shrewd humor; both were brimful of that mirth
which, according to Dr. Johnson, always measures the size of
a man's understanding.

With this quiet strain of mirth ran a deep and persistent
undertone of pity and tragic tenderness. The mystery "of all
this unintelligible world" weighed heavily on both their minds.
"The poor human race," was a phrase often on Mr. Duke's
lips. This matchless humor and womanlike tenderness had
their common origin in the naturalness and humanity of the
man, in a heart that sought the widest good and loved the
widest joy.

THE EXCESSIVE DEVOTION TO ATHLETICS*

THE RECENT REVELATIONS to the public of the exaggerated emphasis put upon intercollegiate athletics and the rank abuses that have in late years grown up about the whole system have produced a shock almost as severe as the shock produced by the disclosures of public and private graft. And between these evils and dangers in college sports and the evils and dangers in the business world there is an unmistakable connection; for the excess that manifests itself in college sports is but a reflection of the same spirit that is everywhere abroad in our country. The intensity with which college sports are pursued is a manifestation of the spirit which the American people put into everything; and the craze for the winning games embodies the spirit and methods of trade. The impulses and habits acquired at home are carried into the schools and colleges. But to account for the rise of evils is not to justify them; and for some of the evils that have grown up about competitive athletics there is no justification.

* *The South Atlantic Quarterly, 7* (January, 1906), 44-49.

Thoughtful men have, for some years, felt that college authorities ought to call a halt and set some limit to the all-controlling place athletics have come to hold in American colleges. The American public has lately been in a fair way to hysteria on the subject. What the sober thought of the more reasonable could not achieve seems about to come at the hands of the many, in the great mass of brute force of enraged public sentiment. To lop off some of the grosser evils of college athletics will be worth the cost to the American people of a genuine case of national hysterics. This swift passing from one extreme to another is our characteristic American way of making progress. To come to a just and durable judgment it is necessary to strike a balance. That there are evils in intercollegiate athletics is beyond question. The disclosures recently made show the conditions in some of the prominent Eastern colleges to be worse than had been known to the general public. Football, as the most exaggerated form of intercollegiate games, is being widely condemned. As at present played, the game should no doubt be abolished. The entire country has been laid under obligations to Columbia University for its announced determination to banish the game; and Harvard never did the country a better service than it is now doing by the investigations it is making and the action it will no doubt take in due time. The present game should be killed and some better autumn game allowed to come in its place; maybe Association or Rugby football, in which a larger number of men could take part, and with less risk to life and limb.

There is good in intercollegiate athletics, when properly conducted. They have made considerable contribution to American college life and deserve to be saved from the perils that threaten them and the evils that now actually beset them. The two chief dangers of intercollegiate athletics are excess and the spirit that would win by unfair means. It may be fairly said that these are the two most prominent dangers in American life. The faults which everybody recognizes as belonging to intercollegiate games are therefore not to be charged to any inherent weakness in the system, but are to be taken as manifestations of American life. While, then, these faults must not be regarded as inherent weaknesses inevitably attaching themselves to college sports; yet these faults must be overcome, else they will make college sports more harmful than useful and will in the end destroy them altogether. The situation has grown more intense year by year, and continually the athletic is being substituted for the intellectual ideal. That this excessive importance attached to athletics is doing harm to American education cannot be questioned. And these evils are more pronounced in the larger and older colleges of the East and North. They are evils that have grown out of mere bigness. They have come from great prosperity, like many of the evils in the business and political life of the country. These larger colleges must do something to lighten the strain that is now upon athletics; and something will doubtless be done before long. Perhaps to abolish the gate receipts would produce the desired results.

These pronounced evils of athletics in the larger Eastern colleges have not threatened the colleges in the South. Our evils are not evils of prosperity, but evils of adversity; and they came from lack of organization, from the chaotic state in which so much of our education finds itself. The country has been too poor, the colleges have been too small, and the communities in which the colleges have been located too sparsely settled to give Southern intercollegiate games the vast crowds and immense gate receipts that have produced the fanaticism and wild enthusiasm in the North. And yet athletic conditions have been no better in most parts of the South than in the North. But the unfortunate situation here is attributable to the disorganized state of education, and, as a symptom of this disorganization, it is most discouraging. Southern colleges are growing rapidly, and the entire section is becoming prosperous as never before. Prosperity will soon come to intercol-

legiate athletics; and if to the evils of disorganization, we add
the evils that come from bigness and prosperity, we shall have
a state of things that will be unendurable. It is absolutely
essential that all reputable Southern colleges at once put themselves right in the matter of intercollegiate athletics.

What is needed is a common set of rules for all reputable
colleges. These rules ought to be reasonably fair, and they
ought to be enforced by an intelligent and just public sentiment in the college and out of it. A college that will habit-
ually indulge in sharp and questionable athletic practices
will not develop moral power enough to correct itself, until
it is sternly judged at the bar of public opinion. If profes-
sionals or semi-professionals are sent against amateurs of
another institution, the conditions are unequal if the facts are
known; if they are concealed it is unfair and dishonest. Nothing can be more permanently vicious and hurtful to the college than the practice—not unknown to some institutions in
the North and in the South—of playing men of doubtful
amateur standing and at the same time proclaiming to the
world that the standing of these men is unquestionable. This
instilling into the minds of the educated youth of the country
the doctrine that in order to win it is allowable to indulge in
sharp tricks will do more harm in the long run than the college will be able to counteract by any good offices that it can
perform. The time will soon come when any kind of shady
practice in athletics will be regarded as dishonorable. The
time ought to be at hand when it will be a discredit to any
college to send out teams that are composed of men who are
not genuine students and amateur athletes; when to send out a
team not composed of amateurs and concealing the facts will
be treated like any other form of common dishonesty.

A common set of rules ought to be in force at all reputable
colleges, because there can be no just comparison when the
competitors do not meet on even footing, and the results must
always be unsatisfactory. I believe it is entirely wrong for any

college to allow its teams to go against other college teams that are not composed of real students and amateurs. The better organized Southern colleges have already taken this position. Northern colleges can do a distinct service to the cause of decent athletics in the South by taking the same stand in games played on their Southern trips.

These common rules should be definitely formulated and should be widely known. The rules should be the result of accumulated experience, and they should represent the best thought of the best institutions of learning in the country. But it must be admitted that rules of themselves will not be effective. Laws must be backed by enlightened public sentiment, and where this public sentiment does not exist no rules can ever be availing. There ought to be among reputable colleges a gentleman's understanding to live up to the rules and to send out as representatives only men who have a right to be on college teams. Unless this sort of sentiment exists in a college, it will become a breeding place for sharp practices and dishonesty; and for this state of things, the faculty and the governing board cannot be held blameless.

Another serious need is some comprehensive organization to which disputed matters may be referred. In the South there is an organization of this sort, and it ought to be initiated in other parts of the country. The Southern Intercollegiate Athletic Association was organized some twelve years ago and it now has some twenty-odd members comprising the better colleges of all the Southern states except Virginia and North Carolina. Trinity College alone represents these two states in the organized movement for the betterment of athletic conditions in the South. For the backwardness of the two states named, the University of Virginia and the University of North Carolina must divide a large share of responsibility.

This association is making an honest effort to better the athletic conditions in the South, and it has had conspicuous success. I can see no serious objection any Southern college could make to joining this association. It is better to join it and try to strengthen it than to remain on the outside and cavil at it. I am sorry to say my observation has taught me to believe that objections to joining such organizations are nearly always disingenuous. This association has adopted a body of rules that proscribe all who are not genuine students and amateur athletes. To an executive committee is referred the question of eligibility of the teams of the twenty-odd colleges that compose the association. Thus it secured an impartial board in the place of an interested athletic committee to pass upon the eligibility of every man who represents his college in an intercollegiate contest. So far as I have been able to observe this board has always been composed of fair-minded and sensible men.

There are still left a few colleges that manifest an evident dislike to the Southern Intercollegiate Athletic Association. They are as a rule colleges that make no effort to regulate their athletics, and want to befoul the general atmosphere by making other colleges seem dishonest as they themselves. There have been some sad manifestations of this sort of spirit within recent years. Some of the same colleges that have manifested this spirit have manifested also a shameful lack of common honesty. On some occasions paid coaches have played against other college teams. At other times ineligible men have been played under assumed names. There has even been a rumor that in one of the important football games played in the South this past season twelve men were run in at one time. We in the South are justly proud of the sense of honor and spirit of chivalry that manifest themselves in so many phases of the life of this gentle and generous people. By some strange perversity, men honorable to the minutest detail of conduct in all other matters, in this one thing become sophisticated and unwilling to meet issues squarely.

But if there are Southern colleges that have good reason for remaining outside the Southern Intercollegiate Athletic

Association, they ought to publish to the world their attitude on the subject of intercollegiate athletics; and their teams ought to conform to the requirements now in force in well-regulated American colleges. Or else they should not claim to stand on the same footing with amateur college teams. The colleges that fail to do their duty ought to be outlawed by all colleges that stand for decency in athletics as in other things, by intelligent and fair-minded newspapers, and by right-thinking men everywhere.

THE STANDARDIZING OF SOUTHERN
COLLEGES*

FOR FORTY-ODD years educational conditions in the Southern states have been thoroughly chaotic. It is not that much heroic service has not been rendered in the cause by self-sacrificing and high-minded men and women, or that much good work has not been done. The workers have been willing and capable, and, the circumstances considered, much has been accomplished. Yet it remains true that there has been almost a total lack of system during most of this period in nearly the entire territory, and to this day our whole scheme of education is in what seems to be, in certain of one's moods, a hopelessly disorganized state. Even the colleges and so-called universities—institutions of the higher learning—which in other parts of the country have made most progress, are here still so badly disorganized that many of them have not only not yet begun to solve the great educational problems of the time, but they have not seemed even to realize the existence of these problems. Before we can begin to effect a solution of

* The South Atlantic Quarterly, VII (October, 1908), 299-307.

our problems we must recognize them and see them in the perspective of right standards and true ideals. Public opinion must work through laws, customs, and traditions; and before public opinion can become effective these laws, customs, and traditions must be well known and widely accepted. We need first in this matter of education to set up among us high standards and right ideals. Whatever influence then helps to standardize Southern colleges at the level of the best American academic traditions is a distinct contribution to educational progress and to Southern civilization.

And this standardizing process is slowly but surely going on. There are in the field at least five agencies that I wish to mention. First in point of time is the Association of Colleges and Preparatory Schools of the Southern States, organized twelve years ago with a membership of six colleges, and now composed of nineteen colleges and thirty-seven schools. This association exists for the promotion of better educational standards and ideals, and it has from the beginning been an influence for good. But up to the present time it has moved too slowly. During the current year many of the colleges belonging to the association have advanced their admission requirements, and now a majority of them maintain respectable standards for admission and for graduation. The association orders colleges belonging to it to demand for admission to all degree courses at least ten entrance units. At the recent meeting in Birmingham, November 7 and 8, the necessary one year's notice was served that at the next annual meeting the by-laws would be so changed as to require fourteen units of all applicants for degrees. Fourteen units constitute the minimum amount of preparation which the Carnegie Foundation accepts as four years of high-school preparation, and is about the requirement for admission to the better colleges of the country. This change in the by-laws will no doubt be made one year hence; for the majority of these colleges will, of their own initiative, require in 1908 the fourteen units.

The second agency I wish to mention is a movement started by the Southern Methodist Church ten years ago. In the year 1898 the General Conference of this church created an educational commission to consist of ten practical educators who should have full authority to formulate minimum requirements for admission and graduation, these requirements to be enforced by all colleges affiliated with the church. Since that date the commission has met at least once during each quadrennium and has prescribed standards by which all colleges affiliated with this church have been classified. The commission met last August at Old Point Comfort, Virginia, and there adopted a standard more advanced than heretofore in force. Especially in the entrance requirements does this standard show an advance over that of other years. There are hereafter to be two classes of colleges, A and B; and the requirements for admission are to be enforced in part in 1908 and in full in 1910. In 1908 colleges of the B class must require 9½ units, colleges of the A class 12 units. In 1910 colleges of the B class must require 12 units and colleges of the A class 14 units. This standard when put into full effect in 1910 will place the colleges of class A, in the matter of admission requirements, alongside the strong colleges of the country. The definitions of units are practically the same as those of the Carnegie Foundation. Institutions falling below class B are not to be rated as colleges at all. Colleges are to offer but two bachelor's degrees, A.B. and B.S.; and the requirements both for admission and graduation demanded of candidates for the two degrees must be equivalent. A college must have seven professors, a course of four years in arts and sciences, and an income of $5,000 exclusive of tuition fees. To belong to Class A a college must have an endowment of at least $100,000. This seems to me to be the most serious and far-reaching attempt yet made by Southern men at the standardization on a large scale and at a proper level of Southern colleges. The church, too, is provided with the machinery and the men to make these regulations bear effectively on the colleges concerned, and marked improvement in the quality of work done by these colleges should be an immediate result.

A third agency, important though its influence on college standards has been indirectly exerted, is the General Education Board of New York, of which Frederick T. Gates is chairman and Wallace Buttrick, secretary. This Board has set up no educational standards to which colleges that would seek its aid must conform. But it has made wise and statesmanlike efforts to strengthen some of the more promising colleges; it has had on exhibition in its office carefully collected data on Southern colleges; and it has done something towards bringing Southern colleges into contact with educational methods and men in other parts of the country. And all these things have had a tendency to lift the general level and so to raise the educational standards of Southern colleges.

But the agency which of them all has had the most immediate and perceptible effect is the Carnegie Foundation for the Advancement of Teaching. The foundation adopted a definition of a college and a standard of entrance requirements, and declined to put on the foundation any institutions that did not conform to its standards. The desire to be placed on the Carnegie Foundation has influenced a few Southern colleges to raise their standards. But the foundation has exerted a still more potent influence. President Pritchett made a thoroughgoing study of American colleges and published the results. He gave each college a rating on the basis of its admission requirements. This publication has had a wide circulation and has exerted an unprecedented influence in the South. The influence has reached almost every one of the better organized colleges throughout the entire Southern states. Its influence is very marked and very real, both on the Association of Colleges and Preparatory Schools, as seen at its recent meeting in Birmingham, and on the Educational Commission of the Methodist Church, which met at Old Point Comfort in August; and an examination of Southern college catalogues for the current year will show a very widespread response to President Pritchett's publication.

The last agency which I shall mention, and the one which is intrinsically the most interesting and ultimately the most important, is the small number of individual institutions that have through all the cross purposes and warring forces of our years of educational wandering been courageous and far-seeing enough to stand and call aloud, as the voice of one crying in the wilderness, for a better order of things, and that have not hesitated to sacrifice in so great a cause the prestige of numbers and the more immediately satisfying compensation of tuition fees. These colleges have stood as beacons of light along the hard road of progress and as bulwarks of strength against which the intellectual confusions, and even at times the surging passions of the hour, have dashed themselves in vain. To such colleges—and they have been found in all parts of the union, North and South—the country owes a debt of gratitude it can never pay.

These five forces, though different in origin and different in the method and sphere of their operation, are all working together towards one end, the making of stronger, better equipped, and more serviceable institutions of the higher learning throughout the Southern states. And nearly all the better organized colleges have been affected. Improvement is everywhere evident and is sure, I think, now to go on rapidly. Movements in our time when once set forward are quick and far-reaching in their results.

This standardizing of our colleges and bringing them into the great currents of present-day American life is calling sharply to our attention the main educational problems of the age. Of these one of the first in importance is the right adjustment of the college entrance requirements to the high-school curriculum, and the strengthening of the lower schools all along the line. The differentiation of school from college and the clear marking out of the comain of each will remove much confusion in our thinking, and do more than anything else can to destroy educational sham and pretense. An educated public opinion will make sham colleges impossible. Such will have to go or else remake themselves into useful preparatory schools.

Already more people are coming to understand what a college is and to distinguish between real education and the sham and pretense that have gone under the name of education. The South has now a number of colleges that in standards of work, in ideals of excellence, and in the quality of the men who teach and who are taught are thoroughly respectable, even when judged in the light of the great colleges of the world. Colleges of this sort are of inestimable value in Southern civilization. They will set the pace for our intellectual life, and through their influence on the lower schools and through the leaders of the people which they supply, will have a large share in shaping and moulding the structure of our entire civilization. The colleges themselves are being rapidly refashioned and, in a period of flux and change now, they are nevertheless taking a setting and direction that are apt to fix their character and work for many years to come. It is of the first importance, therefore, to make sure that they are faced in the right direction.

It is a distinct gain to have our best Southern colleges maintain for themselves standards for admission and graduation that are truly national and that put these colleges in this respect on a footing with the standard colleges of the country. The maintenance of such entrance standards will call for the building up of strong secondary schools and will lead to the perfecting of an educational system thoroughly organized from top to bottom, which is a crying need of our time. The distinction between school and college will become widely familiar and each will be honored so long as it faithfully and honestly does its appropriate work. The pathetic and fatal striving of an institution that could be a useful school to lift itself by its own boot straps into the college class will become rarer. The tragedy of the boy put through one of these so-called colleges and ruined by the delusion that he has been educated will gradually disappear. Honest and unpretentious work will become the rule, and there should follow a general accession of public intelligence and intellectual integrity. For all these reasons I hail with peculiar pleasure the signs so rapidly multiplying of educational progress.

All these efforts, however, so active at this time, to raise standards and otherwise put Southern colleges in line with first-class colleges elsewhere, while in the main highly praiseworthy, are at the same time accompanied by some tendencies that are discouraging. There is, for example, the plain danger that colleges in the rush to keep up with the upward trend may set themselves standards higher than they can live up to; and this would lead straight to the pretense and dishonesty in education from which we are seeking to free the country. The time has come, in my judgment, when every Southern college should demand of all entering students that they shall have completed a high-school course. Just what the entrance standard may be depends upon the stage of development reached by the high schools in the section from which students come. But in all cases the college should demand the high-school diploma. The adoption of this policy will, for some years to come, keep down numbers in all colleges in the South Atlantic states. But it is the business of colleges to seek first the common good rather than their own selfish interests; and the college that pursues a different policy in the matter of admitting students will henceforth probably do in this one way about as much harm as it will be able to do good through all its other efforts. This policy once fixed, the college must enter earnestly into the fight for improvement of high schools now going on so promisingly all over the South. But on the other hand an unseemly scramble to see who can put down in a catalogue the highest entrance requirements is of course a thing to be avoided.

Another danger is that colleges in their effort to conform to educational standards and to types of organization that prevail elsewhere and are there regarded as ideal, may unfit themselves for doing the very service to which they seem by circumstances to be ordained. A college must be at least in part the product of development and not a forced growth; and it should follow the lines of its own development and not be made to form itself on some wholly extraneous model.

This is one danger I fear may follow from the admirable first annual report of the Carnegie Foundation for the Advancement of Teaching. I regard President Pritchett as one of the most competent and conscientious educational experts in this country. His painstaking and thoroughgoing investigations of American colleges and his eminently discerning and fair treatment of so many of our educational problems, place the entire country under obligations to him. Especially has he treated with the fullest knowledge and sympathy the large class of colleges in the South that are considered denominational. The exact valuation of this kind of college gives him considerable concern, as it does every sincere student of Southern educational problems of this generation. The conditions of Mr. Carnegie's gift exclude from the benefits of the foundation all colleges in any way connected with church or state. President Pritchett's admirable discussion and the position taken by the foundation raise in acute form the question as to the best type of college organization for present Southern conditions.

Practically all the older colleges in America came into being either through the church or state. In New England, especially, most of the colleges originally so founded have passed completely from church or state control. In the South still nearly all colleges are either controlled by the states or churches, or they are affiliated with churches. It will be admitted, I think, by all that wherever colleges are needed and have not been established by private benefactions the church or state that builds a true institution of higher learning has done a service to society. And if church or state has been wise enough to found such an institution, and in order to ensure its continuity and efficient government has through its charter given over the institution to a permanent and self-perpetuating board of trustees, then such church or state ought to have the highest endorsement of expert authority and educated public opinion. And in the failure to provide, where there has been failure to provide, such a board lies, it seems to me, the only just objection to state or church colleges as such. It matters little what the origin of a college is; the government of it is important because on this depend its chances for perpetuity. In the long run of years there can be no security for a college which in its actual control is too close to the untrained mass of people, whether this mass is represented by a state government subject to popular will or represented by a church organization that reflects too immediately the changing moods of the multitude. The Carnegie Foundation is eminently right in refusing endorsement to colleges that in their governing boards are not sufficiently removed from possible popular interference to insure a continuity in their development. Our experiments in democracy have not yet been sufficient to make us feel sure of the future of our institutions of whatever character. Uncertain of the future as we must be at best, no wise or thoughtful man would choose to give his life or money to the service of a college, unless he felt that it was not needlessly exposed to the chances of some great popular cataclysm, unless he felt that it would probably endure and continue to do good long after he had ceased to work. To believe in the future of America at all, or for that matter to contemplate human life with any degree of patience, one must believe that the people wish to do right and in the long run and in the main will do right; but this does not mean that they have the expert knowledge to manage a college any more than it means they are competent to argue a point of law before the Supreme Court of the United States, or to treat an acute case of pneumonia.

I think President Pritchett is mistaken in his expectation that a considerable number of these colleges will break connection with the churches that have created and fostered them, even where there would be no legal complications in the way. If a tendency of this sort should ever manifest itself here, as it has in other parts of the country, it would, I believe, be due to changed conditions. I do not look to see this come to pass unless the churches should show a complete misunderstanding of their duty and opportunity to promote the highest and truest education of the people. In any event the change would be a response to circumstances and not a deliberate purpose on the part of the colleges to turn their backs on old and tried friends in order to be placed on a foundation from which they expect financial rewards. I cannot myself understand how men with a right feeling of gratitude or a fine sense of fitness could deliberately take such a step. The step may come, as it has so often come in the past, but it must be due to a natural and inevitable process of development. I feel that even the appearance of evil will deter most Southern colleges from taking this step. A general movement of this sort would be distressing and I hope we shall at least be spared this spectacle.

The colleges built and promoted by churches and governed by efficient and permanent boards form a most useful type of college in the South in this generation. Whether it is to be the final, highest type I do not know, and I do not now care to discuss. Every Southern college in our time must be distinctly an educational propagandist; and for this sort of propaganda an aggressive, influential church is a most useful agency. The college that is well equipped for its work, that stands on its merits and in no sense invokes partisan or sectarian feelings to rally its constituency, that is by its charter safeguarded against the dangers of mob opinion and the possibilities of inefficient control, that is at the same time brought by its origin into sympathetic relations with a great religious organization which through the college is not seeking to project a breeding place for partisanship, sectionalism, or sectarianism, but is seeking to build up an institution for the education and elevation of the people—the college that is thus protected from any possible domination of the ignorant or the vicious and that is yet thus held close to the highest service of the people, ought to be a mighty power in the cause of truth and civilization. To stand for the highest ideals and even fight for them when necessary and at the same time to keep in close, sympathetic relations with the people whom it would serve is, I think, one of the most difficult problems that a Southern college in our time has to solve. But both these things must be done by the college that would be of the largest service to society. And in working out this problem, as in working out many other problems, the church can help the college immensely.

The college that leads and is not willing to be a mere time-server must often turn a deaf ear to the siren voices of political expediency and pliant opportunism. Minds unpracticed in cogent thinking usually seek to catch the nearest way and follow the line of least resistance. The college that aspires to a leadership of ideas and ideals in the service of the republic must at times resist with all its power the mighty local influences that would sway it from its true course. Only the college that is strong enough to survive these fearful testings can fulfil in our civilization the mission that great colleges should fulfil. Such colleges must also occasionally rouse themselves to the more ungracious task of resisting the imposition upon them from the outside of ideals and ideas that would not be most serviceable under existing conditions. The type of college that should be standardized for Massachusetts may well be wholly unfit for North Carolina.

Supported and stirred by the fresh impulses and aspirations, everywhere evident, that spring from the rebuilding of our civilization on the firm foundation of widespread material prosperity and well-being and from the renewing through courage and hope of the unconquerable spirit of the South, the stronger and better organized Southern colleges that are wise enough to set for themselves high standards and ideals, that have vitality enough to throw themselves into the doing of the hard tasks of society, and that are courageous enough patiently to go their own way and fulfil their own destiny in their own appointed time—such colleges have an opportunity rare among men to do in this generation a piece of constructive work that will be of lasting service to Southern civilization and to the republic. Any temptation to turn aside from this path of duty must be withstood, it matters not whether the temptation has its origin at home or abroad. And President Pritchett himself has raised this note of warning, which I have wished to emphasize.

EDUCATION AND CITIZENSHIP IN A DEMOCRACY*

IN A DEMOCRACY EVERY MAN is an important and essential factor in the building or destruction of the nation; yet the leadership of ideas and ideals must come from a relatively small body of picked men. This body of picked men must be developed through some process and by some method. One of the processes to which most men look with hopefulness is education. Unless the schools and colleges can make a large contribution to this high leadership of ideas in the service of the republic, then education has a small mission in America; for education, like wisdom of old, must be justified of her children. The ranks of this chosen body have always been thin and are recruited with difficulty. Not every man who goes through school or even who has a college diploma enters this company of inspired and inspiring leadership. Education, like every other human agency, shows many failures.

There are certain admirable qualities that ought to belong to every genuinely educated man, whether his education was

* *The South Atlantic Quarterly*, VII (January, 1908), 1-10.

acquired through the processes of formal training or in the school of experience. Every educated man ought to have breadth of view and comprehensive sympathies. Man in his state of nature is a gregarious animal; in the next place he is a member of a clan; and in a later stage of his development he is an adherent of a faction, a sect, or a party. This blind championship of neighborhood interests, community feelings, inherited prejudices, and preconceived opinions, transmitted as it is from primitive conditions, is an inborn bias that is hard to resist; and the ability to see the other man's point of view and to enter into sympathy with him who holds antagonistic beliefs is the surest mark and the final test of a cultivated man. The natural tendency to clannishness, partisanship, and separatism has caused many a man in the past to devote to party or sect or faction gifts that were meant for mankind, and is responsible for the religious wars and persecutions of the Dark Ages which make up one of the saddest chapters in human history, as it is also responsible for the later warfare of science and religion, itself almost as destructive as the feuds of faith in the past. It is responsible, too, for sectionalism which curses all peoples, for the dissidence that sets men into warring camps, arrays the country against the town, creates social, literary, financial, and hereditary castes, breeds intellectual Brahmanism, and fixes impassable gulfs between innumerable factions that ought to stand shoulder to shoulder in the conflicts of modern life. That education is a failure which does not give one a speaking and working acquaintance with men good and true in every class and station. We have in our time lost something of the old ardor and intensity of other times; and we must make up for this loss by sympathetic and aggressive coöperation on the part of all good men in every cause that makes for progress and improvement.

Educated men ought to have the ability to think straight and to think through to right conclusions. This ability can only come from rigorous training of the mind and from what

I shall call cogency of character. We need in this seething democracy to place a higher value on the mind, on the discipline of hard and constructive thinking, and on the practice of separating the operations of the intellect from those of the emotions. Our susceptibility to periodic attacks of national hysterics, the oft-used power of sensational newspaper and alarmist popular leaders to "insurrect the public mind," and the lack of sound, hardheaded thinking among the masses leave us a prey to any wind of doctrine that may blow, whether it be a free-silver craze from the wild plains of Kansas, or an anarchistic propaganda from the back alleys of New York or Chicago. More than once in our history this emotional insurrection has threatened the wreckage of this republic; and there will never be any security against this sort of danger except in a large body of men with trained and solid mental capacity. Educated men and educational institutions ought to form a bulwark in this democracy against which the intellectual confusions and the surging passions of the hour shall beat in vain.

Close akin to, but not identical with, this power of accurate and just thinking is soundness of judgment, which applied to the conduct of life constitutes wisdom, that most useful gift vouchsafed to men on earth; and this wisdom is not the product of intellect alone, but comes out of a full harmonious character, and at its highest becomes a sort of moral instinct that almost compels a man to live his life wisely, just as the natural instinct compels the bird to build its nest. This highest wisdom, as I understand it, includes, first, the intuitive knowledge of men, which exposes cant, detests charlatanry, exalts true character and genuine excellence everywhere and is the best guaranty against the reign of the charlatan and the demagogue —for whose growing America probably affords the best soil in the world; and secondly, it includes the instinctive recognition of the eternal fitness of things, which discriminates between the important and the unessential, which discerns the means to reach the desired ends, and so prevents the waste of talents and effort that has rendered ineffectual the lives of so many gifted men.

Boswell quotes Dr. Johnson as saying: "Sir, you know courage is reckoned the greatest of all virtues; because, unless a man has that virtue, he has no security for preserving any other." Perhaps nowhere so much as in a democracy is courage necessary to preserve other virtues and make them efficacious in the community. Here where everything is in the end determined by public opinion it is of the first importance that the individual man shall have the courage to speak the thoughts that are in him and, when the time comes, to stand up and be counted, whether girt by friend or foe. As has been more than once pointed out, aristocracy tends to promote the growth of courage, but the leveling tendencies of democratic life do not foster the growth of moral courage. Every forward movement in a democracy is the result of striking an average of the intelligence and moral sense of all the people. It is difficult, therefore, for a democracy to find and develop its strong men and to give them the opportunity to exert their power. But a democracy can never be stronger than the individuals that make it up, and the individuals must act as individuals and not in the mass. Individuals swallowed up in the mass become the mob. Hence the need of courage in action in a democracy. But further than this, it is impossible to think straight without the courage to face the issues of one's thinking. Without courage, thinking can have no moral energy; and as citizens of a democracy we are concerned with the moral energy of ideas rather than with their intellectual purity.

This is a political year and we are reminded that in the mere matter of casting votes all over America we need not only honesty and intelligence, but also robust courage. In practical questions of government and political parties in a Southern state today, what should be the attitude of one who has no relations to politics other than those of an intelligent and interested citizen? Causes perfectly well known have produced here one great political party and one dominant school of thinking. This is our political inheritance; we should use it conservatively, and from our traditional position should make no departure unless we are convinced that we are moving towards something unmistakably better. But are not patriotic and courageous men when making up their minds how to vote coming more and more to ask what will be best for us and our section, and best for our nation, rather than settle questions as if they were matters of course, offhand and in obedience to ancient sentiment? This abandonment of old issues, this burying of whatever is dead in the past, and the replacing of these old issues with candid and fearless searching after what is best for us and our section, would bring open argument and free discussion about business interests, politics, questions of our history, and all other matters of debate. There would be no toleration for the attempt to hush men's voices, as if by silence any defect in our society or limitation in our civil or social order might be overlooked. Wrong always needs exposure; for the more it is covered, the more it festers. Intelligent and fearless public opinion expressed through free speech and untrammeled ballots is the safeguard of a democracy. Before we can prosper as we should we must free ourselves from every vestige of political cowardice, and overthrow all attempts through abuse, through social ostracism, or through any other means, to browbeat one man into another man's way of thinking. We must be brave enough to vote as we think, without regard to the opinions of others and without regard to any consequences that may come to us through registering at the polls our real convictions on local and national questions.

I do not mean to imply that this conception of the franchise would necessarily change any man's actual vote; but it would change the attitude of many of us towards the ballot, and would intensify the sense of responsibility that is imposed by the right to vote upon every thoughtful and conscientious man.

It is a commonplace of American politics that this duty to cast an intelligent and conscientious ballot is held too lightly by educated men. And this is one of the perils that beset popular government.

An educated man should not only have, in as large measure as may be, sympathy, ideas, wisdom, and moral courage, but to make his influence widely effective for good in a democracy he must have the power of expression either through his speech or by pen. The noblest form of self-expression, as it is also the surest revelation of character, is that which runs itself out through the fingers into one's work, whatever that work may be. Only the man who has found adequate expression of himself, either through the product of his hand or his brain, can reach his complete development. It used to be said that one who has command of three languages is three times a man. I am not sure of this, but it would seem to be true that one is thrice great if, like Leonardo da Vinci, distinguished painter, sculptor, architect, engineer, and musician, he is a consummate practitioner of three arts through which he may develop and express himself.

How is this developed individual to project himself into society and make his influence weigh down the scales on the side of progress? Apart from the transcending power of noble example, this can be done only through ideas, and ideas are best promoted in this democracy by men who can think clearly and write with distinction or men who have the gift of speaking with conviction and power. To bring about improvement we must convince the minds and appeal to the hearts of men; for nothing but opinion and sentiment can effect great permanent changes in a people. To change the complexion of a civilization there must be a slow, gradual change in public opinion. By public opinion I mean the conscious and unconscious thinking of men about duty and conduct, and the embodiment of this thinking in prevalent ideals of life in such a way as to shape the collective and individual character of a

[231]

whole people. To be effective for good this public opinion must be intelligent, fearless, and free. And this honest, robust, wholesome public opinion can grow only in an atmosphere of liberty and perfect freedom. The minds of men must be absolutely free to accept truth and defend it without the possibility of coercion or persecution.

The duty of every educated man then is simply this: to discover the truth and by every means consistent with the doctrine of liberty to make the truth prevail. The disclosure of truth and the embodiment of it in the life of men and in the shaping of institutions is the record and formula of civilization everywhere. This discovery and practical application of truth has been distressingly slow, and the gradual ascent of man has been a perpetual travail. In a sense each generation, and for that matter, each man must discover the truth for himself. Truth in itself is an entity. Yet we can know it only in its applications; that is, as we ourselves are related to it. It cannot therefore be passed along like some valuable commodity from individual to individual and from generation to generation. It breaks through the clouds of surrounding darkness only as individuals from age to age have the vision to see it and the altruism that makes them proclaim it to others.

This discovered truth, in another view of it, may be regarded as a seed. Plant it in the minds of men, it germinates, grows, bears fruit, some thirtyfold and some an hundredfold. The man who has long views, who discovers truth, who will plant it and patiently wait for the harvest, is the wise man: and happy is the age or nation that has such men; for, as the Hebrew proverb puts it, where there is no vision the people perish.

This projection of the individual into society can be done only through ideas and never through force. This does not imply that we are not to combat error. We are to resist evil to the utmost of our ability, but let us make the effort in ways that will do permanent good. We cannot force men to accept our view or to be what we think they ought to be; we must convince and persuade them. It is allowable to smash error in every way that does no violence to the doctrine of liberty. This requires the more patience because liberty is, as we all know, everywhere abused. But after all, the world will, on the whole, gain by liberty, for without it virtue could not exist. It ought forever to be insisted, however, that true liberty implies wisdom and justice.

The patient waiting for the harvest often calls upon us to allow the wheat and tares to grow together; it is in a sense a toleration of evil. But there is no utility of error. All truth is wholesome; all falsehood is hurtful. It is never right to do evil that good may come of it. While error then must never be accepted as good, yet it may be and often is necessary to wait to strike it down, and we must be careful not to do good in a way that evil will come of it. I raise the question, Why is it that a religious age is always followed by irreligion, a generation of inspired and imaginative poets by an age of prose and reason, an era of prosperity by depression? Is not this ebb and flow in human history that every student has remarked due to the tyranny of the majority, to the tendency at these flood tide periods for the men and styles that dominate the epoch to force everything their way and to whip all recalcitrants into line, with a consequent reaction in the opposite direction? Is not human nature so constituted that the tyranny of the majority will always lead to reaction or to revolution? And is it not true that all reforms promoted by force and not by ideas have done far more harm than good? If the answer to these questions that I get from a study of history be correct, then it is always foolish and wicked to attempt to run roughshod over the judgment or to bully the moral sense of men. For good people, in all ages, this seems to have been and still seems to be the hardest lesson to learn; and especially is it hard for a gentle and generous people like the people of the South, who live by fine and disinterested sentiments, rather than by shrewd considerations of forethought and self-advancement. But Southern history, one would think, should have taught us at least this never-to-be-forgotten lesson. The mighty builders and founders of this republic were largely Southern men, and for generations the South furnished more than her share of leaders in every line of effort. But as time went on and as Southern men gave their minds more and more to the defense of their peculiar civil and political order of things, as their thinking became solidified and forced to move in fixed grooves, the conditions of our civilization at length ceased to produce the great minds of the earlier period. We were set upon this hard road by uncontrollable circumstances, and we finally ran in a superb and awful way upon the sudden and sharp disaster of civil war. This solid crystallization and consequent stagnation of public opinion has been one of the persistent evils of slavery. And we still need to give a kindlier and freer hearing to all schools of thinking and a more patient consideration to minority opinion.

We not only need this open, rational, dispassionate discussion of political questions; but we need the same attitude of mind towards all questions of debate, however acute or vital they may seem to us to be. Any sort of constraint of opinion, whether it be tacit or overt, breeds an unhealthy intellectual atmosphere; and a sound and wholesome citizenship cannot be built up in miasmatic intellectual regions. As educated men we have the precious privilege of engaging in the age-long task of purifying the air and creating a better social, civic, and political climate of opinion.

Most of these duties are performed by the educated man in the very process of making all he can of himself. This complete development of oneself is a direct contribution to society, and the indirect influence from example of a successful man is above all the precepts of the unsuccessful and ineffectual. But there are at least two things that educated men should seek to promote among the people at large.

[234]

America's chief contributions to civilization have been in the production of wealth and physical well-being, and the wide dissemination of these among the great masses of men. Here lie the two glories and the two dangers of American civilization. To have added enormously to the wealth of the world and to have given all men the chance to work and live, provided only that nature has sufficiently endowed them with strength and energy to enter into their political rights and to use their opportunities for uplifting themselves, must stand as a memorable addition to the forces that make up modern life. But this swift and startling increase in wealth has led to materialism and this industrial and political democracy has augmented the possibilities and dangers of the crowd. To teach the age the uses of wealth and to cure the permeating evils of an untrained democracy, is the call of America today to her educated men.

It is not an easy task to teach the right uses of wealth to a country engrossed in material tasks and dominated too largely by material ideals. Educated men by example and precept ought to teach those who have wealth that wealth carries obligations of service to the community, that it is a talent to be used for the widest good; that wealth is not a good in itself, not an end to be sought for its own sake, not to be selfishly hoarded or enjoyed, but to be used; not to be made the supreme aid, but to be properly subordinated to the higher uses of life.

The evils of the mob—of an ignorant, undisciplined, and therefore vicious democracy—are imminent and threatening. But the road this country must travel will surely lead to more rather than to less of popular liberty, and the unwholesome restiveness of the present can be permanently cured only by the fitting of the masses of men for enlightened self-government and by removing in right and fair ways whatever of abuses may exist in the business, social, and political life of the American people. This is a stupendous task—to school the mob in a democracy which is itself the government and which can only be lured and led, but cannot be controlled, by the wise and patriotic men who are able to see the true ends of national existence and can discern the ways that lead to national and individual greatness; to develop the masses, to make them strong enough to maintain their rights against obnoxious wealth and desperate poverty, and at the same time reasonable enough to give perfect respect to the rights of others, even those better off than themselves; to make men too intelligent to be led by designing demagogues; in short to construct out of American citizens themselves a mighty tower of strength against blind ignorance as well as against sordid materialism—this is the stupendous task set before educated men in this democracy.

Be it always remembered that wealth is power, though it may be sometimes misused, and in the end wealth will make for a higher civilization; that democracy is the goal of humanity, though it is as yet struck through and through with permeating evils, and democracy will finally achieve the greatest good to the greatest number.

Emerson said, "We judge of a man's wisdom by his hope." In this democracy we often need to be reassured by the hopefulness of the wise; for our national life at times looks like a seething caldron, to pessimistic minds even like a veritable slough of despond. The final duty of educated men, especially of educated young men, is to bring hope and forward-looking thoughts. I have read that on the coins of old Spain there was a device in which the shield of Castile and Leon was supported by the pillars of Hercules, which marked the limit of the Old World. But the motto spoke of no limit. "Plus ultra," it ran—there is more beyond, and what that more might be no man could know. So forth men went in search of El Dorado and of the fountains of eternal youth; and they found America. "Plus ultra" seems the best motto for America at the opening of the twentieth century (as may it be a fitting

[236]

motto for each succeeding century)! There is on every hand manifest a spirit of unrest, but withal in the main a spirit of hopefulness. In business, government, religion, education, and society there is a widespread feeling that we stand at the very threshold of a new era. What is just ahead of us no man can know. But if enough enlightened and high-minded youth can be sent forth with courage and hope to go beyond the limits of past experience in search of a new El Dorado, we may expect, not in some far western island but here in our own time and country, to find a greater America.

THE CONSTRUCTIVE PHILANTHROPY OF
A SOUTHERN COTTON MILL*

FOR THE PAST several years during my vacations I have had occasion to observe a cotton mill in South Carolina that is doing much to improve the living conditions and to raise the standard of life among factory operatives. Because it seems to me to have lessons for other mills and for thoughtful people everywhere who are interested in human progress, I shall try to set forth simply and without ornamentation just what is being done by the management of this mill, the Victor Manufacturing Company at Greer, for the welfare of the employees and their families.

In this mill village the church is fortunately a center of influence. The divorce of the working people from the church has not come about here as it has in some other sections of this country, and if the church is wise it never will come about. The company has erected a commodious church building for the use of all denominations. A union church has some disadvantages, but it also has some decided advantages: for one

* The South Atlantic Quarterly, VIII (January, 1909), 82-90.

thing it tends to mitigate the excesses and the evils of denomi-nationalism, which in isolated and ignorant communities often constitute the chief hindrance to the influence and helpfulness of religious bodies. The danger lies in the tendency for religi-ous tolerance and catholicity to pass into lukewarmness and complete indifference; but this has not happened at Victor. The Methodist and Baptist denominations, the only churches that have constituencies in the community, maintain large and active church organizations. The company gives a residence and two hundred dollars a year to the pastor of any mill church who lives in the village. The mill officers thus help and en-courage the churches, but the congregations are left to rely largely on their own self-direction and self-help. Each has an earnest and efficient pastor, who seeks to shepherd his people and to build them up in their bodies, their minds, and their characters. Still more can be done by the churches as men better trained and more nobly consecrated to the highest good of their fellows enter this field. There is now an urgent need for the right kind of men in this work, and the call will con-stantly become more insistent. The wise cultivation of the religious natures of men will do more than any other one thing to promote a sense of brotherhood and co-operation and to break down the barriers that separate men into factions and produce all kinds of friction in business, in politics, and in society. The manufacturer or social reformer who neglects this agency for order and human brotherhood is very unwise. At Victor there is an eager desire to promote the religious well-being of the people and a fixed purpose to bring the best wisdom of this generation to the service of the children of the light. The success with which the churches are carrying on their work augurs well for the prosperity of the community and for the continuation of the friendly relations that exist be-tween the employers and employees.

The mill maintains for nine months in the year a kinder-garten and a school that offers instruction through four grades.

It is supported out of the mill treasury, supplemented from the public school fund of the state. The officers of the mill select the teachers and give the school a wise general supervision. A much wiser school management is thus secured than is usual in small towns where chance or politics or personal caprice so often determines the destinies of the local school. The teachers canvass thoroughly the homes of the village for children of school age, and everything short of a compulsory law is done to bring all the children into the school. An admirable schoolhouse, built by the company, stands on a commanding hill and is furnished with playgrounds and attractive surroundings. I recently passed from the playgrounds of this mill school to the playgrounds of a neighboring village school, and could not perceive any noteworthy difference in the dress, health, or apparent happiness of the children of the two schools. Wisely managed and well taught, this school affords excellent opportunities for an elementary education.

Efforts to instruct and improve this community are not confined to the church and the school, but the management is constantly on the lookout for any new agency that gives promise of doing good. Already there is a club house for men, called the Lyceum and containing a library, reading room, smoking room, bowling alley, games and lodge rooms, and other means and appliances that fit this building to be a center for the social life of the men of the village. The building is kept open at suitable hours during the day and at night. The reading room is supplied with newspapers and magazines which, I have observed, the people read, and the library affords sufficient opportunity for pleasant and improving reading. A teacher from the mill school is on hand each Saturday afternoon to give to such as may wish it expert advice about books to read. The keeper of the building informs me that the books are widely used, and my own observation goes to confirm his statement. Through the reading room, the library, public lectures, and entertainments, the people of this mill

village have a better chance at self-cultivation and enlightenment than is in reach of the general population of the Southern states outside of cities and larger towns. Besides, the club
rooms furnish a place for social foregatherings in surroundings
that are bound to have a civilizing and uplifting influence.

There is also a commodious and expensive building lately
erected by the company for the use of the women and children
of the village. This clubhouse has a gymnasium, baths, assembly rooms, and living quarters, with all modern conveniences
that make the building a model of its kind. Here are the
headquarters of the Y.W.C.A. workers, the general secretary,
the domestic-science teacher, and the kindergartner, three well-
trained and competent women who give all their time to religious and welfare work for the women and children of the
community. The general secretary is engaged in efforts aimed
directly at the physical, intellectual, social, and religious development of women and of children of seven years and up-
wards. The domestic-science teacher has classes in cooking,
housekeeping, and sewing. The kindergarten teacher has
charge of the children under seven years of age. By means of
classes for mothers, classes for girls, sewing circles, night
school, library, and reading room, these women seek to
promote in the community better ideals of living. They live
in the building, and not only give instruction, but actual object
lessons in cooking, housekeeping, sewing, and the domestic
arts in general. The women and girls of the village have
shown a remarkable eagerness to make a wise use of their
opportunities. At the organization of this work for them one
hundred members were enrolled. Subsequent additions and
the large regular attendance supply additional evidence that
these extraordinary advantages will not go unimproved.

All these facilities for self-improvement that are provided
by the mill and made available for everybody are doing much
to enrich the lives of the people, yet there is perhaps on the
mill itself no obligation to create these opportunities out of

its own funds other than the duty that rests upon every man to do what he can to make the world a better place in which to live. But the mill does owe its employees certain primary duties. It is in common honesty bound to pay a living wage, to consider the interests of the laborer as important as the interests of the stockholder, to create wholesome conditions and, as far as may be, attractive surroundings in which the laborer may live and work. Of these voluntary benevolences and primary duties the Victor Manufacturing Company has done the one, and the other it has not left undone. The operatives are well paid. The wage is higher than the wage paid the ordinary day laborer in the community. The age limit and the working hours are humane and reasonable. The families live in comfortable houses. Good water and the utmost possible cleanliness produce sanitary conditions. The mill itself is beautiful and well kept. The grounds about it are covered with grass and set with trees. Available open spaces are turned into attractive parks. All over the company's property, by use of trees, grass, vines, and flowers, the village is beautified. Every device approved by the best experience has been used to encourage the householders to grow flowers and to cultivate herb gardens. A pasture free of charge is kept for the use of all families that have cows. Sufficient open space is available for those who wish to raise chickens. All these conditions make possible a satisfying home life for every family that will make the most of its opportunities. The people of the mill are beginning to own the houses in which they live. The company is dividing up into lots a near-by tract of land to sell to such mill people as wish to purchase land on which to build residences for their own occupancy. To give the people this further stake in the community will go far towards reforming completely the nomadic life of the factory population, which is a great evil, but which has never been so serious at Victor as at some other mills. The mill happens to be located on the outskirts of a small, thriving town, where social distinctions are little stressed. This fortunate circumstance and the genuinely human, unprofessional attitude of the management towards the people have prevented the growth of social castes and bitterness, and have welded the community into an unusual oneness of aim and sympathy.

Through school, library, public lectures, private instruction, personal sympathy and example, through wholesome conditions and attractive surroundings, the management is seeking to educate and elevate not only the children of the community, but also the whole population, grown-ups as well as the young. Through all these processes and by the use of these most approved methods, I believe a general tendency is being created that is improving and uplifting the community. A higher standard of living is being set, and this will be a controlling influence in many an individual life and in many a home. The tonic effect of ideals and the shaping power of new ideas and new ways of doing things are vague and intangible, but they are pervasive and mighty. There are many people who will do better when they are shown how to do better, but the instruction must come in a way that attracts their attention and in a form that is obvious to their minds. For this purpose a valuable idea put into successful operation is above all formal teaching and abstract advice; things seen are mightier than things heard. Take a simple matter like the matter of cooking. For generations the cooking among the less well-to-do classes in the Southern states has been atrociously bad; whether it is better in the same class in other parts of the country, I do not know. It shows little if any tendency to improve. Now I can see no reason why the sort of efforts put forth at the Victor Mills should not even in one generation bring about a much better grade of cooking in that community. And if it does, that will be as valuable a reform as could be brought about. Mean biscuits have probably done almost as much harm as mean whiskey. So also may improvement be made in housekeeping and other domestic arts, as well as in the training and religious education of children.

Because of the rapid and wide dissemination of ideas through the press, because of the open-mindedness of the American people, and because for intellectual and spiritual purposes the whole country has become one great community—for these reasons movements of this sort in our time, when once started, are swift and far-reaching in their results. Southern farmers have been the class most conservative and least accessible to outside influences in this most conservative section of the country. But now agricultural papers, bulletins of state and national experiment stations, and the experience of other farmers are bringing about a better grade of farming; and better roads, improving country high schools, and the rural free delivery of mails are helping to raise the general level of life among the large rural population of the South. In the creation of a better public opinion and publishing abroad better ideas about agriculture and farm life President Roosevelt's country life commission will no doubt be useful. The enrichment of American country life is much to be desired, especially in the Southern states, where we are, and I hope may remain, largely an agricultural people. But we are destined to become more and more a manufacturing people. This, too, is well, for any country is better off for varied industries. The increasing factory population of the South is creating hard problems that must be worked out or the whole people will suffer. To work out these problems is a high and patriotic duty. The problems are intricate and difficult of solution. They cannot be solved in a day or a generation. The duty of the well-to-do towards the less well-to-do is a matter that has puzzled thoughtful and unselfish men from the beginning of civilization till the present. Much has been learned from the experience of the past. And I believe poor people in America today have a better chance than anywhere else in all time. Much still remains to be done, but this is not going to be done by crude, unfair, or evil-minded agitators, or by well-meaning but ill-informed sentimentalists. The working out through actual experience, step by step, as is being done by the Victor Mills, of the hard problems of factory life is worth more than any amount of vague theorizings of idealists.

The right working out of these problems by this and other such mills will be helped or hampered by public opinion and the legislation of state and national governments. What shall be the attitude of a state like South Carolina towards the material progress which is the most impressive fact in the South Carolina of our time? Shall the state take the reactionary position that this material progress is to be hindered in every possible way, and through the leadership of demagogues shall the masses be arrayed against the classes and railroad and manufacturing enterprises be harassed at every step? Or on the other hand, shall human life and well-being be sacrificed in the interest of greed and wealth? If the state takes the first position it may expect to breed a poor, cheap, and disgruntled people. If it assumes the second attitude it may look for an era of gross materialism and ultimate decay. The legislation of the state affecting labor and capital has been in the main conservative and wise. Further legislation will doubtless be needed from time to time. It should be enacted not in response to the demands of selfish interests or to the demands of agitators or of ill-informed idealists. The manufacturer who does not regard the interest of the laborer as well as the interests of the stockholder is a selfish capitalist, and the legislator who does not regard the interests of the stockholder as well as the interests of the laborer is an irresponsible demagogue. The selfish capitalist and the irresponsible demagogue are two of our great national perils. The selfishness of the one intensifies the recklessness of the other. And because of the extreme radicalism of the demagogue the conservative owner of property often fears legislation and resists reforms that would be useful to himself and to society. Bad legislation comes from both extreme radicalism and ultra-conservatism. Legislation affecting capital and labor ought to be the result of the best wisdom of the legislator who respects the interests of the stockholder and the capitalist who respects the interests of the laborer, the two working together for the common good and not for the sole benefit of one class or another.

It is not the ambition of the officers of the Victor mill to make it a model to be kept on exhibition for their own gratification, for the delectation of the reformer, or for the enlightenment of other mills. It is run as a business proposition on purely business principles. All these reforms have been inaugurated not solely to increase dividends, but on the theory that in the end they will pay, that the output will be larger and better as the quality and character of the laborer is improved. It is to be hoped that the experiment will prove to be profitable. Otherwise the example set by this mill will be wasted; for no business can be run on a losing basis. It must either pay or go to pieces. It is so far the testimony of this mill and of all who have given the experiment a fair trial that money spent in improving the quality and character of the laborer is money well invested from a business as well as from a humanitarian standpoint. There are other mills that are doing the same sort of work; for example, the interest of the Pelzer Mill in the well-being of its employees for years, manifested in so many ways, has been widely commented upon. But at Victor efforts are being exerted in more directions and more wisely than at any other mill that I happen to have observed. The Monaghan Mill at Greenville has been a leader in modern welfare work, and for being first in time and first in ideals holds a sort of primacy among South Carolina cotton mills. When the way has been made plain by the successful experience of such mills as these, all the better mills will be glad to undertake more and more of this kind of work, and the weaker ones as a matter of self-preservation will be forced into it.

This is in no sense a paternalistic or socialistic, un-American plan to do for people what they might better be left to do for themselves. Everybody must admit that it is easier for the average man to live the right sort of life if he is placed in favorable surroundings. The most individualistic social reformer must realize that the improvement of the environment of a man's life creates a better opportunity to improve the quality of the man. The officers of the Victor Mills are not laboring under the delusion and I certainly do not share in the delusion that environment itself will change a man; but it will make easier the cultivation of his intelligence and the improvement of his character which will produce in him a higher order of manhood. To supply the setting for this higher order of life is easier than to find and apply a means that will with any certainty produce the right kind of man. After all is done, it of course remains with the individual to determine whether his opportunities shall be improved or neglected. And I have observed on the part of some in this mill village the same neglect of opportunities that I have observed in colleges and everywhere else. But as elsewhere, many are taking advantage of them and improvement is unmistakable. There are manifold signs that this village is the home of a busy, contented, healthy, and happy people.

If this improvement can be extended here and reproduced in other mills, if the mills in the state can be wisely managed, and if legislation and public opinion continues to safeguard the interests of the stockholder as well as the interests of the laborer, I believe there is before the state a great future of industrial prosperity and industrial peace. And this will bring wealth to the manufacturer, well-being to the laborer, and to the commonwealth freedom from the labor wars and the conflicts of classes that have cursed the older centers of manufacture in this and other countries.

A SOUTHERN VIEW OF LINCOLN*

WE IN THE UNITED STATES continue year after year to honor the memory of Abraham Lincoln, not so much, I think, for what he did, of vast significance though that has been to the future of his country, as for what he was, for those fine traits of character that made him the "first American of his century." A fine character like Lincoln's is not so adequately preserved in the history of his achievements or in his influence upon our institutions as in his sayings, his messages, and his speeches, the best of which have embalmed and treasured up the life blood of this master spirit. Lincoln's sayings, homely and shrewdly just as they are, have perhaps for Americans more interest and value than the familiar talk of any other man of the English race, with the possible exception of Dr. Johnson as reported by Boswell. Lincoln's little masterpieces, the Gettysburg Address and the second inaugural, are, it seems to me, for their felicity and finality of expression among the most perfect, I will not venture to say greatest, of all the speeches

* Read before the Trinity College Historical Society on the centenary of Lincoln's birth, February 12, 1909.

in the English tongue. There is a critical dictum to the effect that prose is never finished. And as a matter of fact, there is the smallest quantity of prose that has that quality of being ultimate and inevitable, which is of the very essence of perfect poetry. But the Gettysburg Address has for a long time seemed to me to be as finished and inevitable as Whitman's "O Captain! My Captain!" or Keats' "Ode to a Nightingale." In addition to its beauty and perfection of form, it has also the sustained emotional power of the very greatest poetry. This piece of prose fulfils completely Milton's definition of poetry: it is simple, sensuous, passionate. There are many "purple patches" in Lincoln's other writings that show the same beauty of form, the same directness and concentration, and that are pitched in the same emotional key.

It may seem strange to some readers that a man who had no formal training, who according to his own statement never attended school as much as one year, who studied imperfectly English grammar after he was twenty-three years old, and who spent all his life in battling against hard circumstances and doing hard tasks—that even such a man should have written prose that for its literary qualities can without exaggeration be given rank with the best work of the supreme masters of English style. But it is not so strange as it seems. Lincoln was as well prepared for his task as Shakespeare and Burns had been for theirs.

In a general way, it may be said that Lincoln's fitness to be a great writer lay in the fact that he was a great man. "The style *is* the man," and it is therefore probably true, as Edward Fitzgerald says in one of his letters, that "all who have the best to tell, have also naturally the best way of telling it."

But in several ways Lincoln had had admirable special preparation that will help us to understand his mastery of English prose style. In the first place, he had an artistic temperament that gave him a keen relish for the joys of mere living and also a keen sense of the tragedy of life, that was susceptible to delicate effects of light and shade and responded swiftly to the appeal of mirth or of pathos. For Lincoln's matchless humor and winning tenderness had a common origin in the naturalness and humanity of the man, in a heart that sought the widest good and loved the widest joy. This sensitive temperament was a part of his endowment. It made possible the Gettysburg Address; and it was likewise responsible for the lifelong melancholy which forms the mysterious side to Lincoln's nature. Like every other man who has ever struck off deeds or words of universal currency, he coined his heart. A deep distress had humanized his soul and effected a complete purgation of his passions. His experience was his richest asset of wisdom. All this experience, self-oblivion, suffering, and human sympathy are crystallized in the Gettysburg speech, and without these it could never have been made. He must first have drunk the cup of life to the dregs.

In Lincoln's case this sensitive artistic temperament was found in rare combination with a native strain of humor and homely wisdom. The poet who has a strong sense of humor is thereby saved from the grotesque absurdities that mar so much of the verse of the young and permanently unbalanced poets of the past century. Lincoln's early love of humor and poetry may be discerned in these boyish lines of his:

> Abraham Lincoln
> his hand and pen,
> he will be good, but
> god knows When!

He made other attempts later in life to write poetry. But his taste in poetry was not faultless. For his favorite poem was the lugubrious "Oh why should the spirit of mortal be proud," which he repeated at every opportunity during a period of thirty years.

Lincoln was not simply a fine-souled man with a sensitive feeling for good and beautiful things in nature and in human character; he had the artist's gift in words, the rare sense of the value of words, not simply to express thoughts but also to suggest emotions. In inspired moments his style has the natural magic, the conjuring power, that resides in the words of the great poets and great orators of all ages. This power to make words connote emotions as well as denote ideas was native with Lincoln, and it was consciously cultivated, too. His revision of speeches shows this clearly. For his first inaugural Seward, after working it over twice, submitted this conclusion: "I close. We are not, we must not be, aliens or enemies, but fellow-countrymen and brethren. Although passion has strained our bonds of affection too hardly, they must not, I am sure they will not, be broken. The mystic chords which, proceeding from so many battlefields and so many patriot graves, pass through all the hearts and all the hearths in this broad continent of ours will yet again harmonize in their ancient music when breathed upon by the guardian angel of the nation." Our presidents have been in the habit of taking suggestions of this sort for their state papers; and Lincoln kept this conclusion, in substance. But he made significant alterations in its form, stamped the words with his own individuality, and gave to them the touch of perfection: "I am loath to close. We are not enemies, but friends. We must not be enemies. Though passion may have strained, it must not break our bonds of affection. The mystic chords of memory, stretching from every battlefield and patriot grave to every living heart and hearthstone, all over this broad land, will yet swell the chorus of the Union, when again touched, as surely they will be, by the better angels of our nature." Seward's rough draft has practically the same ideas as Lincoln's perfected peroration, but, for all the identity of thought, the one is the lumbering product of a literary mechanic and the other the consummate workmanship of a supreme artist in words.

Thus with the tenderness of his great heart reinforced by the touching appeal of consummate art he made his final bid for the love and loyalty of the seceding states. It is but a part of the irony of life that the womanlike tenderness of this gentle-hearted man could not at once have been welcomed by the better angels of our nature, but rather like the shrieking wraith of pity in one of his own favorite books must stride the blast of horrid war and ride upon the storm, till the tears of thousands and tens of thousands should drown the wind of angry passions. This civil war with all that preceded it and with all that has followed in its wake, has been stupendous and abiding in its curse; but now, when I contemplate his character, I seem to be sorry most of all that my people, by the cruel mockery of war, should ever have been made the enemies of such a man as this.

Lincoln not only had training in the art of writing, but he had fed his mind from some of the great books of the world. He had access to the English Bible. That he read this is evidenced by the effective use he made of it, especially in his familiar talk throughout his life; but, his stepmother quaintly says, "He sought more congenial books." From early life in his log cabin days he had read Aesop's Fables, from which he may have got his captivating art of illustrating his points with homely stories after the manner of Aesop; for Lincoln, like Sancho Panza, had his proverb ready for every occasion. He read *Robinson Crusoe, Pilgrim's Progress,* the history of the United States, and Weems' *Life of Washington.* To the list he later added Burns and Shakespeare. These few books he knew well, and they entered into the web and woof of his intellectual and spiritual constitution. He early had a thirst for knowledge, and he used his spare moments for reading. These few germinal books, read with zest, nourished his mind, cultivated his taste, and served as models, so far as a man of original power has models, on which his own style was formed. This loving use of books is the sort of reading that moulds and makes men. Thus it is, he that receiveth a prophet in the name of a prophet, shall receive a prophet's reward.

But Lincoln's best training for writing and speaking was got in the school of experience. Life after all is the best preparation for writing. The man who lives his life keenly is most apt to have the ability to make his words winged with vividness and convincing power. This gift is partly a matter of temperament, but it results too from living one's life intensely, from throwing oneself into one's life, from taking a keen, sharp, intense interest in everything that lies about one. Hence the value of living a healthy, human, normal, and whole-souled existence; hence it is that life for all of us is a far greater thing than learning; and hence it is that the editor of an American magazine has said that he is more apt to find men who can write readably and interestingly about things with which they are familiar, among men of leisure and men of affairs, than among professional students. They live more, are in closer touch with things, and therefore they write a more vivid and concrete style. Literature cannot be made to order. There is a sense in which it may be said that it must come out of the life of the time. The individual and the age working together produce literature. The best writing has not usually been done by the professional man of letters; but the great literature of the world has been turned off by the job. So Shakespeare wrote, and so Dante and Milton. They all had ulterior objects in view, and were not writing for purely literary purposes. Theirs was not art for art's sake, but art in the service of great causes. This, in my judgment, has as a rule been the genesis of genuinely great writing. Lincoln did not write from literary impulses, though he did use literary skill; but his art was made to serve the great causes of men. It was incidental to his life and therefore has the appearance of being accidental. Thus his style at its best becomes simple, ultimate, and inevitable; and for its classical and abiding qualities some of his writing takes rank with the best prose of all time.

Then, too, the best there was in Lincoln was aroused by great occasions. Few human beings are sufficiently energized.

In the case of most of us our spirits are dull as night; we live at a poor, dying rate. Beset as we are by human limitations, what we need most of all is to be freed, aroused, and expanded. In moments of heightened activity the spirit of a great man is fired to an inordinate energy and is inspired with a power not ordinarily at his command. Such a man was Lincoln at Gettysburg. Nature and art had done everything for him. He had on the whole armour. He was endowed by nature with rare gifts, he had had years of self-schooling, he was under the inspiration of a momentous occasion. He made a brief speech that spoke the heart of the nation.

The qualities that enabled Lincoln to make this speech— fineness of character, intimate sympathy with all manner of men, long familiarity with suffering, invincible rectitude, an eager desire to devote himself to the relief of man's estate— the same qualities made it possible for Edwin M. Stanton, without undue exaggeration, to say of his martyred chief as he lay in death: "There lies the most perfect ruler of men the world has ever seen."

PRESIDENT ELIOT AND THE SOUTH*

PRESIDENT ELIOT OF HARVARD UNIVERSITY, after forty years of service in the cause of American education, has announced his resignation to take effect not later than May 19 of the present year, and his successor has been elected. Almost simultaneously with the announcement of his resignation there came from the press his *University Administration,*† a volume which is the result of forty years of successful experience in educational reform, and which is sure to abide as an authoritative handbook on the subject.

President Eliot's resignation and the publication of *University Administration* may be said to mark the end of an era in American higher education. He has made of Harvard a true American university, and, at least in so far as university organization is concerned, it is apt to have an increasing influence throughout the entire country. And this influence will not be confined to the management of universities. President Eliot

* *The South Atlantic Quarterly,* VIII (April, 1909), 184-191.
† *University Administration.* By Charles W. Eliot. Boston and New York: Houghton, Mifflin & Co., 1908, 266 pp.

[255]

has not only undertaken the task of educational reform from top to bottom, but he has given his attention to many of the great problems of American society. To all these educational and social questions he has brought wide knowledge and keen analysis, and also the unmistakable purpose to be of service to his country. For his ability and his service in the cause of education and in many other good causes, he is today justly ranked among the most influential citizens of the republic.

We have lately had the enheartening spectacle of a President-elect of the United States choosing to spend in a Southern city the months preceding his inauguration, in order that he might study at first hand our conditions and come into close contact with our people. Now we have a foremost private citizen of the country, as a sort of crowning event of his professional career, making a tour of the Southern states. That Mr. Taft should have elected thus to begin his term as President of the United States with special attention to the Southern states, and Mr. Eliot thus to close his service as president of Harvard University, is a most unusual tribute to the progress of the present South and the possibilities of the immediate future. Both these are farseeing and patriotic Americans. Besides, President Taft has at heart the good of his country, and President Eliot has a wise care for the welfare of his university. President Taft's attitude and President Eliot's coming among us to gain intimate knowledge of Southern people signalize the fact that there is a new day in the South. It is most gratifying, too, that both these men appear to understand and appreciate the better things in Southern society, and both seem to be in sympathy with our best public opinion. Both accept as inevitable under existing conditions and, so far as I know, give complete assent to the doctrine of the social segregation of the races in the Southern states; and both favor the elimination of illiterate voters, so long as the unfit of all races are treated alike. On these two fundamental propositions the best public opinion of the North as illustrated in these two distinguished men and the best public opinion of the South are agreed. In this agreement may be found the basis for a more complete understanding between the two sections than has existed for half a century.

Mr. Taft's stay in the South the past winter was everywhere hailed with joy and popular enthusiasm. Mr. Eliot is just now finishing a veritable triumphal march through the South. It is not simply the inborn and inbred hospitality of Southern people that causes them thus to welcome two leaders of public opinion in the North. After a half century of isolation they are glad to be understood and sympathized with by representative men from the outside. This new experience will be salutary; and we may hope that it marks the end of sectionalism in this country; that henceforth all Americans, North and South, shall become national in their sympathies, their ideals, their civic, political, and educational undertakings. Not that each section will not continue to cherish its own peculiar ideals and excellencies, but that each will understand the other sufficiently to work together for a common Americanism. If after this any sort of Southern isolation remain, it would seem to be the fault of our leaders and moulders of public opinion.

If President Taft and Dr. Eliot represent, as I think they do, the most intelligent and influential public opinion of the North at this time, then the Southern reactionary will no longer find justification for himself in the misunderstanding and misrepresentation of us, often ignorant and sometimes malicious, that have been in some parts of the country all too common now for many years. The way is, therefore, perfectly clear for all intelligent and right-minded men to take a fair and reasonable position on all questions that concern the country.

More than ever before, the true interests of all sections, races, and classes of Americans are in the main identical. We are all equally bound to do justly and love mercy. All of us in this democracy—white, brown, red, and black—must go up or down together. The plain duty of us all is to help everyone of whatever race or condition to rise to his fullest possible growth. Thus only may the country as a whole move forward. The end of it all we cannot see. To thoughtful men some of our problems look dark, but this next first step is perfectly clear. If Southern men fail to see this duty and obligation they will fail of a great opportunity, and for such failure there could no longer be an excuse.

The voice of the reactionary harking back to the past will, of course, continue to be heard both in the North and in the South; but this is of little consequence, if, as I seem to see evidence for believing, the best public opinion in the North and in the South are now agreed in fundamental questions. Interests will clash, ideals will differ, prejudices and provincialisms will abide. My hope is, however, that it will henceforth not be the South against the rest of the country, but the South as an important portion of the nation bearing its part in the councils of the nation, giving and taking, able to hold its own, willing to abide by majority rule, and sharing in all the privileges and responsibilities of the government as our fathers did. I do not wish to seem to be too hopeful. I see many obstacles still in the way; but this complete reintegration of national sentiment and national sympathy, I am persuaded, is the privilege of this generation of Americans. Shall we be wise enough to enter into it?

President Eliot's speeches through the South have not been confined to educational topics; they have dealt sanely and wisely with almost every phase of our life. From the teaching and example of such a man there are some valuable lessons that Southern people ought to learn. We ought to learn, in the first place, the value in our democracy of the right kind of education. Our ideal must be to give every youth the opportunity to develop himself to the full limit of his capacity. All money properly expended for education is a good investment, from a mere business as well as from a humanitarian standpoint. Money should be more wisely invested than it has been in the past and much more liberally. We need an educational system thoroughly organized from top to bottom and made strong and effective in every part of it. There can be no lasting educational reform that does not extend all along the line.

As President Eliot has so often said, this reform must begin at the top and thence extend itself down to the lowest grades. Hence the need of strong institutions of higher education. In the South we not only need such institutions for educational leadership, but we need them to lead and mould public opinion on every question that concerns our welfare. We need colleges that are strong enough to lead public opinion and that are not content merely to follow it. At every crisis in our history during the past hundred years, such colleges would have been of inestimable value not only to the South itself, but to the whole nation. We need colleges that will serve the great causes of men and not be subservient to local and passing feelings and prejudices; colleges that do not reflect too immediately the changing moods of the multitude, but view the local and the transient from a wide, sweeping standpoint. Colleges to be of the highest worth to us must be free from partisanship, sectionalism, and sectarianism in all their forms; and at the same time they must be wholeheartedly devoted to the truest good of their own people. My own opinion is that a supreme need of the South today is a number of strong colleges that are free from all partisan or sectional bias and hurtful provincialism, that see life steadily and see it whole, not fitfully and in segments of truth; that have their eyes on the high but far-distant goal of excellence, and travel towards it through good and evil report; that know no temporizing, truckling, or compounding with fears.

This ideal Southern college, whether established by state, church, or private benefaction, cannot be made to order. It must be a slow growth. It has taken President Eliot forty years to change a provincial New England college into a true

American university. Through these forty years he has tried to work out Harvard's career in good part with reference to the time and place in which it has found itself. He has not attempted to create the materials with which he has worked, he has only used them; they have been the gift of history. While he has been developing Harvard College out of existing conditions into a real American university, the attempt has been made at Johns Hopkins to transplant to American soil a full-grown German university. This latter experiment has been useful, but except in the medical school it has not been successful. An attempt in the South to imitate a university like Harvard would be equally foolish and prove equally unsuccessful. We cannot transplant. We must build for ourselves in the light, of course, of our own experience and in the light of what has been done elsewhere. This cannot be done by clinging blindly to the past and resisting all change, but must be done by patient and wise experimentation. This method is slow, but is the only sure method; and impatience of human progress finds its just reproof in President Eliot's own memorable saying that "nature's patient ways shame hasty little man."

By wise and patient experimentation President Eliot has made himself the leader in the building up of a great American university. He leaves Harvard well on the road to a satisfactory settlement of the questions that concern professional education. The law school has been called the best professional school in the world. The medical school bids fair to be equally good. The graduate school of arts and sciences and the scientific schools are well established. But many problems concerning the college have not been settled even during President Eliot's extraordinarily successful administration. Some of the hardest of these problems are left for his successor and for all of us who have to do with colleges. Ten or a dozen universities like Harvard will probably be all the institutions of that kind the country will ever need. But all over America there is need of the American college that produces men matured and cultivated in body, mind, and character, and produces this result as surely and satisfactorily as the law school now trains lawyers or the best trade schools turn out skilled workmen.

The method of wise and patient experimentation that President Eliot has applied to the building up of a great university we need to apply here to the development of colleges that will be best suited to our conditions, of agricultural and trade schools that will train for the sort of life and work our youth are to enter upon, and of a small number of high-grade professional schools with standards of admission and graduation as high as are maintained in the most progressive communities in the country.

President Eliot has reminded us that our problems are essentially the same as the problems in other parts of the country (and I am glad to add, he thinks that we are beginning to go about the solution of them in practically the same ways). This is a wholesome lesson for us to learn. Circumstances have caused us to look upon our conditions as peculiar. In dealing with certain phases of what is called the Southern question our thinking still often rests upon the assumption that we are a peculiar people, living under peculiar conditions, with peculiar problems to work out in peculiar ways. In a sense we are, to be sure, a peculiar people, working out our destiny under entirely unique conditions. In fact, this is true of every people and for that matter of every individual. The speech and action of some elements of Southern people would seem to imply that we are free from the operation of the ordinary laws of nature and human progress. We need constantly to be reminded that truth is not partial and of special application, but whole and of universal significance. Whatsoever we sow, that must we also reap. No matter what the provocation may be, if we tolerate mob violence we must in the end expect widespread lawlessness and anarchy. No matter on what grounds we may seek to justify it, any studied unfairness towards any class of people of whatever color or condition among us will do more permanent injury to the oppressor than to the victim. Even in a peculiar civilization like ours, unhealthy political conditions must bring civic inefficiency and decay. These propositions would seem to be axiomatic, but they are not yet universally accepted, especially in our political thinking. I believe that President Eliot's coming among us will help to fix them in our more enlightened thinking and action.

The teaching and example of President Eliot perhaps more than any other American should inspire us with faith in the power of truth when effectively presented to work its own way into wide acceptance without the aid of any sort of force. He has always been content merely to turn on the light and allow it slowly to penetrate every corner of the country. He has presented his ideas and trusted in their own soundness to win ultimate success. He has never attempted to run roughshod over the minds or bully the moral judgments of men. There has been all over the country remarkable growth in toleration of opposing opinion, but there is still further need to purify the air. The victory for religious liberty and toleration would seem among all enlightened men to be complete. We all realize that to make out of religious zeal a whip of scorpions would be morally as bad and practically as harmful as the burning of heretics. We ought equally to recognize that any attempt to turn State pride or sectional patriotism into a rod of correction or that any use of the lash of political opinion is always and everywhere as wicked and destructive as any torture devised by the Inquisition. We can make progress only through ideas, not through force.

President Eliot's teaching and example give emphasis to the duty of educated men in all parts of the country by intelligent discussion and by wise use of the franchise to help on the causes of good government. He has himself taken much interest in questions of government, especially in questions of municipal government. He is not a partisan, but he has the courage to vote for the principles he believes best and for the men he regards as most competent, whether Republicans or Democrats. He was among the leaders in Massachusetts who favored Mr. Cleveland for President, though he has doubtless usually voted the Republican ticket in national elections. It would be a great gain for good government in the South as in all parts of the country if all educated men would take an intelligent interest in questions of city, state, and national government, and if they were courageous enough to vote as they think without much regard to party allegiance. Parties are good things, but so are independent voters. President Eliot has most convincingly pointed out that small groups of intelligent and courageous citizens working together for good causes may achieve valuable results. This cannot be done where men blindly follow political bosses or traditional shibboleths and vote in the mass. If this doctrine should find acceptance in any Southern state, it would speedily lead to improvement in many directions.

President Eliot has more than once remarked that never in his life before has he learned so much in the same length of time as during the seven weeks spent in traveling through the Southern states. There are undoubtedly some lessons that the nation could well afford to learn from these states. But we of the South are not so much concerned to point out these lessons as we are to put ourselves in all respects in line with the progressive men and the progressive sections of our common country.

CONSTRUCTIVE EDUCATIONAL
LEADERSHIP *

A GIFTED YOUNG FRIEND OF MINE, who was graduated from
Trinity College some time ago, like so many others began his
career as a school teacher. When he had taught successfully
for two years, suddenly he quit, saying that he was tired of
teaching other people's children, of pouring his life into other
lives and preparing them for successful achievement, while he
himself had no part in the great tasks of human society. This
conception of the profession makes of the teacher a mere school
keeper, a member of society not much higher in his function
than the maid in the nursery and little different from the peda-
gogue among the Greeks and Romans, whose business it was
to attend the children of his master and combine in mild proportions some sort of instruction with the purely physical oversight of the children. It is this idea of the weak passivity of
the profession which gives occasion for the oft-repeated sneer,
"He who can, does; he who cannot, teaches." The idea is

* *The South Atlantic Quarterly*, VIII (October, 1909), 301-310. In substance,
an address delivered before the North Carolina Teachers' Assembly, Morehead
City, June, 1909.

rather widespread, I fear, and is doing the cause of education as much harm as any other single thing today.

Over against this conception I wish to set the doctrine of the teacher as a worker at the hard tasks of society, as a builder of civilization who, if he be efficient enough, may become a constructive, transforming influence and power like Livingstone or Socrates or Moses. Ideas and ideals are after all the greatest forces in civilization, and from educators and those they educate must come this high leadership of ideas and ideals in the service of the republic. The measure of the teacher's influence is not the amount or quality of intellectual pabulum that he may dole out to docile children, but the sort of guidance he gives to individual minds and to communities, and the moral energy that he succeeds in producing. The low estimate in which the teaching profession is held will pass, when there is in the profession a considerable proportion of men of this shaping and transforming influence and power, and likewise women who have the constructive helpfulness and intuitive wisdom that will enable them to deal successfully with children as well as with whole communities. This type of teacher is our chief need, rather than technical training, professional standards, and higher salaries, important as are all these. The presence in the profession of a considerable number of such teachers will, in due time and without forcing, bring, if not the wage, at least the dignity that ought to belong to one of the most useful of all occupations.

Men and women of originating and shaping power are needed in all times, but they would seem to be especially needed in times of rapid growth; and there do occasionally come times in the history of nations when the ordinary processes of national development are superseded by more rapid methods and when civilization goes forward at a bound. Such an epoch was the Elizabethan age in England; such an epoch came to New England in the middle decades of the last century; and in such an epoch, I believe, we are living here today.

In spite of all misgivings, most competent men, actually at the work of rebuilding Southern civilization, believe that we are standing upon the very threshold of a new era. The belief itself, even if it were not so amply justified by the facts, would tend to produce the expected result. An age of hopefulness is apt to be an age of achievement.

We are living, then, in a time that is rich in promise and full of hope; and we are engaged in a profession that should not only hand on the torch from the past to the oncoming generations, but should also furnish guidance in that process of readjustment and rebuilding which every progressive age must carry on. In what ways may we, at this particular time and in this particular place, best give this service of constructive leadership?

Our civilization must rest upon the secure foundation of widespread material prosperity and well-being. And this widespread prosperity and well-being in our Southern states depends now, and I hope always will depend, peculiarly upon agriculture. Agriculturally, as in so many other ways, we have scarcely begun to be what we are destined to become. The task of improving the agricultural conditions of this region ought to lie heavily upon teachers, urban and rural, elementary and advanced, and upon schools high and low. The practical application of the sciences, trained experience, and educated public opinion ought all to be brought to bear upon this task of improving rural life. This improvement involves the restoration of the soil, the building of roads, delivering mails, establishing schools, strengthening churches, and altogether making the conditions of rural life more wholesome and attractive, thus bringing back something of the former dignity of the country as opposed to the town. The boy from the farm nowadays goes to clerk in a village store, and feels that he has advanced in his social standing and business opportunity. It was not always so. In the old South the planter took social rank above the tradesman and shopkeeper, just as in England still the landowner is held in high esteem. I am not concerned to see revived the arbitrary social importance of the English country estate or even of the old Southern plantation; but I do wish that this generation should understand the opportunity and duty of getting the most out of the soil, not by exhausting it, to be sure, but by constantly improving it. And in this fundamental part of the rebuilding of our ancient commonwealth I wish to see education lead, not "follow, as they say, for reward."

We are coming also to be a manufacturing state, and this, too, is well, for any people is to that extent better off for having varied industries. But whether this industrial gain is in the long run to promote the good of the whole people will depend upon the success with which we overcome the evils that grow up around manufacturing centers everywhere. Along with their material benefits the rapidly multiplying cotton mills of the state are creating a new set of problems in the settlement of which the school has its place. Ample provision for the proper education of children, and various lines of social and betterment work for adults, are already furnishing in some of the mill villages more improved conditions for living than the average Southern community enjoys. But there is still much to be done in inducing a more enlightened management of the unprogressive mills; in the working out, step by step through actual experience, of the hard problems of factory life; in building up a public opinion that will not sustain the irresponsible demagogue who for his own advantage seeks to array one class against another class; and in making this public opinion equally hostile to the selfish capitalist who has his eye always on the interests of the stockholder and cares nothing for the welfare of the laborer.

This whole problem is new in North Carolina and is being created by the new industrial order upon which we are just entering. We must work out the problem for ourselves, in the light, of course, of the experience of other states and other countries; but, equally, of course, in view of our own actual conditions. And this is just one phase of that larger question, the relation of capital to labor, which is agitating the more populous and wealthy sections of this and the other nations of the world. We were for a time sheltered by our isolation. But we are today being swept into the great currents of American life with all its perils and responsibilities; and we are being forced to take our share in the settlement of national questions. Along with the rest of the country, we are face to face with the difficulty of finding a way to be fair to capital and at the same time just to labor. Institutions of education, if they are manned by teachers, and in turn send out graduates, of ability and fair-mindedness, ought to do conspicuous service in the final working out of this most baffling problem of the age.

Within a brief half century, the part of the country in which we live has been exposed to the shock of civil war, the complete overthrow of the old *régime*, the nightmare of reconstruction, all these followed by long years of convalescence, and now, thank Heaven, by a period of rapid growth. The process of normal, orderly development has thus been interrupted and sent violently "spinning down the ringing grooves of change." This structural break with our past and this startling succession of events have made particularly important and particularly difficult the political readjustment of this generation, and the right mediation of the present between our past and our future. On the one hand we are told, almost vehemently, that we must be true to our past, must respond in unbroken solidarity to the old-time shibboleths and traditional political leadership; and, on the other hand, that we must divide, that it is always better for a state or a nation to have two parties. Amid the warring voices that are already heard in the land and that are sure to grow louder as the years go on, what shall be the attitude of mind of those who ought to guide in every onward movement of this changing age? Need we be either reactionaries or revolutionists? I do not believe that by precept or example we are going to seek to tie this generation to the dead past. Nor do I believe that we will break completely with that past and seek to build up a society that may seem to be ideally good but that is completely divorced from our history. We are not going to be blind adherents of the past, and we are not going to be mere opportunists seeking a temporary gain here and there wherever it may be found, but without any guiding principles of thought and conduct. In this period of political unrest the leaders of the minds of men ought, by considerate public discussion and by conscientious use of the franchise, to bring into our public life a spirit of perfect fairness and honesty, and ought to create a moral necessity that each man shall do his duty exactly as he sees it, free from any sort of coercion through inflamed public opinion, through social ostracism, or through any other means.

Upon those who are to lead this generation in the things of the mind and the spirit rests the further duty of mediation between the religious conservatism of this region and the great intellectual ferment of the age. Again our problem is to keep the good of the old and adjust it to the needs and conditions of the new time. No phase of our problem of readjustment is more delicate or more important. Material progress, enlightened government, and popular education are not enough to insure our well-being. If in our eagerness to progress in these directions we neglect the cause of religion, we shall be like the foolish man who cut off his right hand in order that the left hand might be strengthened. We need and shall always need to cultivate a virile and aggressive religious faith, if we are to have a stable and vigorous civilization; and it is highly important that we shall make education and religion mutually helpful and both contributory to human progress.

These are all difficult undertakings (I could mention a good many others), and each one is rendered more difficult by the indifference and outright opposition of certain sections of the public. Those who are comfortably resting in their indifference and those who, through ignorance, prejudice, or selfishness, oppose progress, are in the habit of saying that the preacher should "preach the gospel" and the teacher should take no part in disputed questions. To break down this indifference and to overcome this opposition can never be the work of "docile bairns of knowledge" or humdrum pedagogues. It calls for men of insight, enterprise, daring, and for women of tact, patience, resourcefulness. The true benefactors and heroes of every society are those who do its difficult tasks. And the highest approval of the public will be best earned, and in the long run most surely won, by the teachers who courageously and wisely apply originating and constructive ability to doing such things as are most needed to be done in the communities in which they live and work.

But even aside from these public duties there is abundant room for the use of the teacher's enterprise and originating faculties in the narrower field of formal education, in the completion of educational organization, the perfecting of educational machinery, and the infusing of a life-giving spirit into this perfected mechanism. In proposing to educate all the people, this country is, under the circumstances, entering upon the most stupendous project that any nation in all history has ever undertaken. And we cannot afford to fail; for the perpetuity of democratic institutions and the survival of democracy itself demand the proper training of all classes of people. This necessity for popular education is coming now in North Carolina to be widely recognized, and the new demands make a new and insistent call for farsighted leadership. I can only touch upon the larger aspects of this great question of education, leaving out of account the multitudinous details of educational reform.

We are undertaking to provide universal education; and what is meant by universal education? So far as I can see, it does not mean that educational processes will ever, fallibly speaking, be so perfect or so perfectly adjusted to all kinds of individuals that everybody will be adequately trained. Universal education can mean no more than that there shall be accessible to every child the advantages of the elementary school, the grammar school, and the high school; that at each of these three stages the instruction shall be as perfectly adapted to the needs of the pupils as human ingenuity can devise; that each of the three grades of instruction shall not only provide what the pupil needs at that stage of his development, but shall lead up to the next stage; and that, for the benefit of those who can continue their education, there shall be the same sort of articulation between the high school and the college. To put within reach of every child the opportunities of the elementary school, the grammar school, and the high school, is the main concern of universal education; and in this supreme task every bit of strength the state can command from all sources should be concentrated. In this undertaking every enlightened man and woman, no matter what his or her particular views may be, can in one way or another take part. To consolidate all the forces in the state for this purpose and to utilize them so that the largest and most beneficent results may follow, is a beautiful vision of the future, that with us all should abide and command. But this vision, like every other beautiful vision that implies the perfectibility of human society, looks far to the future. To establish schools wherever they are needed, to provide competent teachers, and to enrich and perfect the school curriculum is a work that calls for the best wisdom of this generation. The establishment of schools and supplying teachers will require time and the liberal expenditure of money. We all realize, I am sure, that a most difficult undertaking awaits us in the working out of a school curriculum. Whatever this curriculum may finally be, there is one thing it must do. The instruction in the elementary school must be equally good for those pupils who will enter the grammar school and those whose schooling ends at the first stage; the instruction in the grammar school must be good for those who will enter the high school and those who cannot;

the instruction in the high school must be adapted to the needs of those who can go on to college and of those who must go immediately to work. Any school course that does not supply this condition will be fatally defective; and the condition is not impossible of fulfilment, for there is a vital unity in all sound education.

The mere proposal by a state or nation to educate all classes of people must have an enlarging and liberating influence on the character of those who propose it. To seek the widest good and love the widest joy is an ennobling aspiration; and to undertake to make the benefits of education universal must tend to develop nobility and greatness in individuals, in states, and in nations. And if it is successful, universal education is bound to increase enormously the efficiency of the country; for to train all, and to give room to all for the fullest development, not only raises the general average, but is the one certain method to find the most capable. This is the kind of natural selection that democracy is to use, and it is the only law of the survival of the fittest that can be permanently tolerated by a humane society. The purpose to promote universal education is one of the most encouraging features of our democracy.

Higher education has been carried on longer in the state, and the colleges are better equipped for their work than the mass of public schools. (Under colleges I include all the higher institutions of education). With the industrial revival and the new educational impulse of the present, I believe our colleges have a rare opportunity to do for this generation a formative and lasting service. I am not sure, however, that the colleges are fully living up to their opportunities. I shall call attention to three particulars in which reform appears to me to be most urgently needed.

A glaring defect of American civilization is our national mania for bigness and blind faith in numbers. The true college is the home of excellence, and one would expect that the college would be the last place to be affected by the vicious doctrine of numbers or the fatal confusion between bigness and greatness. And yet higher education is threatened by just this danger; and from this source, I think, come some of our most serious evils. At least ten years ago every college in the state should have taken the chances of reduced numbers and refused admission to all students who had not completed a high-school course. I should not speak of this now, if I felt sure that there had been made an end to this evil. It has been reformed indifferently, no doubt; it should be reformed altogether. It is just as injurious to individuals, just as destructive to schools below, just as subversive to discipline and fatal to any thoroughgoing system, to admit to college students who have not completed the high-school course as it would be to admit to the high school students who had not finished the grammar-school course. Without the perfect articulation of high school and college we can never have genuine educational progress. It seem to me the only reason why this reform cannot be had at once is the unwise desire on the part of colleges for ever increasing numbers.

Insufficient control in the colleges, and especially the excessive desire for numbers, have led to the wild exploitation of athletics, from which the whole country is suffering. I believe heartily in athletics when properly carried on; but every one of us who has considered the question at all knows that there are athletic evils in North Carolina colleges that cry aloud for reform. And athletic abuses are closely bound up with the lack of intellectual and moral discipline and the general looseness of undergraduate life, concerning which complaints are coming from all quarters today. In many American colleges these evils are partly due to the too rapid growth of the colleges and their inability at once to adjust themselves to changing conditions. It sometimes looks to me as if we might be in danger here of deliberately adopting some of the evils that curse other sections and from which circumstances have kept us free.

The craze for bigness brings another evil in its wake, that is, the resulting tendency for colleges to be concerned primarily about their immediate interests—more students, bigger buildings, increased appropriations, larger gifts—rather than to give themselves wholeheartedly to the service of great causes. This kind of striving must benumb the noblest aspirations and make impossible the truest success of colleges; for colleges, like men, are subject to the immutable law of greatness through service.

In addition to schools that fit our youth for the life and work upon which they are to enter and also prepare for college such as can continue their education, and in addition to colleges that send out graduates trained and matured in body, mind, and character, we need a small number of professional schools with standards for entrance and for graduation as high as are maintained in the most progressive sections of the country. To no professional school, whether law, medicine, divinity, teaching, technology, should the entrance be easier than to the A.B. course of the best colleges. For the so-called learned professions the admission requirement in the stronger institutions should be not less than two years of college work. The time has come in civilized countries when no man should be allowed to enter one of these professions without adequate and thorough preparation. The creation of proper standards for all the professions is a direct product of a rational system of education.

Then, too, some such organized system will be necessary before plans for popular education can be carried on successfully or on a sufficiently large scale; and the perfecting of such a system is one of our first duties. But no one, I suppose, thinks that any organization is of much value except in so far as it furnishes the means by which competent men and women may work effectively. Unquestionably the teacher's best opportunity to build enduringly is in constructive teaching. The one sure way to promote the causes that I have spoken for tonight and others equally important that, doubtless, have suggested

themselves to you while I have been talking, is to build progressive ideas into the mind and character of the youth of the
State. Those who have command of this source of power must
not mistake themselves or be mistaken by others for innocent
pedagogues and school keepers. Affording, as it does, opportunity for the exercise of first-rate ability and for useful service, life for us, we ought to feel, is not a weak and passive
thing, but a great and noble calling.

CONSERVATISM AND PROGRESS*

THE SOUTHERN STATES HAVE had a peculiar history. Originally settled more largely perhaps than any other part of
America by people who in the mother country belonged to the
ruling classes, they naturally had a large share in the making
of this nation. But for causes that are well understood the
early predominance of these states has not been maintained.
Through no fault of his own and through no special fault of
Southern white people, the African Negro, that hapless child
of evil destiny, broke early upon the scene of American history.
And the South has had to pay dearly for the privilege of developing, first through slavery and then in freedom, this backward race into the full blessings of Christian civilization. The
price is not yet paid in full, for though slavery, the "one structural error of the fathers," has been destroyed, it is still stupendous and abiding in its curse. Thus the victim of uncontrollable circumstances through so many long years of suffering and hard struggle now comes at last into an era of growth

* *The South Atlantic Quarterly*, IX (April, 1910), 188-194.

and prosperity—the South is attracting the attention of thoughtful men everywhere. In this time of change we are beset on all sides with advice and proffered assistance. We are told that we need to be cured of the hookworm; we need a new kind of education for the masses and a different sort of organization of our colleges; we need to change our politics; we need a new religion. In this paper I shall seek to inquire into the relations between conservatism and progress, especially as they concern a people like the Southern people today.

As Edmund Burke has pointed out, the legal doctrine of inheritance furnishes a sure principle of conservatism. By our law a son inherits property from his father. He holds the property, uses it, and, if he be wise, improves it and transmits it to succeeding generations. Thus he looks backward to his ancestors and forward to posterity, at the same time being true to both and also true to himself. The doctrine of inheritance does not exclude the principle of improvement; it implies it. It leaves acquisition free, as Burke said, but it secures what has been acquired. This is the true principle of conservatism: to hold on to the inheritance from the past but keep free to improve it and transmit it to posterity bettered by each generation.

This is the wise method of nature. Change should always be gradual and slow, growing out of the past and into the future. Thus in every stage of human development there would be nothing wholly novel and nothing wholly obsolete; organized society in all its forms and with all its institutions would be a sort of family inheritance, all fit and confederated with themselves. By this process the bad would be constantly eliminated and the good from whatever source constantly introduced. Only by this way of conservative progress can nations travel to prosperity and peace. Spain, once the proudest and most prosperous nation of Europe, by force and persecution for centuries beat down all change and so thwarted all progress. The result has been stagnation and national decay.

The French Revolutionists, on the other hand, cut loose from the past and attempted to build anew a civilization that had no basis in the ancient regime. They so staggered the French nation that it has not yet recovered from the shock. In the whirlwind of revolution they sought to build a house that had no foundation. Spain typifies for us false conservatism and France radical change. Both were wrong. Spain tried to stand still, forgetting that time itself, as Lord Bacon said, is the greatest innovator, and time in its course alters things; and it is as bad to be behind the time as to be ahead of the time. In either case the time will be out of joint for the nation. This is the meaning of Bacon's fruitful saying that a froward retention of custom is as turbulent a thing as an innovation. Conservatism may thus become, as it has often become, as disturbing an element in society as radicalism. One is too far behind, the other too far ahead, and neither is of a piece with the age.

Spain did not adapt itself to changing conditions, and so became the laggard nation of Europe. The French Revolutionists found French society constituted in a way that was wholly displeasing to them. Instead of seeking to reform, they overthrew; instead of using the materials of their country which nature and their history supplied them, they demolished the whole social structure and tried to build up in its place one that to them seemed ideally good but one that was completely divorced from the past of France. The wisdom to preserve and the ability to improve they did not possess. They were iconoclasts and destructionists rather than founders and builders of civilization. A great and enduring nation cannot be built up so, but it must be built on a long historic past. Civilization is not a forced growth or manufactured product but a natural development, and the development must be along lines of its own and not made to form itself on some wholly extraneous model. Any other conception of national progress rests upon inexperience and ignorance.

PHOTOGRAPH FROM BLANK & STOLLER

PRESIDENT FEW ABOUT 1936

Likewise each individual, if he be wise, accepts a large share in the accumulated experiences of mankind, and works out his destiny in good part with reference to the time and place in which he finds himself. He cannot create the materials with which he must work; he can only use them. They are the gifts of history. Corresponding to medieval Spain and revolutionary France, men divide themselves into two classes, conservatives and radicals; and in neither class is found the highest wisdom. Let me illustrate from a sad chapter in American history. From 1830 to 1860 our Southern political leaders were too conservative, the moulders of public opinion in the North too radical. Calhoun stood for a literal interpretation of the Constitution, he was true to the past, and the logical validity of his position is generally conceded by competent historians today. But the environment in which he and his contemporaries lived prevented a growth in them of the national feeling which circumstances fostered in other parts of the country, and so, while historically correct, they were put into the wrong by the logic of events. The civilization of the nineteenth century was against the institution of slavery, and the institution of slavery was against the civilization of the nineteenth century. We all know this now and we all rejoice at the issue of the Civil War, although in the conflict of arms we lost. But our leaders of those days, living in an atmosphere colored by the institution of slavery and tempered by a conservative view of the Constitution, did not keep pace with the innovations of time, with the progress of ongoing events. And so they fell out of line with the age. Again, a froward retention of custom, that is, ultra-conservatism, was as turbulent a thing as innovation, that is, radical change. And Garrison, Phillips, and the New England abolitionists were the radicals, who broke with the past and became the victims of fixed ideas. They were essentially revolutionists, and to make their ideas prevail they were willing to destroy the Constitution and overthrow the government. "Extremes in nature equal ends produce." The ultra-conservatives and the extreme radicals were alike disturbing elements. The extremists on both sides went on; and soon there was war and death and mourning in the land. But the extremists did not have their way. Wise leaders, like Abraham Lincoln and Robert E. Lee, were able through storm and blood to guide the nation to its true goal. The government was preserved, the Constitution in its main essentials was saved, some of the evils of our civilization were eliminated, and our country goes on to fulfil its mission.

I have thus indicated at some length through the analogy of inheritance what seems to me to be the spirit in which a man or a nation should seek to promote individual or national progress. But what is progress? My conception of progress may, I think, be inferred from the principle of conservatism which I have suggested. If a wise conservatism means the keeping of all that is good in our inheritance from the past, then true progress is the using of this inheritance not in a spirit of blind adherence to the past but with the purpose to improve wherever certain improvement is possible. We may improve upon our inheritance from the past through the introduction of new principles and new elements, or through making advances over what has gone before in knowledge and in the methods of doing things, by studying what has been and what is in order to mould known principles and elements into newer and higher forms. As thus understood, progress is another name for normal and healthy growth; that is, development out of existing conditions into something unmistakably better.

I would define progress, then, as the growth out of existing conditions into something unmistakably better. In the first place, progress means growth. In this world failure to grow or cessation in growth, which scientists call arrested development, leads straight to stagnation and death. Witness Spain and many other communities and individuals that we are familiar with. This growth, in the second place, to be normal and healthy must be a growth out of existing conditions; it must be the fruitage of a well-established past; it must be the flowering of experience. Any other so-called progress produces half-baked radicals that run amuck up and down the earth, that fit nowhere and are fit for nothing, veritable Ishmaelites whose hand is against every man and every man's hand against them, and who for the peace of society might well be driven into the wilderness with their mother, the Hagar of confusion and every evil work. Here belong the French Revolutionists, the fiery-eyed anarchist and nihilist. And finally, the change, if it is to mean progress, must be into something unmistakably better. Here much of our so-called progress fails. All forms of progress are alike in this, that they are all modes of change. Progress always implies change but change does not always mean improvement. Change in itself is not a good thing. Our inherited institutions, beliefs, and customs ought to be kept intact, except in so far as they can be improved. An inordinate love of novelty and an itching newfangledness produce giddy and superficial character. A great structure must rest upon a stable and enduring foundation.

Another reason why we should be cautious in making changes may be inferred from Spencer's well-known law of evolution: Every active force produces more than one change —every cause produces more than one effect. This scientific law of progress appears to hold everywhere; and it seems often to happen that the resultant effects may be some good and some bad. The growth of civilization itself is not an unmixed good. We are all familiar with manifold evils of civilization, and some of them would seem to be inherent evils and not excrescences that may be sloughed off with the further growth of civilization, just as according to Macaulay the remedy for the abuse of liberty is not less of it but more. If all change is so beset with dangers and if progress itself may seem almost a doubtful good, we should be very careful to hold tight to the fundamentals of life and adopt change only when it clearly leads to genuine progress and certain human betterment.

The world moves, but it seems in certain of one's moods to move very slowly, and to men of a critical rather than a creative temperament it seems to move hardly at all. How has this moderate degree of progress been attained, and how may continued progress of the race be attained? Progress is never an accident, and it is never a blind onward movement that has no sufficient cause and no intelligible explanation. The world grows better, even in the moderate degree in which it does grow better, only because people wish it to be better and take the right steps to make it better. Man is himself the agent of all his improvement. As John Morley has said, "Society can only pursue its normal course by means of a certain progression of changes, and these changes can only be initiated by individuals or very small groups of individuals." And these changes should be well considered, gradual, slow, and I need hardly add, I think much less radical than Mr. Morley would often have them to be; but it is true that these changes must all come in the future as they have all come in the past through individual initiative and individual effort. This is the doctrine of individual responsibilty that needs always to be enforced. The individual cannot safely lose himself in the mass. Each one is solely responsible for himself, his thinking, and his conduct. We have in history inspiring examples of what single men have been able unaided to do.

The Southern states as we know them today are the product of an interrupted and broken past. Originally progressive and prosperous, the deadly disease of slavery was early fastened on the body politic. Then came the tragedy of civil war, after which the historical crime of reconstruction, followed by the tedious years of recovery, and, now by a revival of prosperity and hope. From the nature of things, then, our growth has not been and could not be in all respects wholesome. Without praise or blame for the past or present, the living or the dead, let us, free from reaction and free from radicalism, look our condition squarely in the face, determined to cherish what is good in our civilization, hold fast to it, improve it in all possible ways, and hand it on to those who come after us.

THE COLLEGE IN SOUTHERN
DEVELOPMENT*

IT WOULD SEEM TO BE APPROPRIATE for me, on an occasion like this, to give as clearly as I can my conception of the place of the college in Southern development, and coming closer home, to say plainly what I think Trinity College should undertake to do. This last is the easier for the fact that I have, during the past fourteen years, sustained intimate relations to the administration of the College, and with that administration have been in complete accord. I find now that the way has been marked out by my predecessor and that the College has only to go on to the completion of the tasks it has already set before itself.

The structural break with the past caused by the Civil War and succeeding events has made difficult and important our political readjustment and the right mediation of the present between our past and our future. But apart from any considerations of history and without regard to any theory or school of politics it must be plain to us all that, in a democracy where everything is determined by majorities, every intelligent man

* *The South Atlantic Quarterly*, X (January, 1911), 1-8. The inaugural address delivered in Craven Memorial Hall, November 9, 1910.

should carefully inquire into the merits of all questions upon which he is to cast his ballot and should vote his matured convictions, rather than settle these questions as if they were matters of course, offhand and in obedience to ancient sentiment. In the part of the South with which this college is immediately concerned, freedom of speech and freedom of action in politics are today complete. But here as everywhere else in the country we need to intensify the sense of responsibility that is imposed by the right to vote upon every thoughtful and upright man. And here perhaps more than elsewhere in America we need the courage and moral energy which compel a man to speak the thoughts that are in him, and, when the time comes, to stand up and be counted, whether girt by friend or foe. Just as for many years it has been teaching, Trinity College will continue, both by precept and example, to teach this sort of resolute doing of one's public duties.

Upon the college in the South rests the further duty of meditation between the religious conservatism of this region and the great intellectual ferment of the age. Again the problem is to keep the good that has come to us out of the past and adjust it to the conditions and needs of the present. The influential place which the church holds in the South I should like to see not only abide, but grow and extend; for it is the business of the church to guide the spiritual forces that control the world. The Southern college, if it be wise enough to understand its opportunity, will work in hearty co-operation with the churches. It will not seek to make friends with the churches for the purpose of using them as billboards on which to advertise its wares; it will not court their good will in order to rally its constituency; but in all sincerity it will labor with them just to the end of strengthening and sweetening human life. The aim of Trinity College is stated by the words on its seal, "Religion and Education"; not two but one and inseparable: religion that comprehends the whole of life and education that seeks to liberate all the powers and develop all the capacities of our human nature.

One of our first tasks is the material uplifting of the section, the development of all kinds of business, the creation of wealth, and the building of vital forces of civilization. We are now in the midst of a great industrial awakening; even in the old business of agriculture a new day has arrived. In solving the problems of the new industrialism education has a part to play; and I am not now thinking of industrial education. For while every individual ought to be trained with some reference to the kind of life he is going to live, yet I for one do not wish to see money-making set at the heart of the education of Southern people. Greed is already perhaps our characteristic national vice, and it does not need the fostering of education. Southern people are poor and ought to be encouraged by every right method to get their share of the wealth and physical well-being that have been more widespread in other parts of America, but to educate a race of mere money-makers would hurry in an era of sordid materialism that would be a more deadening blight to right and worthy living than ignorance and poverty have been. Let us have wealth and the training of wealth producers; but let us not give to industrial training an undue emphasis in the education of youth.

Of all the confusions and tragedies that followed the Civil War in the South, perhaps the most pathetic have been the chaotic educational conditions of the last half-century. There has been progress in the direction of a rational system of education, but we are not yet out of the wilderness. In all educational reform the college should furnish its full share of leadership. And this means that it must not be content to ride upon whatever may happen to be the popular wave, but it must resist fads and bad tendencies, as well as encourage and direct tendencies. Trinity College will always throw itself unreservedly into the doing of the supreme duty of the hour. A while ago it was at any cost to break the shackles of politics and traditionalism. Today it is to put within reach of every child the opportunities of the elementary school, the grammar school, and the high school. This task is made extraordinarily difficult by the double system of education that must be maintained for the two races; and in this great task every bit of strength the state can command from all sources for the next ten years should be concentrated. To consolidate all the forces in the state for this purpose and to utilize them so that the largest and most beneficent results may follow is a proposal that should command the heart and hope of all enlightened men and women.

I have sought to emphasize my belief that our colleges should give themselves to the doing of the hard tasks of society, and that educated men should do their full stint of work. Attention ought also to be paid to the gentler side of Southern civilization. The hospitality, the graciousness, the beauty and purity of the social life were the best characteristics of the old order. The grace and charm of our elders in their best estate have gone, and have been succeeded by much that is crude and raw in our life. In the discipline and invigorating of mind, in the formation of tastes, and in the amendment of manners which come through the right kind of education will be found the surest nourishment for the poise and fineness of temper that make cultivated men and high-bred civilizations.

These are some of the ways in which a college may promote the interests of society, if it is controlled by wide sympathies and a spirit of constructive helpfulness. It is not, however, among the direct aims of the college to educate publicists or ministers or skilled workmen or teachers, but to send out graduates who have been trained for efficiency and who are equipped with trustworthy character. The college that is doing most to produce these qualities of efficiency and character is rendering the largest service to the world. These are precisely the qualities that are needed in politics, in the church, in business, in education, and in society. Many lines of business and some other forms of endeavor in America have grown faster than men have been developed to manage them. And this failure of American civilization to develop an adequate supply of efficient and trustworthy men gives whatever of justification there may be for the belief held by a good many foreigners and others that our form of government is breaking down at some points.

There is a feeling rather widespread, though I am not sure it is just, that the college of today does not make as surely for efficiency and character as did the college of other days. The college has certainly in some ways gained, and perhaps in others it has lost, ground. The old curriculum with its fixed studies and severe disciplines has been liberalized and enriched. American colleges have grown and have improved their facilities for education until, in the matter of educational opportunities, the best of them are perhaps unexcelled in the world. But it is becoming increasingly clear that it is not enough for the college to provide even the richest of opportunities for its students and then unconcernedly leave them to use or neglect the opportunities as they may see fit. Ways and means must be found to make education take effect. The educational appliances must somehow be brought into live connection with undergraduate callowness. There is a saying current in German universities that one-third fail, one-third go to the devil, but the remaining third govern Europe. This survival represents too great a loss of human life. Freedom of opportunity must mean freedom to go to destruction, but in the case of college youth, freedom must be hedged about with restraints. The fine old phrase "cure of souls," if extended to include cure of minds and bodies, would define the function of the college.

The four years in college ought to be very happy years in every man's life—happy not because he spends them in idleness or luxury, but because they are years full of effort and achievement, of generous friendships and inspiring ideals, full of youth and hope. A normal man, if he once gets a taste of it, enjoys vigorous work and wholesome living. The educational

opportunities offered by the prosperous colleges of the East or
the big state universities of the West, are unquestionably far
superior to the opportunities that can be offered by the struggling colleges of the South. But there are evils of prosperity
as well as evils of adversity. And, despite all our limitations,
it is probably no more difficult for us than for them to secure
vigorous intellectual work and wholesome living; in fact, I am
encouraged to believe that the conditions are ripe for the building of some great colleges in the South. But we shall have
to profit by the experiences of colleges elsewhere—by their
successes and by their failures. Especially must we learn how
to bring the processes of education effectively to bear on a
larger proportion of students. The growing importance that
secondary concerns hold in the thought of undergraduates is
more and more tending to obscure the true ends of a college
course. If we will take command of the situation before the
tyranny of public opinion is fastened upon us by students,
young alumni, and communities taught to demand this sort of
entertainment at the hands of colleges, then I believe it will
be possible for us to shift the center of interest from athletics
and other equally irrelevant undergraduate absorptions on to
the intellectual pursuits and wholesome recreations that are
proper to college life. This shifting of the center of gravity
will be helped by adequate regulation and due subordination
of athletics; by demanding strict attendance upon college
duties; by exacting a reasonable amount of intellectual work;
and by enforcing rigorous standards of scholarship. In developing our colleges we have the chance to put upon self-cultivation and wholesome living an emphasis they do not now
usually get in American colleges.

Our opportunity consists partly, too, in magnifying the office
of the teacher. For its teachers the college needs men of ideas
and power rather than experts in the several branches of learning. The almost exclusive use of scholarship tests in the selection of teachers is, in my judgment, one of the gravest defects

in American colleges and even in the greatest American universities. Scholarship enters essentially into the making of a good teacher, but so do also a genuine interest in young men and some gift for teaching. Graduate-school ideals have worked themselves down into the college to the serious detriment of the college. I have nothing but praise for the painstaking investigation and thoroughgoing honesty that belong to the best scholarship of our time. Unceasing search for truth is necessary to insure the continued progress of the race; and every wise man will keep an open mind towards truth in all its phases. I, of course, believe in perfect freedom to teach and freedom to learn. But I do not regard the speculative pursuit of new truth as the main end of college education. The search for truth is in itself profitable, but the search is most profitable when it results in finding truth and in making the widest applications of it to human life and human conduct. An undergraduate ought not to be ever learning, and never able to come to the knowledge of the truth. The thin air of high speculative knowledge cannot nourish hardy and robust manhood. Probably everybody knows truth enough to save his life if he would use what he knows. Some things, after all, are known, and there is no need for a man to stop and build his own bridge every time a bridged river crosses his path. If a perfect college curriculum could be framed I believe it would insure to every student familiarity with the best that has been wrought out of the experience of the race and close contact with such studies as are fitted to produce in him "soberness, righteousness, and wisdom"; and then it would leave room for individual tastes and aptitudes.

To give the proper oversight of the studies of undergraduates is not enough; their living conditions, their conduct, and their habits must be looked after. The minds need rectifying, but just as often the lives need to be renovated. What profiteth a man though he speak with the tongues of men and of angels and leave college a dyspeptic; though he understand all knowledge and have the habit of spending money that does not belong to him, or be confirmed in any of the other fatal vices that beset college youth? Conduct, as Matthew Arnold has said, is more than three-fourths of life. If their work is to be of the highest value, colleges must find and control the motive powers that lie at the basis of character. I admit it is hard to keep other things equal; but, other things being equal, the so-called small college, with its intimate contacts and direct methods, probably has the best chance to do the sort of teaching that forms as well as informs.

If the Southern college is to be a leader for conservative progress in this generation, it must be given a free hand. To stand against reaction on the one side and radicalism on the other, it needs a great deal of power. It must by its organization be safeguarded against the dangers of mob opinion and the possibilities of inefficient control. To stand for correct ideals and even fight for them when necessary and at the same time to keep in sympathetic relations with the people whom it would serve is, perhaps, the most difficult problem that a Southern college in our time has to solve.

Regard for the voices of political expediency and pliant opportunism has time and again proved disastrous to the Southern states as it has often proved disastrous to other American states. Minds unpracticed in cogent thinking usually seek to catch the nearest way and follow the line of least resistance. The college that aspires to a place of leadership in the service of the republic must at times resist with all its power the mighty local influences that would sway it from its true course. To have faith in the future of America at all, or, for that matter, to contemplate human life with any degree of patience, one must believe that the people wish to do right and in the long run and in the main will do right; and more and more we are going to rely upon the people. But this does not mean that they have the expert knowledge to manage a college any more than it means that they are competent to argue a point of law before the Supreme Court of the United States, or to treat an acute case of pneumonia. The susceptibility of a pliable democracy to periodic attacks of national or sectional hysterics, the oft-used power of sensational newspapers and alarmist popular leaders to "insurrect the public mind" ought in the colleges always to find bulwarks against which they beat in vain. Only the college that is strong enough to survive these fearful testings can fulfil in our civilization the mission that great colleges should fulfil.

Such colleges must also occasionally rouse themselves to the still more ungracious task of resisting the imposition upon them from the outside of ideas that would hurt them. There are competent and conscientious educational experts in our time who seem to ignore the fact that a college must be in large part the product of development and not a forced growth; and that it should follow the lines of its own development and not be made to form itself on some wholly extraneous model. Forced conformity to types of organization that prevail elsewhere and are there regarded as ideal would unfit Southern colleges for doing the very service to which they seem by circumstances to be ordained. Against this subtle danger I believe that Trinity College will set itself with all its might.

Another temptation from which our colleges should turn is the temptation to strive for bigness. The vicious doctrine of numbers has, I think, never been more overworked than in American institutions of education. The desire to be big rather than great is responsible for many of the evils from which American colleges are suffering today. Some of these evils are temporary and due to quick growth and inability of the colleges at once to adjust themselves to the new conditions. We at the South have not suffered from this cause, but we are in danger of deliberately taking over some of the evils from which circumstances have kept us free. One result of this overeagerness for size and numbers is the ruinous tendency for colleges to be concerned primarily about their immediate interests—more students, bigger buildings, increased appropriations, larger gifts —rather than to serve, and when necessary even to suffer for, the great causes of mankind. This kind of striving must benumb the noblest aspirations and make impossible the truest success of colleges; for colleges, like men, are subject to the immutable law of greatness through service. The greatness of a college depends not upon the size of its plant or the number of its students, but upon the quality of the men who teach and the quality of the men who learn, upon its ideals and its influence.

We here have no ambition to be miscalled a university; we are not even concerned that this shall be a "big" college; but we are immensely concerned that it shall be a shining place where high-minded youth may catch aspirations to true character and genuine excellence, and whence into this vast experiment in democratic government that is being tried out on the American continent, there shall go a long succession of men who have been trained to think straight and to think through to right conclusions, and made strong by the power to know the truth and the will to live it.

FORCE AND RIGHT IN THE GOVERNMENT
OF THE WORLD*

FORCE AND RIGHT ARE the governors of this world—"force till right is ready," wrote Joubert in striking phrase. And force and right do each have their place in the government of the world, in every form of organized society, and in the life of every individual. The more primitive the society is, the larger is the place that force must have; the more enlightened it is, the more does right prevail. But in all human societies force must frequently be called upon to hold the field till right arrives. Likewise the more primitive the man, the more must force be relied upon; the more enlightened he is, the more may he be trusted to the guidance of his own inward sense of right.

To find the proper relations between force and right has been and still is a difficult problem both in the management of human societies and in the conduct of individual lives. In a general way it may be said that force can be applied to conduct, never to opinion. Conduct may, and often should, be made to conform to standards outside of itself, while there can be no

* *The South Atlantic Quarterly*, X (October, 1911), 314-322.

possible compulsion of the mind. The power that moves it must be inward; it is moral compulsion, the compelling sense of right. This sense of right resides in the heart, and so it is that out of the heart are the issues of life. Discipline and coercion of the body are sometimes necessary, but the soul loses its tone and health as soon as force supplants right there.

Even in the field of conduct, where force must sometimes be applied, it should always be so used as to lead to its own ultimate supplanting by right and should be given over as soon as possible; the prescription is, "Force till right is ready." The inexperienced boy needs to be hedged about with restraints, but the restraints should be so administered as to fit him for the responsibilities of manhood. There is no doubt that a certain amount of compulsion must be used in the government of a child. He is without the safeguards of experience and acquired wisdom, and for a good many years of his life his safety depends upon authority. But this authority should always be exercised in such a way as that he may be gradually prepared for personal liberty. He needs to be so sheltered and so guided that his growing experience will lead him out of the helplessness of childhood and the innocence of youth into the undisputed strength of manhood; for liberty, if it is to be useful to the individual himself or to society at large, must be preceded by character.

Doubtless too much authority always does harm, but our danger today lies in the opposite direction; for the use of force, and the heroic treatment of the good old times, seem to be gone forever, and there is at present an unmistakable tendency towards hurtful looseness in American homes and in all grades of American education. This growing slackness in the home and in the school, unless checked, will undoubtedly develop not strength but weakness in the men and in the citizens of the future. The severe discipline and fixed programs of the old education needed to be relaxed and made more attractive, but the movement in this direction may be carried too far. The effort to make the path of duty always easy and alluring to human beings is foredoomed to failure. No man in the conduct of his own life can rely at all times upon his enthusiasm and genial sense of youth, but he must often hark back to the "Stern Daughter of the Voice of God."

The new education is relying too much upon the interest of the pupil. To be sure, it is an unspeakable gain that the child shall like his studies and be thoroughly interested in his school; and the improvement made here has made this a happier world. But where interest flags, as flag it sometimes must, the pupil must be taught to do hard and disagreeable tasks, and taught to do them until he even learns to love to do them. Again it is "force till right is ready." As a college officer who has had considerable observation, I feel sure that the premature and injudicious lifting of the weight of authority in American homes and schools and the effort to make the life and education of the child always easy and attractive are breeding a softness and lack of the real stuff out of which men are made that bodes no good for the future of our country.

I have considered thus at length the place of force and right in the proper development of the boy into manhood, not only because it is a matter of concern to men in all generations, but because it typifies the whole religious and political history of mankind. Just as in the experience of the individual the boy is prepared, through the restraints of a well-regulated home and a well-ordered education, for the liberties of developed manhood, so in the religious history of the race, supremely exemplified in the Hebrew and Christian religions, the compulsion of law comes before the freedom of grace. In the old dispensation men were held by the restraints of the Law; in the new it is the Truth that makes us free.

One incident in the life of the Founder of Christianity forms the most striking possible contrast between the utter futility of cruel force and the invincible power of right. "And while he yet spake, lo, Judas, one of the twelve, came, and with him a great multitude with swords and staves, from the chief priests and elders of the people." Judas, with the enraged mob, on the one side, a perfect embodiment of hideous cruelty, set over against the blameless Saviour of Mankind—if ever force in behalf of the establishment of truth was justifiable, surely this was the time. But Jesus Christ had proposed to be the founder of an everlasting state and the legislator of a world-wide society, and therefore at the very outset of his public career he had deliberately determined to build his empire upon the consent and not upon the fears of mankind; for I believe the marvelous story of his temptation is best understood if we suppose it to have been at least in part caused by his growing consciousness of supernatural power and by the incitement to employ force in the establishment of his Messianic kingdom. In response to this temptation then, he said, "Get thee behind me, Satan." So at the end of his earthly career he proclaims this perhaps most novel and revolutionary of all his teachings, "All they that take the sword shall perish with the sword." This in no sense teaches or remotely implies, I think, the weak latter-day doctrine of passive obedience and nonresistance. For it is only a little while before this, when he found the money changers and the traffickers in small merchandise turning the temple of God into a den of thieves, that he cast them out. To control such conduct he was not above the use of force; for we are told that he made a scourge of small cords and with righteous indignation he drove the thieves from his Father's house. This last incident seems to be in keeping with the belief that in human societies force must sometimes be applied to conduct. But the former incident in extraordinary circumstance and by revolutionary teaching emphasizes the futility of force in the permanent establishment of right among men, and is in its originality strong evidence of the incomparable, the divine wisdom of the Great Teacher.

And this lesson of the Founder has been of all his lessons perhaps the hardest for good men to learn; for goodness im-

[297]

plies moral warmth, and in the presence of evil it is not easy to hold in check the passion of purity and the enthusiasm of virtue. And so it has happened that in the past two thousand years force has too often been mistakenly brought to the support of right. After three hundred years of bloody persecution the Christian Church came to perhaps the most dramatic and exultant moment in its history when Constantine the Great joined its ranks and gave to the scattered and stricken Christians the security of state protection and put back of them the authority of a great name. But this moment of seeming triumph instead of ushering in a new day proved to be the beginning of a long night; for the heathen element of force here entered into the church, long to remain in the vast and elaborate system of coercion which ensued. This was kept up longer in Spain than elsewhere, and its dire effects are well illustrated by the history of that country. Spain tried to stand still, forgetting that time in its course alters things and that nothing is so turbulent and disturbing to society as the strain to keep things fixed in a world which is controlled by the law of eternal progress. In the effort to beat back all change Spain thwarted all growth and became the laggard nation of Europe; it held childishly to its religious inheritance from the past and refused to allow it to be touched by the spirit of progress, which is a part of all healthy human life—religious and every other sort. The nation starved its religion almost to death; and it has persisted, to be sure, but as a shriveled infant with the grotesquely ancient face and the low vitality of premature old age.

This heathen element of force dies hard. It assumes many shapes and manifests itself in many ways. In our time even liberalism has called to its side a mild form of force, and on a wide scale we today are beholding the illiberality of liberalism. This boasted liberalism wears an ugly face, and by human perversion it seems to breed another and opposite form of force— a sort of obstinacy on the part of good men, a reaction into what Arnold of Rugby called "that natural but most deadly error of human indolence and corruption, that our business is to preserve and not to improve." This false liberalism and this reactionary and ultra-conservatism are alike disturbing elements in all societies.

The danger in the coercion of religious opinion lies in the inevitable and violent reaction into irreligion, as for example, in the case of the French revolutionists. For they would dethrone not only the king, but God as well. But even more dangerous is a certain polite and invincible indifferentism which is apt to follow coercion, and which is everywhere the arch enemy of the truth. The action of force and the reaction from it into indifference and neglect, I think I can illustrate by a brief reference to one chapter in the history of education. Up to the time of the establishment of our republic, education had everywhere rested upon a religious or, at any rate, a moral basis. But unfortunately force had got in its deadly work and religious tests were rigorously enforced upon the teachers and the taught. This attempt to force religious education down the throats of the unwilling led inevitably to a swing of the pendulum to the opposite extreme, that education has nothing to do with religion or even with morality. There resulted provisions in state constitutions that put a most serious handicap upon American public education. The opportunity to teach the Bible and Christianity, free, of course, from all compulsion and free of every vestige of sectarianism, would be in every grade of education of inestimable value. The general proscription of religious, and therefore practically of moral, teaching in American public education is a national calamity the magnitude of which is not yet fully appreciated by the country. And this gigantic and far-reaching defect in our civilization is a powerful proof of the evil of all force in religion.

So also in the political history of mankind force and right have been the governors of this world. Early societies were unlimited monarchies; government was controlled by the strong. It was the right of might. The general trend has been steadily towards democratic and self-governing organizations of society. This growth has seemed at times distressingly slow. But in the long run the slow growth of democracy has not been an unmixed evil. For while democracy seems to be the true goal of humanity, yet on the whole it has perhaps been a good thing that there have been restraints upon democracy itself. Here again force has at times had to hold the field till right arrived. This principle still holds in the management of inferior and backward races. It is not liberty but sheer cruelty to throw upon a people responsibilities for which they are not ready, just as it would be a crime to give absolute freedom to an inexperienced child. A grave mistake of this sort, as everybody knows, was made in this country when full responsibilities of citizenship were thrust upon the Negro race without first preparing the race for these high civic duties. So in the treatment of prisoners restraints are necessary, but humane societies have yet fully to learn that force should even here be so used as to lead to right, that prison experiences should be not simply punitive but largely reformatory in their nature and effect.

I have just spoken of the use of force in the management of races and individuals not capable of governing themselves, but even when we rise in the scale, in order to insure stability and the steady onward movement of mankind it would seem to be necessary to have a system of checks and balances in every form of government.

It is better that the growth of self-government even should be slow and sure than that it should be rapid and uncertain. We need especially in this country today a system of checks and balances that will bring to bear upon all important questions the most enlightened public opinion as represented by the sober second-thought of the American people.

The breaking down of the system of checks and balances provided in the Constitution by the Fathers would not only threaten the permanency of our institutions, but by making all public life more insecure would render still more difficult the hardest task of a democracy—the task of developing high moral courage in public men. If tenure of office in this government is made too insecure, shall we in the future witness such a spectacle as startled and thrilled the whole country when, in 1878, L. Q. C. Lamar, of Mississippi, in no spirit of defiance to his people, but in unalterable allegiance to the right as he himself saw it, rose in his place in the United States Senate and dared to vote against the instructions of the legislature of his state? Courage and moral energy like this are the glory of our republic, and to foster these qualities ought to be a main concern of all civilizations.

This particular lesson needs emphasis today. We have been insisting upon the rights of men. It is now time to insist on the duties of men. If democracy is to endure, it must exist alongside of excellence, otherwise it will prove to be the most dangerous form of government ever known; for its evils would be all-pervasive. If a king is bad he can be put out of the way, but if the whole people should go wrong where would the remedy lie?

Upon the ancient doctrine of the right of might rests the government of monarchs and kings and the administration of justice by means of the trial by ordeal out of which later grew the use of torture and persecution. These survive still in the abuses of an inflamed public opinion too often brought to bear upon individuals in all societies. If the old right of might assumes the form of the right of mere majorities, then this latest will be the most dangerous form the doctrine has assumed in all its long history.

The preparation of a democracy for self-government is a stupendous task. We need therefore, I say, to stress not so much the rights of men, for they are now pretty well established, but the duties of men. There are grave dangers in the glorification of democracy and in teaching that majorities are always right, whether they are right or not. And dangers too in the kindred doctrine of the perfectibility of human nature upon which state socialism seems to be built—the doctrine that to improve men we need only to improve their environment. Improved conditions do help to improve manhood: but we must not leave out of the account human nature, which is the one stable and unchanging thing in the world. The way to improve society is to train the minds and strengthen the characters of men, to increase the number of those who can think correctly and act in accordance with right.

It is only fair to right to give it an open field. And this demands that the minds of men shall be absolutely free to accept truth as they see it and free to defend it without the possibility of coercion or persecution. I do not wish to be understood as advocating that we should commit the issues of right to the main chance of things and trust that it will be borne on the stream of tendency and taste towards that destiny to which, either against or with our wills, it must inevitably drift. Quite on the other hand, I strongly believe that progress of whatever kind is never an accident, and is never a blind onward movement that has no sufficient cause and no intelligible explanation. The world grows better, even in the moderate degree in which it does grow better, only because individuals wish it to be better and take the right steps to make it better. Man is himself the agent of all his improvement. And this improvement comes about through individual initiative and individual effort.

But this projection of the individual into society can be done only through ideas and never through force. This does not imply that we are not to combat error and resist evil to the utmost of our ability; but we must remember that we cannot force men to accept our view, however dear it may be to us, or force them to be what we think they ought to be, however imperative this may seem to us. We cannot force, we must convince and persuade them.

[302]

This patient waiting for the harvest often calls upon us to let the wheat and the tares grow together; it is perhaps in a sense a toleration of evil. But there is no erecting of evil into good; there is no utility of error. All truth is wholesome, all falsehood is hurtful. While error then must never be accepted as good, yet it may be, and often is, necessary to wait to strike it down, and we must be careful not to do good in such a way that evil will come of it. And in this connection I raise the question, Why is it that a religious age is always followed by reaction into irreligion, a generation of inspired and imaginative poets succeeded by an age of prose and reason, an era of prosperity quickly superseded by depression? Is not this ebb and flow in human history, which every student has remarked, due to the tyranny of the majority, to the tendency at these floodtide periods for the men and style that dominate the epoch to force everything their way and to whip everybody into line, with a consequent reaction in the opposite direction? Is not human nature so constituted that the tyranny of the majority will always lead to reaction or to revolution? And is it not true that all reforms promoted by force and not by ideas have done more harm than good? If the answer to these questions that I get from a study of history be correct, then it is always foolish and wrong to attempt to run roughshod over the minds or to bully the moral sense of men.

TWO HOPEFUL RELIGIOUS TENDENCIES*

WE ARE ACCUSTOMED TO THINK of our age as marked by material progress and widespread physical well-being but by a corresponding religious decadence. Despite superficial appearances I think it is possible to show that this popular belief rests upon a misconception of the true spirit of the age. I shall attempt now to point out only two of the hopeful religious tendencies of our time.

The first of these relates to the steadily changing manner of interpreting the Bible, to the increasing feeling that it is to be read not slavishly according to the letter that killeth, but in the light of the spirit that giveth life. While the Christian religion had back of it centuries of preparation, still it is not a growth in the ordinary sense of the word. It is today what it was in the beginning—"the faith which was once delivered to the saints." It rests upon an unchanging Bible. Though the Bible has through the shifting social, civil, and intellectual ideals of nineteen centuries remained quite unchanged, yet the

* The South Atlantic Quarterly, XI (April, 1912), 153-157.

understanding of it, the interpretation and the practical application of it have changed from age to age.

The interpretation of the Bible is a growth, and the history of it has striking resemblances to the literary history of some of the greatest of human documents. The beautiful simplicity, fine self-restraint, and universal truth of Homer have at times not been enough to escape the devastating effects of what seems to be in average human nature an inevitable craving for literalness; and for generations the Homeric poems were actually supplanted by a prosaic commonplace that claimed to give from an eyewitness the facts of the Trojan war. As late as the Elizabethan age, in his translation of Homer made famous by Keats's memorable sonnet, Chapman, lacking spiritual vision, had the temerity to handle the sacred vessels of Greek art with the substantial grasp of the barbarian. And even Pope, great poet though he was, with his dull literalness and formidable heroic couplet, thought to amend the morning freshness and the divine liquidity of the older poet's verse, simple as if it were singing itself in the streets of Athens amidst her primitive, vigorous sons by the sources of the river of time. While Homer's poetry has by modern criticism been restored in the full integrity of its text, it is still too often the pitiable victim of a mousing and pedestrian scholarship.

The literalists have time and again tried to improve on the wisdom and consummate art of Shakespeare, the loftiest of all the singers that time is heir to. These literary formalists by false standards of excellence so perverted the tastes as to obscure from many generations of Englishmen the richness of Shakespeare in truth to the universal and his ministry to the imaginative reason and to all the elements by which the human spirit, if it would live aright, has chiefly to live.

To come to a document with which Americans are more familiar, the Constitution of the United States, though expounded by a slowly changing body that is supposed to be remote from the moods of the multitude, has yet felt the tendency of the age to abandon word-by-word interpretation and to put the spirit above the letter; for, as Mr. Dooley half seriously observed, the decisions of the Supreme Court always follow the election returns.

There has likewise been a period of strict construction of the Bible. A willingness to rest in the literal meaning rather than to find and apply its universal significance has many a time played havoc with the Scriptures. This Pharisaic tendency to give to the literal, the temporary, and the local, the place that belongs to the spiritual, the abiding, and the universal, has often not only completely distorted the meaning of the Bible but it has vitiated Christian life. And by it the fine enthusiasm for goodness has been turned into heat for some favorite interpretation or some particular form of belief. This religious intensity, good in itself but diverted by a wrong interpretation of the Bible, has unfortunately been reinforced by another trait in human nature. Man in his state of nature is a gregarious animal; in the next place he is the member of a clan; and in a later stage of development he is an adherent of a faction, a sect, or a party. This blind championship of neighborhood interests, community feelings, inherited prejudices, and preconceived opinions, transmitted as it is from primitive conditions, is an inborn bias that is hard to resist; and the ability to see the other man's point of view and to enter into sympathy with him who holds antagonistic beliefs is the mark and final test of a cultivated man. The natural tendency to clannishness, partisanship, and separatism has caused many a man in the past to devote to party or sect or faction gifts that were meant for mankind, and is responsible for the religious wars and persecutions of the Dark Ages which make up one of the saddest chapters in human history, as it is also responsible for the later warfare of religion and science, itself almost as destructive as the feuds of faith in the remoter past. It is responsible, too, for sectionalism which curses all people, or the dissidence that sets men into warring political camps, arrays the country

against the town, creates social, literary, financial, and hereditary castes, and fixes impassable gulfs between innumerable factions that ought to stand shoulder to shoulder in the conflicts
of modern life. We have in our time lost something of the old
ardor and intensity of other times, and these were in themselves good. We must make up for this loss by sympathetic
and aggressive co-operation on the part of all good men in
every cause that makes for progress and improvement. We
must acquire a speaking and working acquaintance with men
good and true in every class and station.

I am not here arguing for the destruction of religious denominations and political parties. They will always have their
place, I doubt not. But the old partisanship, bitterness, and
unfairness, now so fast passing away, ought to pass completely.
Churchmen of all denominations ought to work heartily together for the good of their fellows; and citizens, especially
now that we are entering upon what promises to be an uncommonly bitter national campaign, should bear in mind that patriotic men of all parties are equally concerned in the welfare
of our common country. Every Christian man and every good
citizen, I believe, must have breadth of view and comprehensive sympathies. That these are coming is one of the hopeful
signs of our time.

Close akin to the first is the second sign of promise of which
I will speak—the tendency, in recent times so pronounced, to
shift the emphasis from correctness of creed to soundness of
life. I do not mean to intimate that sound living does not still
rest on sound thinking. But the erecting of an ancient confes-
sion of faith into the seat of authority has produced a false
conservatism, an insistence upon regularity of experience and
profession that have at times made religious sects a clog on
human progress. This insistence too on correctness of creed
rather than vital religion is apt to breed empty profession and
orthodox formalism—an intellectual and spiritual sluggish-
ness that is froward in its retention of outworn forms rather

than conservative of the simple, essential spirit of Christianity.

The shifting of emphasis from formal profession and correctness of creed to one's actual work and the spirit in which one works has for a good while been steadily going on, and has today become almost completely effected. And no greater incentive to true religion could be given than to make universal the standard that judges men, not by what they profess to be and believe, but by the amount of Christian service they give and by the spirit in which they give it. The only check I can see to the complete setting up of this standard throughout Christendom is an assertive so-called liberalism that, decrying all creeds, makes some good and earnest men react in the opposite direction. Of course dogma has its place in religion, and the tendency of which I speak does not make for the weakening of this, but for a shifting of emphasis from creed to life. It is not that we may have a new creed but a new and fuller life; a religion not like that of the Middle Ages, a matter of the intellect, but like that of primitive Christianity, a religion of the whole of life. This extension of the scope of religion makes it not a consideration for the future but for the present, not for one day in the week but for every day, and for all men. This conception of religion held by the devouter souls of all times is being more widely accepted and is resulting in the widening of religious activities. "The salt of the earth" touches more of human life; "the light of the world" shines further.

These tendencies do not rest on the discovery of new truths but on the old eternal verities made strong again by being stripped of intellectual confusions that through human imperfections have gathered about them in the passing of the centuries. But the two converging tendencies do create a new opportunity for the church in America in our time, an opportunity to touch life at more points than ever before. A few years ago Christian America united in efforts for an old-time revival of religion. The result was in a form perhaps unlooked for; for it was, I believe, a wave of reform that reached every phase of national life. This movement created by the conscience of the country has been taken up by self-seeking men and with characteristic American excess has in many cases gone to all kinds of extremes; but at bottom it is sound and is symptomatic of that saving quality in the nation that is to preserve it.

The slackening of the coherent force of creeds and the less ardent communion of minds in convictions of a common belief will be more than made up for by a spiritual union and by the bond of a common service.

Now, I hope that no one will think I have been preaching a gospel of good works. I realize with great distinctness that what one does depends absolutely on what one is; and the "what is" is therefore first to be attended to rather than the "what does." The chief business of the church will always be to keep the sources of life fresh and strong, and the fruits may be depended on to be sound and growing. "Seek ye first the Kingdom of God and His righteousness, and all these things shall be added unto you" is not only an authoritative promise but is a truth enforced by all experience. This is the true religion of the past and the religion of the future.

Resting upon old and everlasting truths I have ventured to sound this note of encouragement because we are so accustomed in our time to hearing pessimistic jeremiads, because there is hesitancy and uncertainty in so many directions, and because our minds are brought so constantly into touch with the mire and poisons of the world that Christian America needs to be reassured by renewed faith and hope. My faith is that a religion like this will lift the race from the low ground of intellectual miasma into the uplands of the liberty of the true sons of God.

WILLIAM GARROTT BROWN*

WILLIAM GARROTT BROWN in the exile of a long illness died at New Canaan, Connecticut, October 19, 1913. In his untimely death the cause of letters in America sustained a serious loss; for while his field was American history and politics rather than literature, he yet possessed in a remarkable degree the equipment of a man of letters. It is idle to speculate concerning his achievement had the circumstances of his life allowed the full development of his talents. One thing is certain; he had to a degree rare in our time and country the ability to think clearly and to write with distinction.

The facts of his life are easily recited. He was born at Marion, Alabama, April 24, 1868, the youngest son of Richard Wilson and Mary Cogwell (Parish) Brown. His father's family had come from Virginia, and his mother's from North Carolina. He graduated from Howard College in 1886 and afterwards served as instructor in the Marion Military Institute, both institutions being at that time located in his native

* The South Atlantic Quarterly, XIII (January, 1914), 69-74.

village. In 1889 he entered the junior class at Harvard University. He took his A.B. at Harvard with the highest honors in history in 1891. He continued his university studies in history and allied subjects. He received the degree of A.M. in 1892 and for the eight following years he held a position in the Harvard Library. During the year 1901-02 he was lecturer in American history.

An inherited tendency to deafness and growing ill health were a bar to an academic career; and writing became his profession. Never really sound of body, he ten years ago developed tuberculosis. Before he discovered it the disease had so strong a hold on him that it could not be overcome, and henceforth he had to fight for his life.

Brown was born and spent his early life in Alabama, before that state had had time to recover from the bad effects of the Civil War, the worse effects of Reconstruction, and the long convalescence that had to follow these. He thus shared in this "saddest fact in all the world"; and he felt himself to be, as he once wrote, an heir to all the sorrow and all the tortured pride of it. In a very peculiar sense, then, for him the time was out of joint; and it was the cursed spite of his life that he, like any other serious-minded man, felt a call to set it right.

One of the most remarkable pieces of writing he ever did is his essay called "The Foe of Compromise," in which he makes a finely scrupulous inquiry into that something which "forever rises up in men, as men like Garrison and Morley and the radicals of other times, have risen up in all societies, to fight with compromise, whatever form it takes." In this essay is embedded a great deal of Brown's own character. He had within himself the same sort of longing for a completeness which life cannot give. He too wanted better bread than was ever made of wheat. This straining to see life whole kept him from "that peace for which mankind, in all lands, all languages, to all their gods, forever pray."

[311]

These circumstances and the response of his temperament to these circumstances were in his case peculiarly unfortunate. "For," as he wrote in his well-known preface to *The Lower South in American History*, "my true task like many another task of many another man, must wait for better days: for days of confident mornings and calm evenings. Such his days and nights must be, and firm his will must be, his mind at peace, his silence undistracted, who would enter into the body of this civilization which I have tried to intimate with outlines, and make it live again through these and other of its times and seasons, he also living in it, and dying in it and rising in it again."

These confident mornings and calm evenings never came; and yet Brown achieved results of lasting significance. His published volumes include *Official Guide to Harvard University*, 1899; *A History of Alabama*, 1900; *Andrew Jackson*, 1900; and *Stephen Arnold Douglas*, 1902, in the Riverside Biographical Series; *The Lower South in American History*, 1902; *Golf*, 1902; *A Gentleman of the South*, a novel, 1903; *The Foe of Compromise and Other Essays*, 1903; *Life of Oliver Ellsworth*, 1905.

During the last decade most of his writing was for such periodicals as the *Youth's Companion*, the New York *Evening Post*, the *Atlantic Monthly*. And for six years he wrote the political paragraphs for *Harper's Weekly*. He kept this up until the sale of the *Weekly* to Norman Hapgood a few weeks before his death; and he made a national reputation for that paper, although his hand in it was unknown to the public. When the worst came and he had to do his reading and writing in bed, neither Robert Louis Stevenson himself nor any other knight of the pen ever gave himself to his work with more wholehearted resignation or heroic devotion. When his health broke down Brown was engaged in writing a life of General Grant. He was also at work on a "History of the United States in Our Own Times." Several striking chapters from this were printed in the *Atlantic Monthly*. The material for both these works was destroyed in the burning of Kenilworth Inn at Asheville, where he was at the time living.

Brown and I lived together at Harvard College during the years from 1893 to 1896, and we have been intimate lifelong friends. I feel that I have perhaps been too close to him to speak justly of his talents, his character, or his achievements. I am going to quote recent statements from three men of national reputation. Bliss Perry, for many years editor of the *Atlantic Monthly* and well-known author, closes a short tribute to Brown in the *Harvard Alumni Bulletin* for October 26 with this striking paragraph:

The men who knew him tried to define his indescribable charm of speech and behavior, but they fell back helplessly upon some such word as "thoroughbred." His courtesy was exquisite. He bore his handicap of deafness with the finest dignity, and with a deprecatory humor which was delicately perfect. But his deafness was a serious obstacle to an academic career, and he turned finally to literature,—only to discover that he had to battle, and as it proved, in vain, against tuberculosis. He made for ten years a gallant fight, which has just ended. No one can say what he might have accomplished with unimpaired health and a longer opportunity, but those who knew him believe that William Garrott Brown would have gone very far. And if he had never accomplished anything, they would have loved him none the less.

Edward S. Martin, literary editor of *Life* and author of many books, in the *Harvard Graduates' Magazine* for December has written:

Brown's loss of health was a national misfortune. His historical and political equipment was very unusual indeed, and coupled with his talent as a writer and his very noble and disinterested character, made him a rare man for whom distinguished employment was certain to have sought if only he had had the physical powers to undertake it. It is surprising what scarcity there is in our time and country of men qualified to undertake such employments as offered to him. A contemporary speaks of him as "the

[313]

man of most promise as a historian turned out by Harvard's Historical Department in the last 25 years."

In the recently published letters of Charles Eliot Norton there is reference to Brown in a letter to Samuel G. Ward, of Washington, the friend and correspondent of Emerson.

I was interrupted the other day, and had no chance to resume my letter before the arrival of three interesting guests who came from Colorado Springs, from Chicago, and from Alabama (by way of Cambridge) to take part, on last Thursday, in our Annual Dinner. I have sent to you a report of the speeches on that occasion, and, though you will not approve altogether of their doctrine, you will be interested in the manner in which it is set forth, and especially in the substance of the speech (which was not delivered) of my young friend, Mr. Garrott Brown, of Alabama. Perhaps you have seen some of his recent articles in the *Atlantic* and other magazines, or his lately published volume on "The Lower South in American History," a volume well worth reading.
He is a man of refined nature, sensitive, modest, of high character, and a strong and a cultivated intelligence. His studies of the South have special value from his intimate knowledge of the field, and from his inherited sentiment for the old conditions, and his clear appreciation of the new. He is greatly hampered in social relations by deafness, but he is so entirely a gentleman that his disability stands little in his way. I commend his book to you.

Mr. Perry's words suggest something of Brown's remarkable personality. Something of this "thoroughbred" quality is found ingrained in all his writing. His style has distinction; and when on occasion it rises to the height of some great argument it becomes charged with a sort of eloquence that is rarely equaled in the writing of any other man of our time.
Mr. Martin speaks of Brown's historical and political equipment as having been very unusual indeed. He inherited keen interest in politics. He had been steeped in it in youth in his native Alabama and went to Massachusetts just at the time of the national resurgence of the Democratic party. He was

actively engaged in the organization and management of the Harvard Democratic Club in the Cleveland campaign and did a great deal of speaking throughout Massachusetts for Cleveland. He was an ardent supporter of William E. Russell, for four terms the Democratic governor of Massachusetts. He made in one of his essays the keenest analysis of American parties that has ever been written. In *Harper's Weekly* during recent years Brown espoused the cause of Woodrow Wilson both before and after his election to the presidency.

Mr. Norton remarks that Brown's studies of the South have especial value from his inherited sentiment for the old conditions and for his clear appreciation of the new. His "inherited sentiment for the old" and "clear appreciation of the new" gave him an extraordinary fitness for writing about Southern history. He hoped eventually to write an adequate history of our Civil War setting forth the human forces at play in this greatest tragedy of modern times. I have frequently heard him speak with the utmost enthusiasm and conviction about this, declaring that the man who could do it fitly would live as long as Thucydides. We are not likely to have soon among us another man so well fitted for this task; and the ending of his life before the completion of the task makes his death a national misfortune.

I wish to bear this personal tribute to the memory of my departed friend: he had sheer intellectual honesty as I have never observed it in any other man; he had the rare courage to face life squarely, to lead forlorn hopes and to die in last ditches, and when he could see no hope, even the "courage to despair"; he had a genius for friendship, and he was loved by all high-minded men who ever came within the range of his winning personality. America has lost a man of talent, maimed and dead ere his prime. But above and beyond this loss, those of us who loved William Garrott Brown have felt that in his death something of tenderness and beauty and glory has passed from the earth.

SPOKEN AT THE FUNERAL OF JOSEPH G. BROWN, RALEIGH, N. C., JANUARY 31, 1927*

WE ARE A GREAT HOST GATHERED as we are here today for the last time about the body of our dear departed friend. We come from all professions and all ranks of life. We represent many varieties of opinion and experience. But we are all of one mind concerning Mr. Brown. He was one man about whom there can be no serious differences of opinion. We have here, too, a community of feeling. This man's death is the one "touch of nature" that makes akin practically the entire city of Raleigh and a large part of North Carolina.

Why this extraordinary uniformity of opinion and unity of feeling that we see here today? Mr. Brown was a normal man. He had the traits of character that make a universal appeal. We all stand in admiration and reverence before the oneness, the wholeness, the completeness of the man's life and personality and the issues of this harmonious development of the whole man in his activities, his character, and his influence. There were no moral, intellectual, or even physical "insurrec-

* *Duke University Alumni Register*, March, 1927, pp. 78-79.

tions in his kingdom of man." His physical, mental, and spiritual constitution was not a house divided against itself. There was a consolidation of all his resources and a concentration of the last thing that was in him, and all this was always available whenever evoked by the crises of life. Whatever direction he might turn his effort at any given time he was "all there." He succeeded in many ways, and he achieved success because he himself was success.

In business he was very successful. Equipped as he was, how could it have been otherwise? But even in business he worked not primarily for himself—he worked for others; for depositors, for patrons, for shareholders—for the public. Here was a man who spent a lifetime in business, working through approved business methods and achieving business success; and yet he was always concerned more for others than for himself.

He gave himself unstintedly to public service in the best sense of those words. Throughout a long life he served his neighbors in countless ways, the city of Raleigh where he was born and where he lived all his life. He served the state many years and in many ways. He served important causes of the national government, especially during the Great War. Indeed I think he never recovered from the strain of the load he carried in those hard years. All this was done without expectation of reward.

He was pre-eminently a servant of the causes of education. In 1871 he entered Trinity College, now a part of Duke University. From that day until his death he served the institution through every stage of its development and in every sort of way—as loyal son, as patron, as benefactor, as trustee for thirty-four years and as president of the Board of Trustees for ten years. He served other institutions. He was educationally minded. He had the spirit of youth and could work at the tasks of education with an understanding heart. He was the kind of man, the only kind of man, that can succeed or even be useful in intimate work with youth. He deserves to live among those who through guidance and inspiration of the young have most effectively served their day and generation.

He had a deep religious nature and experience. Beginning here at this church in boyhood, out through the state, and everywhere, he devoted his time, his money, himself to the church, to the orphans, to charities, to all good works, "for the glory of the Creator and the relief of man's estate." He was earnest but never narrow; he had intense convictions but was without a trace of bitterness.

What were the products of all this—of his rich inheritance in a strong body, a good intellect, and right tendencies; of his inner moral adjustment; and of the discipline of years rightly lived? One product was a mind that always ran true to form. He was finely adjusted to life and this adjustment gave him a sort of moral instinct that carried him to his tasks with something of the inevitableness of the natural instinct that compels the bird to build its nest and to sing its songs. Thinking back, as I have been thinking for the past twenty-four hours, over many years of intimate association with Mr. Brown and others in tasks and problems that have sometimes been intricate and difficult I have not been able to recall one instance when it seemed to me that he did not think straight and think through to right conclusions. This sort of intuitive wisdom does not come out of the intellect alone but out of the full, harmonious development of all a man's capacities and powers. As we all well know, Mr. Brown had in an unusual degree this precious gift of unerring wisdom.

Another product was an all-pervading goodness. He was rightly in tune with the Infinite, and it seemed to be more nearly natural for him to do right than for almost any other man I have ever known. He lived here all his life. I dare to challenge the memory of any of you and I care not how long you have known him, can you recall many, if any, occasions when you felt that he did wrong?

It has been said that the beautiful is higher than the good because it includes the good—it is the good made perfect. At any rate Mr. Brown's inner character flowered also in beauty, a beauty that showed itself even in physical excellence. He had a clean and fine face that none but a good and wise man could ever wear. He had a personal charm and winsomeness. I recently heard a little boy say the men he loved most were his father and Mr. Brown. This is typical of the feeling of children, of youth, of adults. None knew him but to love him.

The quiet, useful, and happy life of this man is an unanswerable argument for our Christian religion. That sort of living and witness-bearing on the part of Christians and a new emphasis by all our preachers upon the plain teachings of Jesus and upon Jesus himself as the Way of Life, and the Only Way of Life—these are the things for which this troubled age of ours is impatiently waiting; and these, too, are the things that would bring about the greatest revival of essential Christianity the world has ever known.

There's the worth of this man's example, and there's the heritage of his life—sweet, abiding, consoling to all who knew him and who may know of him in the after-years, to you his neighbors and friends, and above all to you, his sorrowing loved ones.

BENJAMIN N. DUKE
THE MAN WHO LIVED FOR OTHERS*

MR. DUKE'S DEATH came after many years of invalidism; and in his last years he was in constant confinement and extreme illness. During these years of his isolation from life we have already been in position to see his career with something of the perspective of history. On some of his last birthdays I undertook to speak of his life in just the way I believed that history would record it in the long after-years. I wrote out for newspapers what I had said on one of these occasions; and he read it. He was good enough afterwards to tell me that he liked it better than anything ever written about him because he thought that every word of it was true. I mention this now to bring out one of the most characteristic things about him—his utter sincerity and his devotion to the simple truth. I use the incident also to emphasize the folly of exaggeration. I shall on this occasion be at even more pains, if possible, than hereto-

* Delivered at a special Chapel service, January 24, 1929. *Duke University Alumni Register*, February, 1929, pp. 50-52. Mr. Duke died at his home in New York, January 8, 1929.

fore to speak words of soberness and truth about our great benefactor and our dear departed friend.

We have in other years found opportunities to pay tribute to the services and to the character of Mr. Duke's father, Washington Duke, and to the services and to the character of his brother, James B. Duke; and since now the last of the three is gone and since their lives were so interlocked, it seems to me that it will be profitable to consider as a whole and in some of their larger aspects the contributions the Dukes have made to civilization. I fully realize that there were many others who had a part in it all, and I know they would wish others to have due credit; but it is the sober truth to say that the industries which they led in developing made a world market for the products of North Carolina farms and so laid the foundations for the later prosperity of the state. The value of this particular service may from time to time have been obscured by temporary confusions in thinking; but I believe it is bound to stand as one of the significant facts in the history of North Carolina. Even more significant is their leadership in the development of hydroelectric power. They had a share in all forms of our progress, but the two I have mentioned, to go no further, will be sufficient to make them for all time outstanding industrial leaders, not only in the state but in the nation.

But progress cannot be built alone on factories and farms and hydroelectric power. It requires also a sound climate of opinion, and to this the Dukes have made the largest contributions. They came up out of the grinding poverty that followed the Civil War. They lived through a period of intense sectionalism and bitterness, but the character of all of them came out untouched by these fires of adversity. They refused to live in a dead past or blindly to conform to the traditions of that past. They were quick to realize that the war was over and that there was a new day in the South. They had the vision to see this new day and the courage to live in the light

of it. This often brought them into conflict with local sentiment. But they went on, and they were always patient and
tolerant of others. In their business, their friendships, their
gifts, they knew no distinctions as to religion, politics, race, or
social class. They had many obstacles to overcome, but they
succeeded in their great undertakings. They not only called
us to better things but they showed us the way. We are indebted to them and to the illustrious examples they have set
us for the promotion of freedom of opinion, liberality, tolerance, and catholicity. To their influence and to their examples more than to any other single thing we owe the sound
and wholesome public opinion here that at this time gives
North Carolina its high place among the commonwealths of
this nation.

Their influence and example have been formative and powerful in another way. The Dukes have been the greatest philanthropists the South has ever produced, and their gifts to
education have been equaled but a very few times anywhere
(indeed but twice, I believe), in the history of the world.
These contributions have come not only from father and sons
but also from grandchildren and other members of the family.
Following in the footsteps of his grandfather, Mr. Washington Duke, and of his parents, Mr. and Mrs. B. N. Duke, Angier B. Duke, like his sister Mrs. A. J. Drexel Biddle, gave
generously to the College during his life, and, dying in 1923,
left it a handsome bequest and other bequests for church and
orphanage support.

These three men were much alike. Washington Duke, I
have always thought, much resembled Abraham Lincoln, particularly in his homely humor, his tenderness, patience, charity
and wisdom. As a pioneer in industrial development, as the
leader in philanthrophy who stands first in time and first in
ideals, as the father of famous sons, he has won a secure place
in the history of the state. James B. Duke had a power of
vision and achievement that made him one of the mightiest

men of his generation, and he takes rank with the foremost philanthropists of all time. Benjamin N. Duke, beginning as trustee of Trinity College in 1889, was the first of them to become interested in the promotion of higher education. He co-operated with and stimulated his father's interest in it, his brother's, his own family's, and other people's. There is a real sense in which he has been a leader and inspirer of the Duke family in their great philanthropies which in the grand total will run from $90,000,000.00 to $100,000,000.00, and this alone would give him a secure place in history.

During the past thirty-eight years and in bequests announced after his death he has himself given away many millions of dollars,—to Trinity College, to Duke University, and to a multitude of institutions, individuals, and all kinds of good causes. His latest notable gift is the Angier B. Duke Loan and Scholarship Fund, totaling $1,000,000.00, and established at Duke University as a memorial to his son who graduated there in 1905. There was to an unusual degree a personal element in Mr. B. N. Duke's giving. All through life he gave not only his money, he gave himself; and he had a wide range of interests and sympathy. Wherever there was a human need his heart responded. He was one of the noblest men that ever lived.

The father and sons all loved their fellow-men, and they had an eager desire to serve others and to serve every good cause. We North Carolinians can never fully know how much we owe to these men, not only for their industrial and financial leadership, for what they did and for what they directly gave, but also for the power of their example, for the ideals they have created, for the tendencies they have started, for the influences and institutions which they have set agoing and which will go on doing good as long as American civilization endures.

The most far-reaching of all their services to civilization is the fostering through thirty-odd years of Trinity College, and finally the building of Duke University around it. Indeed the building of a great endowed university at Durham is an outstanding event in the history of the state and in the history of the country. An endowed university of commanding power has always been the most serious lack in the southeastern states.

Through a period of more than thirty years Mr. B. N. Duke every year gave money to Trinity College in ways and amounts that have made possible the institution as we have known it. He did far more than this. Through a large part of this period he was the support and the inspiration of the men who as teachers and educational administrators have made the institution in the past generation and are here to carry it into the future. For nearly forty years he carried Trinity College and Duke University on his heart. He thought of it by day and by night, and he kept this up to the hour of his death. By the stimulus of his generous gifts and inspiring personality, the College was developed to the point where it might become the center round which could be built the University that his brother's magnificence founded in December, 1924. He will always hold a high place in the history of Duke University and of American education. A great institution must rest upon many shoulders. The man serves it best who most enlists cooperation, who works to get the thing done and cares not who receives the credit for it. Here is where this great-hearted man shines. He will always stand out as an illustrious example of a man who linked his life to an undying institution in which he believed with the whole heart, who stood by it through evil as well as good report, and who sought for himself nothing except to him the sweet and precious privilege of serving his fellow-men.

MAKING EDUCATION MORE CREATIVE*

I RECOGNIZE THAT YOURS is a school of technology, but I also know that it is not just a training or trade school but an educational institution. Since we are meeting tonight under the auspices of an honor society I will ask you to think with me from the educational rather than the technical standpoint. The call today upon American colleges of every kind is, I think, to improve the quality of education.

We need a unified program of education that will consider the interests of the student in his several stages from the primary grades to the university. That is to say, we need what we have talked a good deal about in America and have never had, a genuine "educational ladder." The student, not the subject matter, must become more and more the center of interest and effort. The student must be made more and more to participate in his own education and not remain just a passive learner, must look at his education from a creative standpoint rather than take it in like a jug. He must, too, be brought

* Phi Kappa Phi Address at the Georgia School of Technology, Friday Night, December 1, 1933.

to realize that education is a lifelong process. The new education will stress personal, social, and moral elements in education; and will expect to be judged by its product—fruits in the soundness of men.

But can we bring a larger proportion of our undergraduates beyond the surface of things and into touch with the great essential realities, and so make education more creative—creative in scholarship, in literature and the other arts, in culture, in character, and in service to country, to causes and to humanity? And if so, how can this be done?

A half century ago one of the most promising poets of his generation in England abandoned the writing of poetry and gave as his reason that his age had fallen upon a time of unsettlement and speculative thinking that fitted it for analysis and criticism rather than for creative work of any kind. Eighteen hundred years earlier the foremost prophet of the Christian centuries had sounded a note of warning against the coming of confused and perilous times when men would be ever learning and never able to come to a knowledge of the truth. Was Matthew Arnold right in his belief that a bustling intellectualism, keen and erudite though it be, may nevertheless disturb that poise and silence which must precede all creation; and was St. Paul right in his inspired intuition that a man may learn and learn and yet never be able to come to a knowledge of the truth; and are there any indications that we have fallen upon these "last times" foreshadowed in the words of the great apostle and discerned in the keen analysis of the shrewd English critic?

I have no railing accusation to bring against our age as compared with other ages. Despite frequent lapses (one of them lasted four hundred years and we call it the Dark Ages)—despite that turbid ebb and flow which thoughtful men have observed in all human history, I am persuaded that the main course of tendency and taste is upward and onward forever. Yet if the sons of Martha with the careful soul and the troubled heart may be so cumbered about with much serving that they fail to choose "that good part"; if there is now a peculiar danger that the mind of man may be so careful and troubled about the many unessential things that it fails to find rest in ultimate principles; if, in short, men can be so preoccupied with getting facts as to leave them no leisure to seek the truth, then this circumstance ought to be brought to the attention of all thoughtful people, especially of educational leaders and future educational leaders, who like us today face a time of seriousness and high endeavor but also of extraordinary confusion.

The importance of keeping clear this distinction between the essential and the unessential, between truth and fact I shall seek to enforce with familiar illustrations that, I hope, will be appropriate to an occasion like this. Perhaps the principle can be most easily illustrated by reference to well-known pieces of literature. For example, Keats' sonnet on first looking into Chapman's Homer gives a fine expression of the feeling that one has when one really learns something or accomplishes something—the feeling of "some watcher of the skies when a new planet swims into his ken"; and this is one of the noblest English sonnets, in spite of the fact that the poet in it makes "stout Cortez" and not Balboa the discoverer of the Pacific:

> Or like stout Cortez when with eagle eyes
> He stared at the Pacific—and all his men
> Looked at each other with a wild surmise—
> Silent, upon a peak in Darien.

We have no better example than these lines of that wizardry of words, that natural magic which characterizes English poetry at its highest. And yet to a mind of a too critical bent this historical inaccuracy would ruin the effect of the sonnet, while to a sincere and sensible student of poetry it makes the least possible difference. The point I wish to make is that this error as to fact does not affect the truth of the poem—its truth to art or its truth to life. Again, *Hamlet* is an idealized and universalized world tragedy. It may not be, and is not, true to the facts of Danish history of the twelfth or thirteenth century. The scene of it, as Lowell has said, is laid in a Denmark that has no dates. But it embodies a phase of human experience that will always be true to human nature. It is thereby lifted into the domain of the universal; and so becomes suggestive and interesting to men in all generations. It transcends the world of fact and reaches up into that of universal truth. Those who have the best to say naturally have the best way of saying it; and this universal truth in *Hamlet* is expressed in a final, felicitous, adequate, and enduring form. And for these reasons *Hamlet* will probably stand as a master work among men forever, while its errors of fact are and will be only matters of interest to the curious and the learned.

So, too, the *Iliad* lies beyond the ken of history. But it dallies with the innocence of life in the old age so sincerely, it sees with a plainness so near and flashing, it sets forth the doings of men and gods on the sounding plains of Troy with so simple a beauty and so much fidelity to universal experience that its words echo still. The *Iliad* comes to us out of a far, forgotten past, and is an abiding proof of the triumph of universal truth over historical fact. Wherever there be mere knowledge it shall pass away. It is never the material but the ideal that abides and commands.

I am not seeking to lead you away from actuality, certainly not from reality. All great poetry, like all great art, like great deeds and great character, must rest upon a true view of life. The poet must see life truly, must understand himself and things in general, must have a deep knowledge of life as it is. There can be nothing great or beautiful in poetry or art or life or character that is not ultimately based upon the truth.

> Beauty is truth, truth beauty—that is all
> Ye know on earth, and all ye need to know.

The beautiful includes the true; it is the true made perfect. This "true made perfect" is what great poetry everywhere gives us and it is with the purpose to find this rather than with an inquisitorial yearning for facts that we should always approach the study of poetry.

In reading literature it is always relevant to ask "is it true?" but often impertinent to ask "is it a fact?" And the higher we go in the scale of values the more earnestly need we to give heed to this distinction. In the parable of Lazarus and Dives or the Book of Job it is of course a thousand times more useful to get the kernel of truth they contain rather than to inquire if they are founded in actual historical circumstances. Indeed the bane of Biblical scholarship of yesterday was just this centering of the main interest in the pursuit of facts; in the study of sources, the comparing of analogues, and the indulgence in unsupported inferences, to the neglect of the fundamental duty to find the plain meaning of the Bible and to partake of the spiritual vitality and energy that beat there with the divine pulse of its original.

These are but illustrations; the same sort of confusion has been at work in the field of modern scholarship in general. It grows increasingly difficult to master facts and to find one's way to the truth. A comparatively small body of truth is adequate for the guidance of any man's life. But there is now more uncertainty as to what these truths are. There results a Babel of warring voices and universal confusion of life. The details of knowledge have become so extensive that it requires more grasp of mind to comprehend them. It is easier to be a sort of expert in a limited field of knowledge, but more difficult to be a master of one's subject. The college therefore has increasing difficulty in finding for its teachers true masters of learning, men of ideas and power rather than technical experts in the several branches of scholarship.

The flux of ideas regarding true educational values has led to a lack of solidarity in college curricula and administration that is producing a widespread feeling, whether just or unjust, that the college of today does not make so surely for moral and intellectual efficiency as did the college of other days. The college has certainly in some ways gained, and perhaps in others it has lost ground. The old curriculum with its fixed studies and severe disciplines has been liberalized and enriched. American colleges have grown and have improved their facilities for education until, in the matter of educational opportunities, the best of them are perhaps unexcelled in the world. But it is becoming increasingly clear that it is not enough for the college to provide the richest of opportunities for its students, and then unconcernedly leave them to use or neglect the opportunities as they may see fit. Ways and means must be found to make education take effect. The educational appliances must somehow be brought into live connection with undergraduate callowness.

I have not time now to follow this discussion into the field of social and political reform where we are apt to rely on shifting expedients rather than trust to tried and guiding principles, or into an inquiry into the chief aims of our whole national endeavor, where we overstress the value of deeds, of achievements, of comfort and physical well-being, or into the whole trend of our life, which is to put fact above truth, the temporal and the local above the abiding and universal, the material above the ideal, the mind above the spirit, and so everywhere bigness above greatness. I merely suggest to you how these tendencies must affect colleges and college administration.

Let us try to hold ourselves and, so far as we can, our institutions to the main things; to develop in ourselves and our students the power to know the truth and the will to live it. Vocational and industrial education is to be valued, not primarily because it will make wage-earners and increase the wealth of the nations, but because it may be used to develop competence and character. Scientific studies are of little educational value if they end in a knowledge of the laws of nature, and not in such a fashioning of the affections and the will as to make us live in loving obedience to those laws. In historical, economic, philosophical, social investigations an earnest, even reverent, search for the truth is not high enough motive, but the rule of righteousness in the world. Art should be prized, as even Whitman has said, in proportion to the radiation through art of the ultimate truths of conscience and of conduct. And books for educational uses should be rated in accordance with their formative and sustaining power. Education will begin to fulfil its great meaning and mission when it learns that intellect itself is a function of personality. It must find and control the motives that lie at the basis of all character. The emotions and affections, and that strange precipitation of them which we call the will—admiration, faith, hope, love— these make mankind. And to reach these is the great aim of education.

SPOKEN AT THE FUNERAL OF DR. WILLIAM IVEY CRANFORD, DUKE UNIVERSITY CHAPEL, AUGUST 31, 1936*

IT WAS FORTY YEARS AGO next week when I came to Durham to cast in my lot with this people. The first week I was here I was brought into intimate contacts with Dr. Cranford and his lovely family circle. I had just come from Harvard University, and he had recently come from Yale. I found that he was familiar with the Greek philosophers, that he had been trained in a school of philosophy, and by nature was at home in a kind of philosophy, that does not point humanity the steep and thorny way to invincible pessimism, but rather leads to the calm that alone is joy and the victory that alone is peace. By nature and by training he knew something of the matured wisdom and the sweet uses of philosophy.

He had, I soon discovered, a beautiful and lucid mind, rare as excellence itself, and a spirit as guileless as Nathaniel's. It was easy to fall in love with a man like that. I fell in love with him, and he has held my admiration, my gratitude, and my affection through all the vicissitudes of these forty years.

* *Duke University Alumni Register*, September, 1936, p. 224.

At the Funeral of William Ivey Cranford

I came to know him not only as an individual man, I knew him as a member of the College, and later the University, community. He was loyal, competent, and unselfish—a rare combination and the sort of man that is to an educational administrator as the shadow of a great rock in a weary land.

He was a wise and a good man, than which I can say nothing higher of any human being. "They that be wise shall shine as the brightness of the firmament, and they that turn many to righteousness as the stars for ever and ever." Dr. Cranford shines among the brightest of all those who have here lit their torches and in turn passed them on to others.

The life of this man can have no ending. It is a great and an abiding influence among us and will pass on to those who come after us in the unending succession of sons and daughters that constitutes the precious immortality of a great educational foundation.

We loved him, we admired him, we seek to follow him; for by his beautiful life he has ever lured us to brighter worlds and through his essential goodness has led the way.

An institution like this is a storehouse of learning, with its libraries and its laboratories and its scholars; but it is also an accumulated heritage of high and inspiring personalities, and now another beautiful and noble spirit takes a secure place in the great tradition.

*DOES AN AMERICAN UNIVERSITY HAVE
RESPONSIBILITY FOR THE SOCIAL AND
MORAL IDEALS AND PRACTICES OF ITS
STUDENTS AND GRADUATES?* *

THERE IS GENERAL RECOGNITION of the obligation of a university to seek knowledge and to transmit it, to dedicate itself to the disinterested pursuit of truth and the defense of it at all costs. This University fully recognizes this obligation. But in addition to this, and particularly in times of uncertainty like the present, does this University have any word for you concerning your duties to your country and to the great social and moral causes that undergird the country? It would be in bad taste for me to use an occasion like this for partisan or political discussion. I am going to avoid that, but if telling you the truth as I see it today should seem to you to have political implications, that I cannot help.

I hope you will think of me as a friend speaking to younger friends going out into a time of unsettlement, when old and tried things seem to be giving way to the untried. As I hope all of you know, I am a great believer in youth with its visions, its inexperience and venturesomeness, its purposes and its

* Baccalaureate Address, Duke University, Sunday Morning, June 6, 1937. *Duke University Alumni Register*, June, 1937, pp. 162-164.

hopes. I fully realize that you see the world with young eyes and ought to see it afresh. But seeing the world with your young eyes you will be helped in the effort to understand life if you avail yourselves of the lessons of history, if you know something of what the experience of the race has taught to be most worthwhile and most enduring. It is in this spirit of "friends in council" that I undertake now to tell you something of my understanding as to the responsibility that Duke University feels for the social and moral ideals and practices of its graduates.

You are practically all American citizens, or at any rate if any of you are not, you are interested in the great experiment in democratic government that is being tried out on American soil, in the American dream, as James Truslow Adams has called it, "the belief that it is possible to create an order of society in which, avoiding communistic restrictions upon individual initiative and acquisition, every man and woman would nevertheless have the opportunity of rising to full stature and living the fullest possible life of which they are capable." This belief, cherished by millions of people, while, of course, never fully realized, has nonetheless made this America the greatest republic in history. And the circumstance that practically all of you were born here gives you free and untrammeled citizenship in this republic and lays upon you the corresponding responsibility to use wisely and for the benefit of all mankind your priceless political inheritance; to cherish it, to preserve it unimpaired and even, if possible, bettered by this generation, to transmit it to the generations that are to come.

In times of uncertainty like the present, men have too frequently taken up extreme positions in one direction or another, and have run upon sudden and sharp disaster. They have paid too much heed to the past or too little. They have failed to see and ask for the old paths; or else they have been content not to walk but to stand therein. The world moves and we cannot stand still, yet change should always be gradual and slow, growing out of the past and into the future. Thus in every stage of development there would be nothing wholly novel and nothing wholly obsolete; organized society in all its forms and with all its institutions would be a sort of family inheritance, all fit and confederated with themselves. By this process the bad would be constantly eliminated and the good from whatever source constantly introduced. Only by this way of conservative progress can individuals and nations travel to prosperity and peace.

As Burke long ago pointed out, the legal doctrine of inheritance is an illustration of the right attitude of the present to preceding generations. By our law a son inherits property from his father. He holds the property, uses it, and, if he be wise, improves it and transmits it to succeeding generations. The doctrine of inheritance does not exclude the principle of improvement; it implies it. It leaves acquisition free, but it secures what has been acquired. True conservatism is not simply the holding on to the inheritance from the past but the keeping it free to improve it and transmit it bettered by each generation.

In matters of government the average man has in the past usually looked with too much reverence upon things as they are, and has strained to keep them fixed, until they became unendurable and led to reaction and revolution. But the trend throughout the world now seems to be radical rather than conservative. There has been a sudden emergence of the people in all governments everywhere. Everywhere the people are on the move. There are as a result wider social sympathies than ever known before. From the individualism that has hitherto belonged to civilization we are, temporarily at least, moving toward the communal state of mind, toward a community of feeling, a nationwide, even worldwide thinking in chorus. And there is growing up a respect for this mass judgment that is making it increasingly difficult to breed and sustain individual men with the courage to stand alone, and the

[336]

disinterestedness to serve the common good rather than to promote some form of selfishness or despotism. This is a brief but not an unfair setting forth of the predominant state of the popular mind in this and in perhaps all the great countries of the world.

This set of national and international conditions calls for leaders with courage, vision, and strength of character. But as a matter of fact, American political leaders all too often show an eagerness for office, a meek compliance with what they suppose to be the popular will, an indifference to the voice of duty and the demands of right, a disgraceful huckstering with circumstance; and all this creates a situation that is fraught with peril to our country.

Intellectual and emotional instability are the striking traits of public men and a hospitality of opinion that enables them to agree with whatever the people feel, I will not say think, at a given moment. Playing thus upon a fluent and shifting popular feeling demagogues become more dangerous than ever before in history. When such leader, conscious demagogue or self-deluded, seeks to concentrate power in himself rather than rely upon the checks and balances of representative government, then the next step, and it is an easy one, is dictatorship, either through Fascism or Communism, as the character of the people and the political institutions and traditions of a given country may make easiest at any given time. What is happening in the world today is an open book before you. And even in America vigilance is the price of liberty.

I believe democracy is the true goal of humanity. But if democracy endures it will not be because the people rule, but because through the people right is brought to pass. In weakly yielding to the rule of the people we may easily forget to insist on the rule of right. Truth is a thing to be sought diligently, and it is not to be found by consulting majorities. What we most need now is not leaders so fused with the throng that they are content to drift on the stream of popular sentiment, but rather those who have faith enough in men to risk preaching to them doctrines which at the moment happen to be unpopular.

Against this democratization of government and all other agencies for human well-being, I do not wish to see you react towards the authority that controlled in the past. Ours must always be a government of opinion and not of office, whether elective or hereditary. But this is a time when every educated man, every sober-minded citizen, should reflect deeply on his public duties, and should act in the light of his matured convictions, uninfluenced by the gusts of unwisdom that will arise at intervals in all societies.

It will not be inappropriate, I hope, on this occasion and in this place to call attention to the obligations that rest at this hour upon this intensely American part of the nation here in the Southern states. Southern men had a large share in the founding and building of the republic; and this fact ought to be a constant call to us at this crucial time to take our rightful places in the house which our fathers had so much to do in building. It may well be that destiny has placed into our hands the task of conserving fundamental traits which through us must be put again into the national life before our country can go on in security and strength to fulfil its mission in the world. It is a fact that the South is again today politically in the ascendancy. The chairmanship of the greater committees is in the hands of Southern members of Congress, as also the presidency of the Senate and the speakership of the House. Will our representatives now rise to their opportunities as did those great leaders in the age of the building of the republic? Or will they just respond in unbroken solidarity to old or new shibboleths and political leadership that has the proper label? I particularly hope they will not feel obliged to go with the multitude, but will rather heed the still, small voice of principle, of national honor and integrity. Thus might we achieve again the real greatness of our section and take our rightful places in the house which our fathers had so much to do with building, and contribute our part, as those who lived here before us contributed their part, to the greatness of our common country.

But however important they may be, correct political and social ideals and practices alone will not be sufficient to save this republic. It must be undergirded by the great moral causes that have sustained it from the beginning. Free America will endure so long as it rests upon moral and religious sanctions, and not much longer. It becomes increasingly clear to me that the recent and present distress of this country, as of other countries, is not due so much to defects in particular economic or governmental systems as it is due to a breakdown in the character and intelligence of the people themselves, to a widespread moral deflation, to an inadequate and often false ideal of life under which we have developed a lopsided civilization, with periods of mushroom growth followed by terrible lapses.

The subduing of a new continent here on American soil has developed a turn for practical affairs, a resourcefulness, and a power to bring things to pass that have made this a rich country with widespread material well-being. Do not let the pessimists and the demagogues deceive you: this is not only a rich country, there is here more widespread material well-being than has ever been known anywhere else in the world. And this is good, but this preoccupation with immediate and urgent material tasks has had other results not so admirable. In great wealth and widespread material well-being too many of us felt that we had found our ultimate good; and the whole national ideal and goal came for all too many Americans to consist in making money and in living comfortably, even magnificently, with the body.

Upon this practical materialism and under the influence of ideas current throughout the world there has been building up in this country a materialistic philosophy of life that would neglect the elements by which the human spirit, if it is to live aright, has chiefly to live and would concentrate on the things in this physical existence that seem to the individual to be at the moment most desirable. To this philosophy we owe, among other bad things, the current fallacy that we can make good citizens and good men by continued doles and boondoggling employment.

If we are to survive as a great country with adequate national ideals, this whole theory of life we in America must use every possible weapon to combat. And the best way to combat it is to set over against it another kind of philosophy, to bring about such a comprehension of the whole meaning of life as will create an order of society in which goodness and beauty, righteousness and truth, gentleness and strength can live together and living together can build a nobler civilization than man has yet known, a civilization in which culture and Christianity can work in hearty co-operation and wealth and well-being become more widespread than even America has seen. But this highest civilization still awaits, and must ever await, the power to combine a full and beautiful living with a religion that comprehends the whole of life.

Unfortunately the reactionary and revolutionary points of view appear most often and most pronouncedly when men's minds turn toward this the greatest of all human concerns; and here as elsewhere the one is apt to lead to the other in quick succession. We cannot, of course, be too conservative of the essential things in our Christian religion; but we can be so preoccupied with the retention of outworn forms that we fail to catch the significant in our religious inheritance from the past. This seems to me to have been the besetting sin of the late-medieval church, especially in France and Spain; and it is a besetting sin of the church today wherever there appears a tendency to rest in inherited forms, methods, or processes, to rely upon "things" however respectable or venerable, and not upon principles. This strain to keep "things" fixed in a world which under guiding and unchanging principles is by the law of its creation in eternal progress is unnatural and convulsive to society, and therefore in the inevitable reaction is revolutionary. Our ancestral religion should serve best to illustrate the right relation between the past and the present. It is our richest inheritance, but it must be constantly touched by the spirit of progress. And it will in the future keep alive among us as through all the years it has kept alive a feeling after God and unearthly things that has saved and will continue to save us from materialism and flat despair.

Upon a university like this and upon men and women like you lies heavy the duty of mediation between right religious conceptions and the intellectual ferment of the age. Again, the problem is to take the good that has come to us out of the past and adjust it to the conditions of the present and the needs of the future. Let us do what we can to see that the influential place of the churches as held in America not only abides but grows and extends. For after all is said and done, it is the business of the church to guide the spiritual forces that in the end control the world.

But how can these great results be achieved? Crime statistics and many bad features in our civilization clearly show that they have not yet been achieved. This is not the time to enter into a detailed discussion concerning the ways and means for achieving these high goals of education. The ways are difficult and there might be much difference of opinion concerning them. And, let it be remembered, my subject is the responsibility of the University for building soundness in the minds and character of students. This is just what our present-day education most needs—a sense of responsibility for the conduct and character of students and graduates, the tonic power that would come from an understanding that education is concerned not with what is superficial and accidental, but as Walter Pater said of Socrates and Plato, with the tranquil godship that is in man. The need is not so much for a method as for a spirit that would animate all schooling processes and for a pattern of education that might be followed through all its stages. The task is so great that the school must call to its side the home, the church, and every agency of education.

When all these forces can everywhere be brought to join wholeheartedly in their common task to make a better world by making better men and women in the world, then we may expect to build a civilization with really great and enduring qualities.

AN OLD COLLEGE AND A NEW
UNIVERSITY*

TRINITY COLLEGE, a part of Duke University since Mr. James
B. Duke founded the University by his Indenture of Trust
executed December 11, 1924, goes back in its origins to Union
Institute which began with the academic year 1838-1839. The
Institute was called Union because it was an interdenominational undertaking. In 1851 it developed into Normal College, organized with the immediate purpose of training teachers for the newly created public-school system of North Carolina, authorized in 1852 to confer degrees, and for a time
affiliated with the state. In 1859 it became a college of liberal
arts under the name and investiture that it has continued to
bear.

Looked at in one way, it might seem right to date the beginning of the College from 1852 when it became a degree-
granting institution. But the College and the University built
about it represent a continuous movement that started in the
year 1838-1839, and Union Institute is a chapter in the story
that cannot be neglected. Interdenominational co-operation is

* Address delivered at Duke University Centennial Celebration, Saturday Afternoon, April 22, 1939, *Duke University Alumni Register*, May, 1939, pp. 108-110.

an idea whose hour had not then come. Union Institute was ahead of its day; but it rested on an idea whose hour has now come, and it should be cherished and preserved as a permanent and precious spiritual asset in the life of the total institution. With this interpretation of Union Institute it becomes, not just the first chapter, but one of the most important chapters in the eventful history of the College and of the University.

Some words from the preamble to the resolutions forming the Union Institute Society will show the motive that prompted the founding fathers. The words were no doubt written by Brantley York, the first Principal of Union Institute and a man of considerable distinction in his day: ". . . possessing no small share of philanthropy and patriotism, believing that ignorance and errour are not only the bane of religious but also of civil society . . . we therefore ordain and adopt the following articles and resolutions."

In these few words are intimated ideas that run through the history of the institution since its beginning one hundred years ago down to the present moment. "Philanthropy and patriotism," opposition to "ignorance and errour," concern for "religious and civil society." Without any knowledge of these words, Mr. Duke in his Indenture of Trust by which the University was created, used other words that carried the same idea. "Education . . . is, next to religion, the greatest civilizing influence." "Education," "religion," "civilizing influence," are words that are in complete harmony with the spirit of the Institute that began a century ago.

The first of the bylaws of Duke University, and this was taken over from the bylaws of Trinity College, to like effect set out that the aims of Duke University are "to assert a faith in the eternal union of knowledge and religion . . .; to advance learning in all lines of truth; to defend scholarship against all false notions and ideals; to develop a Christian love of freedom and truth; to promote a sincere spirit of tolerance;

[344]

to discourage all partisan and sectarian strife; and to render the largest permanent service" to the causes of "religious and civil society," substituting at the end four equivalent words from the Union Institute preamble.

Bold strokes all through the institution's history give the impression of romance and the dramatic. As a matter of fact, the destinies of the institution all the way have been the concern of what we in America like to call the common man. A competent American historian has expressed the doubt whether any of the Trustees of Union Institute were planters or slaveholders. As time went on and the College moved to an industrial community here in Durham, the support of it passed more and more into the hands of industrialists, a good many of them influential in the industrial and commercial development of the state and some of them still well known. Finally came the great gift from James B. Duke by which the University was founded. A paragraph from the Indenture will make plain his conception of the relation between industrial development and the promotion of education and the common good:

For many years I have been engaged in the development of water powers in certain sections of the States of North Carolina and South Carolina. In my study of this subject I have observed how such utilization of a natural resource, which otherwise would run in waste to the sea and not remain and increase as a forest, both gives impetus to industrial life and provides a safe and enduring investment for capital. My ambition is that the revenue of such developments shall administer to the social welfare, as the operation of such developments is administering to the economic welfare, of the communities which they serve.

The institution has never been under the dominance of political ideals. It was only involved indirectly with the issue of slavery and the Civil War. On the other hand, it has always been committed to the moral, social, and material well-being of all the people. It is therefore a typical institution of this very democratic state. It has influenced the state more than is generally understood and the state has influenced it. It is also representative of like forces that have built great and abiding institutions of education and of other kinds, particularly in our early history, all over America.

The one request made by the founder of Duke University was that the University "secure for its officers, trustees and faculty, men of such outstanding character, ability, and vision as will insure its attaining and maintaining a place of real leadership in the educational world, and that great care and discrimination be exercised in admitting as students only those whose previous record shows a character, determination, and application evincing a wholesome and real ambition for life."

Is there inconsistency between a university thus committed to intellectual excellence and to the highest educational ideals on the one hand, and on the other hand the older institution that was supported through all its history by average American citizens, a good many of whom by industry and character achieved some success and so were able to build a good college that was from its beginning devoted to the well-being of "religious and civil society"? In other words, can a university be devoted alike to science and to service; is it going to be possible here or for that matter anywhere in this republic to reconcile the conflict between democracy and excellence? Certainly colleges and college graduates should contribute with ever-increasing strength toward the reconciliation of excellence and democracy upon which, I should think, the perpetuity of this republic must finally rest. One reason for not taking too gloomy a view of America is the democratic character of its institutions of education, the persistence through them of the traditions of excellence, and the survival of colleges through hard times and through all kinds of hard circumstances.

Duke University in its organic law is committed to the selective admission of students, and it has definitely adopted the principle of limited enrollment. It will always insist that the best ought to be good enough for any of us; and that however democratic we may be the best is not too good for any of us who are willing to pay the price of effort that it costs. At the same time it will do what it can to keep the door of opportunity open to those who would avail themselves of the best it has to offer; and thus make its educational opportunities as good as possible and, considering the limitations under which it must work, available for as many as possible.

All the way from the words in the Union Institute preamble to the words in Mr. Duke's Indenture education and religion stand together as the words *learning* and *religion* stand together in the Seal of Trinity College, and now of Duke University, just as they have stood together in English civilization and were brought to America from the mother country. The builders of this University have used a style of architecture that links us with the past by merely putting those lines in our buildings which, as Woodrow Wilson said of the Tudor Gothic buildings at Princeton, point every man's imagination to the historic traditions of learning in the English-speaking race. These buildings you see about you have been constructed with the further purpose to provide a place fit in every circumstance of beauty and appropriateness to be the home of the soul of the University and in the belief that these appropriate and beautiful surroundings will have a transforming influence upon students generation after generation and even upon the character of the institution itself. The architectural harmony and strength of the plant is intended to suggest unity and fullness of life. Here stand side by side science and religion—science and scholarship completely given to the full, untrammeled pursuit of the truth, and religion with its burning passion for righteousness in the world—and commit the University to the union of the intellectual and the spiritual in our American culture. This underlying conception of the mission of Duke University has affected the building and organization of every part of it.

On this campus the Chapel, hard by the library and the laboratories and co-operating with the University in its every effort to promote the truth and serve humanity, is not only central, but, with its stained glass, its vaulted roof and noble spires, will dominate the place. This is intended to be symbolical of the truth that the spiritual is the central and dominant thing in the life of man. I am emphasizing this, not only because it is a part of our record, but because it seems to me now to be important. All universities worthy the name have won freedom in religion. Unfortunately, too many people in the universities and out have come to assume that freedom in religion means freedom from religion; and to reassert a strong moral note will not always be easy for universities in our day. It would nonetheless seem to me to be perfectly clear that information, training, learning, scientific research, intellectual culture—any or all of these alone will not be sufficient to save the world of our troubled day. The world needs spiritual regeneration, and our university halls ought to echo with the voice of moral authority.

I have undertaken to trace certain threads that have run through the pattern of this institution these one hundred years. Despite all its outward changes it seems to me to be a fact that it has kept one soul; that it has been guided by the same controlling faiths. But despite this inner consistency its most valuable and persistent tradition has been the tradition of change. Its history has been a succession of crises, one stirring episode after another in a moving dramatic story that came to a fitting climax. Again and again and through all its stages its chief characteristic has been a moral resilience and energy that has enabled it to go forward when the time for going has arrived and at the same time without loss of gains already made. The College did an unprecedented thing when it brought a Northern man to the presidency in the 1880's, in the very shadows of Reconstruction. It showed again wellnigh unexampled courage when half a century ago it was able to get up and move from an isolated site into a growing center of population. When its great hour came, the College, its alumni, and constituents were ready to take on the investiture of Duke University, the latest and greatest chapter in its eventful history.

In the beginning it was a matter of opinion as to whether it would be better to build the University about Trinity College or build a separate university and locate it elsewhere. In the end it seemed best to build it about the College, with its long history, its ideals, and its body of alumni. I am more and more convinced that this decision was right. I should have no confidence in the future of any American university that did not have a good college at its center. There would not be in sufficient numbers those to love it and care for it in the succeeding generations. People in general are more interested in the moral energy of ideas than in their intellectual purity, and the college is the part of the university where the emphasis should be put upon the energy of ideas rather than upon the ideas themselves. The college so becomes the moral center of the university and the graduates of the college may be counted on, as a rule, to give to the university their life-long devotion. Graduates of the schools of arts and sciences, medicine, law, and theology, will do much for the fame and influence of a university, but in the nature of things they cannot be relied on for its support in the same way as may be expected of the graduate of the college.

On this theory of a university it becomes highly important to make the college at the center of the University as good as it is possible to make it. It is true that the goal of college education is today ill defined, as is also the goal of American civilization. If, as many of us think, the aim of American civilization should be deep culture and high moral purpose, then the main purpose of the American college should be so to use the processes of education and the agencies of culture as to make men with intellectual and moral power.

In the years that have intervened since Mr. Duke signed the Indenture of Trust creating Duke University, there has been a good deal of discussion (and some of it has found its way into print) as to whether there is in the southeastern section of the United States a climate of opinion that will sustain a great endowed university. Meanwhile Duke, through its construction and organization program, has steadily gone forward with the building of a university that is in no sense a copy of any existing institution but that is not out of line with the best educational traditions or the best educational tendencies of our time.

I am happy to be able to report that all this has gone on, some of it far-reaching and in its implications involving much that has been characteristic of Southern civilization, without interference from local public opinion and wholly uninterrupted by gusts of unwisdom that are apt to arise from time to time in any democracy. With this experience in mind and with a like experience through many years in the history of Trinity College, I am ready to say that I believe Duke is no more apt to suffer from an unwholesome public opinion than are universities in other parts of America. On the other hand, located as it is in a part of the country that is now in the midst of its building era (taking the long view of it I am optimistic enough to see the current discouragement as an episode and not a catastrophe), this university might conceivably have an unusual chance to produce creative rather than merely critical attitudes of mind, if this distinction will pass muster, and I realize that it may be more a matter of emphasis than an essential difference in type of mind. From this standpoint, Duke University is not only an educational adventure; it is a social experiment of wide significance, and as such it is attracting and will continue to attract the attention of enlightened men throughout the country.

We have received a great deal of advice especially as to the general type of university that we should undertake to build.

We have not been able to take it all, but we are grateful for it all. We are trying to proceed in the light of the best that experience has taught. Duke aspires to be a national university. Indeed it is already a national university in its standards and ideals and in the fact that its teachers come from all parts of America as well as from elsewhere, and its students in about equal numbers from the Southern states and from the rest of the country. But in our undertakings we cannot wholly overlook the circumstance that we are located in the South and owe it certain duties and kinds of special service. We have therefore not been altogether as free as would be a new endowed university in a part of the country where there are many others in the field to make experiments involving the university as a whole. The physical sciences get a disproportionate emphasis in American civilization and American education. There ought to be somewhere in the country universities that place their major emphasis on the humanities, and others that stress the sciences of man as over against the sciences of nature. It has occurred to a good many thoughtful people that Duke should have become a university of this specialized type. Duke should be adequately equipped for research in the human sciences, but I prefer to see this done in an institute within the University rather than undertake to develop a specialized university. The South has not yet made its due contribution towards scientific research and the scientific spirit, and so has lagged, not only in its material, but also in its social and political development. Duke must try to do its part at this point and at the same time strive to become a home of idealism.

From the beginning Duke has insisted that it is to be not a sectional but a national university. Sectionalism has good as well as bad uses, but one of the dangers to the unity and highest well-being of a country like ours is the undue magnifying of sectional peculiarities and sectional interests. This tendency in evidence everywhere among men has at times been strengthened in America by well-known historical causes. One thing that has all along worked against this harmful tendency has been the going of many our picked youth to Northern universities for part of their education and the coming into Southern colleges of young teachers who have been trained in the North and West. It will be even more useful to have students come from the North and West, as they are now coming, for a part of their education in universities located in the South and to have young teachers pass from Southern universities into teaching positions in all parts of the United States. It will be even more significant when Southern universities are strong enough, and some of them are now, to draw to their teaching staffs mature and distinguished men from all parts of the world.

Democracy must more and more look to strong educational centers for the formative influences that are to save it. There is a tendency on the part of governments all over the world today to interfere with teaching. Even in America, and in some of the more enlightened states, we have teachers' oaths, and other threats to honest teaching appear from time to time. American colleges and universities have largely won freedom in religion and freedom in scientific teaching. While there may be occasional economic pressure groups from one direction or another, these wrong influences will be local and temporary. But colleges and universities must all the time be on their guard against the threat everywhere of government enlarging itself at the expense of liberty. In some countries the test has already come. It may come in others. In colleges and universities strong enough to resist new and old sets of pressures freedom may be called upon to take its last stand.

Duke University began its first stage a century ago "possessing no small share of philanthropy and patriotism." It now enters upon its second century possessing the same love of country and love of mankind. This and all other institutions, and our entire region, have suffered from well-known interruptions, at times so serious as to throw a whole section of the country out of line with the main currents of American life. I am sure I speak for all our Southern institutions and our Southern people when, in the presence of these distinguished representatives from the United States and other nations, I say that we are more and more ready and determined to take our rightful place in the house which our fathers had so much to do with building and contribute our part, as those who lived here before us contributed their part, to the greatness of our common country and to the service of mankind.

DOES HISTORY HAVE LESSONS FOR US?*

WE ARE COMING TO THE close of our Centennial year. We have especially this year been looking at the past to see the lessons it has for us in the present and for the future. Those of you in residence this year have had many opportunities to reflect from one standpoint and another about this history. All our talking and essentially our thinking, however, have been from the standpoint of human society and not especially from the standpoint of individuals like you.

In bringing the Centennial year to a close I am going to attempt this morning to bring directly to your attention some lessons that I think history these past one hundred years holds for you. I am not doing this for the sake of history, but in the interest of the individuals who make up the graduating classes of this year. As usual I am this year profoundly interested in those who are to receive degrees and in their adjustments to their life work and success in it. If what I have to say seems too much like fatherly advice, please remember that

* Baccalaureate Address, Duke University, Sunday Morning, June 4, 1939. *Duke University Alumni Register*, June, 1939, pp. 141, 148.

I have been watching young people come and go for a good while, and my desire to be of service to them as they come and go increases rather than grows less with the passing of the years. I wish above everything else just now that I could say something that might be useful to at least some of you as you go from this place.

The history of the past century and for that matter all history suggests to me first of all the lesson of hope. I see no reason why you should be more discouraged about life than have been others who have gone before you. Conditions change but the essentials of living and of success remain largely the same. Find what you think you can do best, fit yourself as well as is humanly possible, then go to work and have the ability to move in a straight line and to stand up under hardships and discouragements. There is something hard and there are many discouraging things about the life of everyone who takes his life seriously. There is no scarcity of opportunities, certainly in professions like those of teaching, preaching, in the whole mission of healing—medicine, nursing, technicians. There is still an abundance of opportunities for those who want to work in some form of business. Most states, maybe all of them, in the American union are not more than half developed, and to that extent are still frontiers. Then too pioneer conditions exist in Mexico, in Central America, and in South American countries. In all these American countries outside the United States it would be good for us and for them if we had more social and business contacts and interchange.

In the strict sense of the word the American frontier is not a thing of the past and the opportunities of youth in the Western hemisphere are still practically unlimited. This may not be in accord with the view that is widely prevalent at this time, but if you look at it closely I believe you will find that it is in accord with the actual facts in the case. It may not be, and in fact is not, as easy to accumulate money as it was a few years ago, but as long as opportunities lie open in the United States and elsewhere in the Americas, no youth should feel that life is essentially harder for him than it has been for others who have gone before him. After all, everybody who really succeeds must in his way be a pioneer.

Still keeping you in mind and reflecting back over these one hundred years of history, I observe one constant characteristic and that is the institution's power to withstand outside pressures. As far as I can discover, it has always firmly set its face on the goal to which it would aim and has not been turned from its course by the whims and moods of the hour. It has chosen to go its own way once having decided on the course it should pursue. Any intelligent study of our past will show that this has always been true.

At an alumni meeting in Washington a few years ago I was asked for a definition of the spirit of Duke University. I undertook this definition, and with this result—it is the spirit of a strong and formative university, removed as far as possible from the pressure of immediacies and dedicated to the long view of truth, devoted alike to science and to service, and inspired by the hope that democracy and excellence can be reconciled in this republic. Whether that be an adequate definition or not, it at least emphasizes the need for the power to resist pressures and to take a long view of truth. Fads and moods go to extremes, and whoever goes with them may expect to find himself always wrong. We must, of course, be a part of the life about us and learn to work with others. Co-operation is a watchword of our time; but after all it is the individual that counts in human society, and we must see with our own eyes, stand on our own feet, and always be ready to stand up and be counted whether girt by friend or foe. Otherwise we may expect to be blown about by every wind of doctrine and swept before every gust of unwisdom that arises from time to time in every democracy.

To be sure, this must seem to you like a counsel of perfection, but it is true that we must be co-operative and at the same time when the test comes be ready to stand firmly for the things that we think are right and high and for the good of the largest number, and this without too much regard for what others about us may be thinking or doing. We must have faith enough in the people to be willing to risk telling them the truth even when it is not agreeable or acceptable to them. Just this has, I think, always been the practice of Duke University and this has been true in all its stages. I hope it may always be its practice and that you and others who are to come after you will follow its example.

Another emphasis in this centennial year has been loyalty to the past. We have taken every means at our disposal to bring out the contributions that other generations have made to the total institution and its causes. This is a lesson that ought to have great significance, especially for us who live in a new country, and a new country that was geographically far removed from the older existing civilizations. It has been easy for us to overestimate the self-sufficiency of a new world and therefore easy to forget our debt to the past. Each generation starts afresh, but it should start with a keen sense of awareness of its inheritance from the past and a willingness to use that inheritance. Under our law we inherit from our fathers but we are left free to use this inheritance and, bettered by our use, to transmit it to oncoming generations. This should also be our attitude toward history. In our world we must conserve in order to progress.

Duke University has been built firmly on the past. In my address at the Centennial Celebration I undertook to trace certain threads that have run through the pattern of the institution these one hundred years, to point out that it has been guided by the same controlling faiths and has kept essentially one soul. I also took pains to point out that despite this inner consistency its most valuable and persistent tradition has been the tradition of change. Built in a consistent framework of the past, always keeping faith with its history, taking every step with the utmost care and with due regard to inherited traditions and yet, steadily progressing in the full light of the present, Trinity College has quietly grown into Duke University, and this growth of a more or less provincial but good college into a national university has been one of the far-reaching and even revolutionary achievements of our time. I take some pride in this achievement, and I venture to emphasize it here today because I think it illustrates the way of all real progress. Let down your buckets where you are, consider carefully what you are, what your past is and your inheritance. See life about you as it is, find your place in it, use the lessons of the past to work out the problems of the present and reach the hopes of the future. Be intelligent and informed and work hard and you will succeed.

This loyalty to the past is important but it must be reinforced by vision and courage in the present. No man can succeed unless he has the vision to know the day of his visitation and the courage to enter into an untried future. This vision and this courage are particularly needed in hours of crisis and change when we must make decisions that have far-reaching consequences. This may seem to you to be another counsel of perfection. Even so, I urge it upon you—be careful, watch your steps, stand in the way and look and see which is the right way to go. When the vision is clear and the direction seems right, then have the courage of your convictions and an unfaltering faith that will carry you to your goal.

In the next place, I call it to your attention that this has been an undoctrinaire institution, not particularly preoccupied with set theories, but always ready to face realities and do the work at hand. It is so easy for a university in one generation to use stock ideas and pursue them relentlessly without too much regard for the institution's total well-being. For an illustration, a distinguished university president seventy-five years ago, revolting against the hard and fast college curriculum that existed then, set out to develop the elective system. With his

zeal for reform he carried that too far and his successors re-
acted from the extreme elective system as at first developed.
Whenever you see a new university president, a new governor
of a state, or a new President of the United States, or any
other important administrator, turn his back on the past and
set out with some sort of new deal that he will follow through
thick and thin, you can know at once that you have on your
hands a politician, or, if sincere, a self-centered man who wants
to make a record for himself without due regard to the larger
good involved. At any rate, if such administration is too much
out of line with the traditions of the university, the state, or the
nation, that administration's success will be limited and temporary. Again I am venturing to insist that sound development
everywhere must be a growth out of the past into the present
and on to the future. Disregard of the past and too much preoccupation with one's own point of view are not the marks of
great leaders or great men. I hope that these will not be
characteristic of you.

The University and the College about which the University has been built, while I hope not exploiting the spirit of
helpfulness as a form of protective advertising, have, nonetheless, made it a point to be friendly and helpful to all those
high or low worthy of help, and friendly and helpful to all
causes worthy of support. It seems to be easy for universities as they grow and prosper to lose something of this friendly
and helpful spirit, at least to lose some of the commoner manifestations of this spirit; and the same, I have observed, is
equally easy for individuals. I hope that Duke may always
preserve the simplicity, the friendliness, and the amenities of
life that ought always to be an essential part of the spirit of a
great institution of whatever kind, and also of great individuals. I hope that you will cherish these finer human qualities
and make them not only a part of your own spiritual constitution but an effective part in your living with others. It will
help you in your own personality, it will help you to succeed,

it will help you to be a co-operative and useful member of society wherever your lot may be cast.

The University in its present stage and in all its stages has been devoted to freedom. It has not, I hope, said too much about this. Why should a free institution or a free man be forever boasting about it or forever defending it? This ought to be taken for granted just as a man who is a gentleman can well afford to let that fact be taken for granted. Freedom is not something to be proud of but something to be grateful for and to be wholeheartedly committed to. It is one of the most precious gifts of the human spirit and without it life itself is always futile. This University will always stand ready to defend freedom whenever and wherever it is attacked; but the University has not been willing, and I hope will never be willing, to fight windmills at the call of irresponsible extremists either in the one direction or the other. I commend this example also to you. You must be alert in your time or you may be caught in one way or another. There are propagandists abroad and aplenty who are seeking to promote extreme ideas of one kind or another, and at present in this country they usually assume to speak in the name of freedom. Too often they are wolves in sheep's clothing. Do not be caught by them unless you are willing to be lambs for the slaughter.

This University in its every stage has striven to avoid being particularistic. It has, I think, sought to do its own special task but has at the same time always kept in mind the larger good that might be involved. It is not sectarian but catholic, not sectional but national, not local but universal in its sympathy and outlooks. Every man's life must also be such if it is to become what a worthwhile human life ought to be. A wholly self-centered life is essentially futile. An individual can become really great only as he builds his life in a background of the universal and in the light of values that are eternal. See life, but see it in its round completeness—in its material, its intellectual, and its spiritual aspects.

As a final counsel of perfection I covet for you, for each one of you, the concentrated strength that will enable you to do well your own special task and a universality of sympathy and wideness of outlook—these constant characteristics of greatness in the spirit of man.

DEMOCRACY IN A TIME OF CRISIS*

IN THE FACE OF SUCH A WORLD as we look out upon today I do not know what I should undertake to say to you. We face hard realities and we must face them resolutely. The things we cherish most are threatened. Wars are raging that might involve our whole civilization. These world conditions will affect us in many ways. Free governments are everywhere being tested as by fire. The dictators again have their hour of glory. There is a revival of the pagan admiration for the "great man." Let us hope that his hour of glory will be brief and that again there will be rough sledding in the world for all Caesars and Alexanders, for all dictators and mighty manipulators of men.

I have, even now, the faith to believe that the great man of the future will more and more have leadership among men because of what he is, rather than by means of control of them through force, that he will lead because of his character and the righteousness of his appeal and not by holding men in the

* Baccalaureate Address, University Chapel, Sunday, June 2, 1940. *Duke University Alumni Register*, June, 1940, pp. 124-125.

bondage of some sort of power derived through birth, position, or the authority that resides in office of whatever kind. That is, greatness will tend, I still think, to lose its pagan elements and have more of a Christian meaning.

I stress this thought at this point because I believe that the universality of the Christian religion is the foundation stone of modern democracy. "Whosoever will"; "Come unto me, all ye" . . . this constitutes the charter of democracy as the world has until now known democracy. From this, by devious ways, came the French yearning watchword of Liberty, Equality, Fraternity, and our own nobler claim to give all a free and equal share in the inalienable right to Life, Liberty, and the Pursuit of Happiness.

The kind of democracy for which I have enthusiasm has been, for me at least, best defined by the great scientist Louis Pasteur—democracy is that form of government which leaves every citizen free to do his best for the common welfare. I would emphasize the words (1) "free," (2) "his best," (3) "common welfare." We cannot overestimate the worth of freedom. Whatever individual, whatever group, and whatever nation sells freedom at any price makes a bad bargain. A free church in a free state is of the essence of the American ideal. They must both be kept free and if the republic in its original and fundamental conception is to endure, they must both be kept vigorous.

In both these directions we have made serious mistakes in this country that we should promptly correct. All churches should, I feel sure, cease to be too much preoccupied with formal professions and correctness of creed and throw all possible emphasis on spiritual vitality and moral energy. Otherwise we may look to see Protestantism a declining force in America, and democracy with it.

Then, too, if we are to keep a vigorous state and nation citizens must not only be devoted to the nation and its causes, they must be brought to participate directly and actively in the opportunities and obligations of citizenship. Unless we come to succeed better than we have until now succeeded, we might live to see America follow the drift away from democracy; and with this steady drift away from democracy we might even live to see freedom for the time perish from the earth. This sort of citizenship will call for enlightenment and character, but most of all for courage. I have had occasion many times to stress this, but it never needed stressing more than now. Courage is the greatest of all virtues; because, unless a man has that virtue, he has no security for preserving any other. Perhaps nowhere so much as in a democracy is courage necessary to preserve other virtues and make them effective in the community and in the state. Here where everything is in the end determined by public opinion, it is of the first importance that the individual man shall have the courage to speak the truths that are in him, and when the time comes to stand up and be counted for what he esteems to be right, though the battle rage and the barbarians beat at the gates. We may at times be neutral citizens, but this is no time for neutral minds. We must have convictions for which we will stand though every free government in Europe should fall; yes, even though the heavens should fall.

Aristocratic societies tend to foster the virtue of courage; but the leveling tendencies of a democratic state do not favor the growth of moral courage. Every forward movement in a democracy is the result of striking an average of the intelligence and moral sense of all the people. While it is easier for a democratic than an aristocratic society to find its natural leaders, at the same time it is more difficult to give them the opportunity to exert directly their power and their wills. They are too apt to be swallowed up in the mass and become followers rather than leaders of men. Hence the need of courage in a democracy. And here is the supreme opportunity for an institution like Duke University to make wise and courageous leaders who will serve, but never be subservient to, the people.

It would be good for politics, for the purity and strength of political parties, and for the peace and security of the state if we could feel that all educated men at least would at the ballot box always vote their own matured convictions and never be influenced by even an unconscious feeling that they must respond in unbroken solidarity to new or old shibboleths and political leadership. Just now we need statesmen who will place the welfare of the country and of humanity high above every other consideration, and we need citizens who will choose and support such leaders. This is the sort of moral and intellectual leadership we must have in this country if we are to hold our place in the sort of world we know. As a nation in the midst of desperately critical circumstances, we need clear heads and true hearts; we must be on our guard against "fifth columns" and "Trojan horses" of every kind.

A genuine democracy will leave every man free to do his best. For myself, I profoundly believe in this republic and the fundamental ideas upon which it is built; and I would have you believe in this—in what James Truslow Adams has called the American Dream, that is, the persistent belief that a whole people without communistic restrictions on individual initiative and acquisition may be free to live their lives to the fullest possibilities. To be sure, this dream has not been fully realized. Perhaps no dream has ever been fully realized in our human world.

Certainly the American way of life did lead to the building up of a great nation in a short period of time. The nation as it has developed has not been without its faults, but the contrast of our country with other countries in the world today ought to bring some reassurance that we have in the main moved in the right direction. A good many Americans in this generation have looked persistently at the faults of the nation and failed to recognize its virtues, and some of them have even espoused other forms of government across the seas that are built on dictatorships of one kind or another. This is a good time to remember Burke's advice not rashly to throw over a system that works even though it may have some faults, in favor of an untried plan even though it may have much, in theory, to commend it.

Citizenship in this republic is a precious heritage. Like any other inheritance it should be used by us, improved so far as we can improve it, and transmitted to future generations. The nation has enemies both on the outside and on the inside. We must be on our guard against the threat, everywhere in the world, of government enlarging itself at the expense of liberty. It could be possible that here in America freedom will be called upon to take its last stand. Always and everywhere it costs to be free men, but freedom is worth all that it costs. One of our great dangers is ignorance of our inheritance and indifference to it, its opportunities and its obligations. This treasure is committed to us in earthen vessels. We must be willing to pay the price of preserving it. For you this may be only work and service; it may involve for you the searching and redeeming experiences of sacrifice and suffering.

It is, of course, not the business of colleges to indoctrinate their students, but all American colleges should be dedicated to country as well as to causes and to humanity. And we should stress today the importance of freedom and initiative and the obligations of every citizen to do his best. One of the worst signs of our times is the well-known fact that there are so many of our citizens who are not trying to do their best, so many of them indeed who are not trying to do at all. As a wag has put it, here is a new incentive for the young in our time—make all you can, save all you can, so that you can help those who won't.

In a sound and enduring democracy every man will be left free to do his best and to do his best for the common welfare. We hear too much in our day about the rights and privileges of free men and far too little about the obligations and responsibilities of free men. We must be left free to do our best, but we must come to understand that we are working not altogether for ourselves but for others as well. We must come more and more to keep in mind the common good. In a democracy that is to last, men must of course be free; they must be free to do their best, that is the best that is possible for them, but just as certainly they must keep a sense of brotherhood, a common fellowship in the common good. Every good member of a democratic society must live his own life, do his own work, attend to his own business, and yet he should also keep ready to help others and live in the hope to do some permanent good in the world.

To keep the balance between this fellowship in the common good and the full use of the guarantees of the liberty of the individual is essential in a free society. The citizen must not only love his country and be devoted to its causes, he must keep a free mind and use his intelligence. We have not had too much discussion about vital questions of our time. Indeed, I think we have had too little, but the sort of discussion we have had has often seemed to me to be irrelevant and apart from realities. Too many people insist on just holding on to what has come down to us from the past. They forget the well-known words, "a froward retention of custom is as turbulent a thing as an innovation." Reaction is as disturbing in human society as radicalism. Extremes meet, and they are alike in being often, if not always, wrong. Real progress is built on the past and grows out of the past. The doctrine of inheritance does not exclude the principle of improvement; it implies it. This is true conservatism—to hold on to the inheritance from the past and keep free to improve it and transmit it to posterity bettered by each generation. Time in its course alters things; and it is as bad to be behind the time as to be ahead of the time. In either case the time will be out of joint for the individual or the nation. One is too far behind, the other too far ahead, and neither is of a piece with the age. Unless there is this wisdom to preserve and wisdom to improve there will be conflict and confusion in every generation.

We have in the past twenty years seen something of the evil effects of this conflict between extremes. "Extremes in nature equal ends produce." The ultraconservatives and the extreme radicals have been alike disturbing elements. When these two extremes go on, both sides set in their ways, there is bound to come utter confusion and destruction in one form or another. The blind lead the blind, and ignorant armies clash by night. When blind leaders insist on blowing out the light there is nothing to do but fight it out in the dark.

Even when these evils do not go to this extent, and they have not done so in America in seventy-five years, there are other though lesser evils. There are those among us who have strong and stubborn convictions, and convictions that are not always well founded. There are others, unfortunately, who have no convictions at all. They live in a neutral world, a vapid and empty world. There have been many of these in the European democracies following the fatigue of the last World War. Upon them ultimately rests a good deal of responsibility for conditions in Europe now. I am sorry to believe that there is too much of this lack of conviction in our own country. It is to the danger in this lack of conviction that I would directly call your attention. No man will strive to be the noblest he can be unless he has convictions that seem to him to be worth struggling for, and without burning convictions none of us will be apt to go far in the confused and uncertain world that we live in. Nobody is going to sacrifice or suffer for anything unless he believes in it profoundly.

I wish that all of you, and all American youth like you, in these times that will try men's souls, might hear loudly ringing in your ears the call to be heroes as well as idealists— heroes because you have the power to stand, in any crisis and at all costs, and idealists because you seek the widest good and love the widest joy.

While, as I have said, it is not the business of colleges to indoctrinate their students, it is the mission of American colleges to dedicate themselves to country as well as to causes and to humanity, and their high mission to provide leadership of ideas and ideals in the service of the republic. Men and women rightly educated by these colleges will make substantial contributions not only to sound thinking and sound conduct upon which a great republic may be built, but they will be contributing to that also which must be ever-present in the consciousness of any democracy if it is to endure—a reasonable ground for belief in itself and in its destiny. We still judge a man's wisdom by his hope. We need now to be reassured by the hopefulness of the wise. The final duty of educated men, especially of educated young men, is to bring hope and forward-looking thoughts.